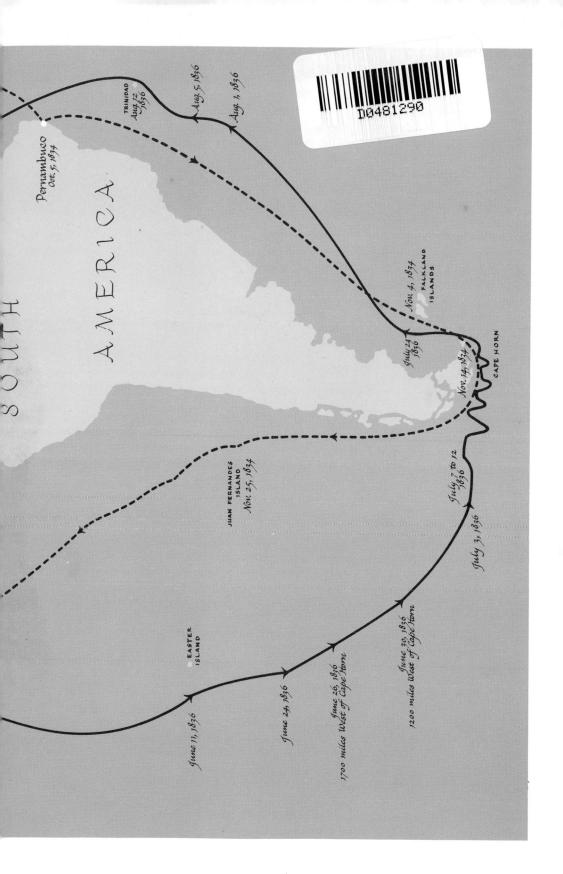

TWO YEARS BEFORE THE MAST

VOLUME TWO

TWO YEARS BEFORE THE MAST

A Personal Narrative of Life at Sea
by Richard Henry Dana, Jr.

Edited from the original manuscript and from the First Edition, with Journals and Letters of 1834-1836 *and* 1859-1860, *and notes by* John Haskell Kemble *with original illustrations by* Robert A. Weinstein, *and illustrated from contemporary paintings, prints and charts.*

The Ward Ritchie Press, Los Angeles, 1964

Illustrated with Drawings by ROBERT WEINSTEIN
Designed by JOSEPH SIMON

⚓

Distributed Exclusively by Lane Book Company, Menlo Park, California

TABLE OF CONTENTS

LIST OF ILLUSTRATIONS

TWO YEARS BEFORE THE MAST

Drawing by Robert A. Weinstein

*and the two ships were covered from head
to foot with their white canvas...*

CHAPTER THIRTY
Homeward bound . . .

At eight o'clock all hands were called aft, and the watches set for the voyage. Some changes were made; but I was glad to find myself still in the larboard watch. Our crew was somewhat diminished; for a man and a boy had gone in the Pilgrim; another was second mate of the Ayacucho; and a third, the oldest man of the crew, had broken down under the hard work and constant exposure on the coast, and, having had a stroke of palsy, was left behind at the hide-house, under the charge of Captain Arthur. The poor fellow wished very much to come home in the ship; and he ought to have been brought home in her. But a live dog is better than a dead lion, and a sick sailor belongs to nobody's mess; so he was sent ashore with the rest of the lumber, which was only in the way. By these diminutions, we were short-handed for a voyage round Cape Horn in the dead of winter. Beside Ben Stimson and myself, there were only five in the forecastle (Ben and I were now in the forecastle, having taken the berths of the men who left); who, together with four boys in the steerage, the sailmaker, carpenter, &c., composed the whole crew. In addition to this, we were only three or four days out, when the sailmaker, who was the oldest and best seaman on board, was taken with the palsy, and was useless for the rest of the voyage. The constant wading in the water, in all weathers, to take off hides, together with the other labors, is too much for old men, and for any who have not good constitutions. Besides these two men of ours, the second officer of the California and the carpenter of the Pilgrim broke down under the work, and the latter died at Santa Barbara. The young man, too, who came out with us from Boston in the Pilgrim, had to be taken from his berth before the mast and made clerk, on account of a fit of rheumatism which attacked him soon after he came upon the coast. By the loss of the sailmaker, our watch was reduced to five, of whom two were boys, who never steered but in fine weather, so that the other two and myself had to stand at the wheel four hours apiece out of every twenty-four; and the other watch had only four helmsmen. "Never mind—we're homeward bound!" was the answer to everything; and we should not have minded this, were it not for the thought that we should be off Cape Horn in the very dead of winter. It was now the first part of May; and two months would bring us off the Cape in July, which is the worst month in the year there; when the sun rises at nine and sets at three, giving eighteen hours night, and there is snow and rain, gales and high seas, in abundance.

The prospect of meeting this in a ship half manned, and loaded so deep that every heavy sea must wash her fore and aft, was by no means pleasant. The Alert, in her passage out, doubled the Cape in the month of February, which is midsummer; and we came round in the Pilgrim in the latter part of October, which we thought was bad enough. There was only one of our crew who had been off there in the winter, and that was in a whale-ship, much lighter and higher than our ship; yet he said they had man-killing weather for twenty days without intermission, and their decks were swept twice, and they were all glad enough to see the last of it. The Brandywine frigate, also, in her passage round, had sixty days off the Cape, and lost several boats by the heavy seas. All this was for our comfort; yet pass it we must; and all hands agreed to make the best of it.

During our watches below we overhauled our clothes, and made and mended everything for bad weather. Each of us had made for himself a suit of oil-cloth or tarpaulin, and these we got out, and gave thorough coatings of oil or tar, and hung upon the stays to dry. Our stout boots, too, we covered over with a thick mixture of melted grease and tar, and hung out to dry. Thus we took advantage of the warm sun and fine weather of the Pacific to prepare for its other face. In the forenoon watches below, our forecastle looked like the workshop of what a sailor is,—a Jack at all trades. Thick stockings and drawers were darned and patched; mittens dragged from the bottom of the chest and mended; comforters made for the neck and ears; old flannel shirts cut up to line monkey-jackets; sou'westers lined with flannel, and a pot of paint smuggled forward to give them a coat on the outside; and everything turned to hand; so that, although two years had left us but a scanty wardrobe, yet the economy and invention which necessity teaches a sailor, soon put each of us in pretty good trim for bad weather, even before we had seen the last of the fine. Even the cobbler's art was not out of place. Several old shoes were very decently repaired, and with waxed ends, an awl, and the top of an old boot, I made me quite a respectable sheath for my knife.

There was one difficulty, however, which nothing that we could do would remedy; and that was the leaking of the forecastle, which made it very uncomfortable in bad weather, and rendered half of the berths tenantless. The tightest ships, in a long voyage, from the constant strain which is upon the bowsprit, will leak, more or less, round the heel of the bowsprit, and the bitts, which come down into the forecastle; but, in addition to this, we had an unaccountable leak on the starboard bow, near the cat-head, which drove us from the forward berths on that side, and, indeed, when she was on the starboard tack, from all the forward berths. One of the after berths, too, leaked in very bad weather; so that in a ship which was in other respects as tight as a bottle, and brought her cargo to Boston dry as a bone, we had, after every effort made to prevent it, in the way of calking and leading, a forecastle with only three dry berths for seven of us. However, as there is never but one watch below at a time, by 'turning in and out,' we did pretty well. And, there being, in our watch, but three of us who lived forward, we generally had a dry berth apiece in bad weather.*

All this, however, was but anticipation. We were still in fine weather in the North Pacific, running down the north-east trades, which we took on the second day after leaving San Diego.

Sunday, May 15th, one week out, we were in latitude 14° 56′ N., long. 116° 14′ W., having gone, by reckoning, over thirteen hundred miles in seven days. In fact, ever since leaving San Diego, we had had a fair wind, and as much as we wanted of it. For seven days, our lower and top-mast studding-sails were set all the time, and our royals and top-gallant studding-sails, whenever she could stagger under them. Indeed, the captain had shown, from the moment we got to sea, that he was to have no boy's play, but that the ship had got to carry all she could, and that he was going to make up, by 'cracking on' to her, what she wanted in lightness. In this way, we frequently made three degrees of latitude, besides something in longitude, in the course of twenty-four hours.—Our days were spent in the usual ship's work. The rigging which had become slack from being long in port was to be set up; breast backstays got up; studding-sail booms rigged upon the main yard; and royal studding-sails got ready for the light trades; ring-tail set; and new rigging fitted and sails got ready for Cape Horn. For, with a ship's gear, as well as a sailor's wardrobe, fine weather must be improved to get ready for the bad to come. Our forenoon watch below, as I have said, was given to our own work, and our night watches were spent in the usual manner:—a *trick* at the wheel, a look-out on the forecastle, a nap on a coil of rigging under the lee of the rail; a yarn round the windlass-end; or, as was generally my way, a solitary walk fore and aft, hour after hour, in the weather waist, between the windlass-end and the main tack. Every wave that she threw aside brought us nearer home, and every day's observation at noon showed a prog-

*On removing the cat-head, after the ship arrived at Boston, it was found that there were two holes under it which had been bored for the purpose of driving treenails, and which, accidentally, had not been plugged up when the cat-head was placed over them. This was sufficient to account for the leak, and for our not having been able to discover and stop it.

ress which, if it continued, would, in less than five months, take us into Boston Bay. This is the pleasure of life at sea,—fine weather, day after day, without interruption,—fair wind, and a plenty of it,—and homeward bound. Every one was in good humor; things went right; and all was done with a will. At the dog watch, all hands came on deck, and stood round the weather side of the forecastle, or sat upon the windlass, and sang sea songs, and those ballads of pirates and highwaymen, which sailors delight in. Home, too, and what we should do when we got there, and when and how we should arrive, was no infrequent topic. Every night, after the kids and pots were put away, and we had lighted our pipes and cigars at the galley, and gathered about the windlass, the first question was,—

"Well, Tom, what was the latitude to day?"

"Why, fourteen, north, and she has been going seven knots ever since."

"Well, this will bring us up to the line in five days."

"Yes, but these trades won't last twenty-four hours longer," says an old salt, pointing with the sharp of his hand to leeward,—"I know that by the look of the clouds."

Then came all manner of calculations and conjectures as to the continuance of the wind, the weather under the line, the south-east trades, &c., and rough guesses as to the time the ship would be up with the Horn; and some, more venturous, gave her so many days to Boston light, and offered to bet that she would not exceed it.

"You'd better wait till you get round Cape Horn," says an old croaker.

"Yes," says another, "you may see Boston, but you've got to 'smell hell' before that good day."

Rumors also of what had been said in the cabin, as usual, found their way forward. The steward had heard the captain say something about the straits of Magellan, and the man at the wheel fancied he had heard him tell the 'passenger' that, if he found the wind ahead and the weather very bad off the Cape, he should stick her off for New Holland, and come home round the Cape of Good Hope.

This passenger—the first and only one we had had, except to go from port to port, on the coast, was no one else than a gentleman whom I had known in my better days; and the last person I should have expected to have seen on the coast of California—Professor Nuttall, of Cambridge. I had left him quietly seated in the chair of Botany and Ornithology, in Harvard University; and the next I saw of him, was strolling about San Diego beach, in a sailor's pea-jacket, with a wide straw hat, and barefooted, with his trousers rolled up to his knees, picking up stones and shells. He had travelled over land to the North-west Coast, and come down in a small vessel to Monterey. There he learned that there was a ship at the leeward, about to sail for Boston; and, taking passage in the Pilgrim, which was then at Monterey, he came slowly down, visiting the intermediate ports, and examining the trees, plants, earths, birds, &c., and joined us at San Diego shortly before we sailed. The second mate of the Pilgrim told me that they had got an old gentleman on board who knew me, and came from the college that I had been in. He could not recollect his name, but said he was a 'sort of an oldish man', with white hair, and spent all his time in the bush, and along the beach, picking up flowers and shells, and such truck, and had a dozen boxes and barrels, full of them. I thought over everybody who would be likely to be there, but could fix upon no one; when, the next day, just as we were about to shove off from the beach, he came down to the boat, in the rig I have described, with his shoes in his hand, and his pockets full of specimens. I knew him at once, though I should not have been more surprised to have seen the Old South steeple shoot up from the hide-house. He probably had no less difficulty to recognising me. As we left home about the same time, we had nothing to tell one another; and owing to our different situations on board, I saw but little of him on the passage home. Sometimes, when I was at the wheel of a calm night, and the steering required no attention, and the officer of the watch was forward, he would come aft and hold a short yarn with me; but this was against the rules of the ship, as is, in fact, all intercourse between passengers and the crew. I was often amused to see the sailors puzzled to know what to make of him, and to hear their conjectures about him and his business. They were as much puzzled as our old sailmaker was with the captain's instruments in the cabin. He said there were three:—the *chro*-nometer, the *chre*-nometer, and the *the*-nometer. (Chronometer, barometer, and thermometer.) The Pilgrim's crew christened Mr. N[uttall] "Old Curious," from his zeal for curiosities, and some of them said that he was crazy, and that his friends let him go about and amuse himself in this way. Why else a rich man (sailors call every man rich who does not work with his hands, and wears a long coat and cravat) should leave a Christian country, and come to such a place as California, to pick up shells and stones, they could not understand. One of them, however, an old salt, who had seen something more of the world ashore, set all to rights, as he thought,—"Oh, 'vast there!—You don't know anything about them craft. I've seen them colleges, and know the ropes. They keep all such things for cur'osities, and study 'em, and have men a' purpose to go and get 'em. This old chap knows what he's about. He a'n't the fool you take him for. He'll carry all these things to the college, and if they are better than any that they have had before, he'll be head of the college. Then, by-and-by, somebody else will go after some more, and if they beat him, he'll have to go again, or else give up his berth. That's the way they did make the spun yarn. This old *covey* knows the ropes. He has worked a traverse over 'em, and come 'way out here, where nobody's ever been afore, and where they'll never think of coming." This explanation satisfied Jack; and as it raised Mr. N[uttall]'s credit for capacity, and was near enough to the truth for common purposes, did not disturb it.

With the exception of Mr. Nuttall, we had no one on board but the regular ship's company, and the live stock. Upon this, we had made a considerable inroad. We killed one of the bullocks every four days, so that they did not last us up to the line. We, or, rather, they, then began upon the sheep and the poultry, for these never come into Jack's mess.*The pigs were left for the latter part of the voyage, for they are sailors, and can stand all weathers. We had an old sow on board, the mother of a numerous progeny, who had been twice round the Cape of Good Hope, and once round Cape Horn. The last time going round, was very nearly her death. We heard her squealing and moaning one dark night, after it had been snowing and hailing for several

---

*The customs as to the allowance of "grub" are very nearly the same in all American merchantmen. Whenever a pig is killed, the sailors have one mess from it. The rest goes to the cabin. The smaller live stock, poultry, &c., they never taste. And, indeed, they do not complain of this, for it would take a great deal to supply them with a good meal, and without the accompaniments, (which could hardly be furnished to them,) it would not be much better than salt beef. But even as to the salt beef, they have hardly a fair allowance; for whenever a barrel is opened, before any of the beef is put into the harness-cask, the steward comes up, and picks it all over, and takes out the best pieces, (those that have any fat in them) for the cabin. This was done in both the vessels I was in, and the men said that it was usual in other vessels. Indeed, it is made no secret, but some of the crew are usually called to help in assorting and putting away the pieces. By this arrangement, the hard, dry pieces, which the sailors call mahogany and 'old horse', come to their share.

There is a singular piece of rhyme, traditional among sailors, which they say over such pieces of beef. I do not know that it ever appeared in print before. When seated round the kid, if a particularly bad piece is found, one of them takes it up, and addressing it, repeats these lines:

"Old horse! old horse! what brought you here?"
" 'From Sacarap' to Portland pier
I've carted stone this many a year:
Till, killed by blows and sore abuse,
They salted me down for sailors' use.
The sailors they do me despise:
They turn me over and damn my eyes;
Cut off my meat, and pick my bones,
And pitch the rest to Davy Jones."

There is a story current among seamen, that a beef-dealer was convicted, at Boston, of having sold old horse for ship's stores, instead of beef, and had been sentenced to be confined in jail, until he should eat the whole of it; and that he is now lying in Boston jail. I have heard this story often, on board other vessels beside those of our own nation. It is very generally believed, and is always highly commended, as a fair instance of retaliatory justice.

hours, and, getting into the sty, we found her nearly frozen to death. We got some straw, an old sail, and other things, and wrapped her up in a corner of the sty, where she stayed until we got into fine weather again.

Wednesday, May 18th. Lat. 9° 54′ N., long. 113° 17′ W. The northeast trades had now left us, and we had the usual variable winds which prevail near the line, together with some rain. So long as we were in these latitudes, we had but little rest in our watch on deck at night, for, as the winds were light and variable, and we could not lose a breath, we were all the watch, bracing the yards, and taking in and making sail, and 'hum-bugging' with our flying kites. A little puff of wind on the larboard quarter, and then—"larboard fore braces!" and studding booms were rigged out, studding-sails set alow and aloft, the yards trimmed, and jibs and spanker in; when it would come as calm as a duck-pond, and the man at the wheel stand with the palm of his hand up, feeling for the wind. "Keep her off a little!" "All aback forward, sir!" cries a man from the forecastle. Down go the braces again; in come the studding-sails, all in a mess, which half an hour won't set right; yards braced sharp up; and she's on the starboard tack, close hauled. The studding-sails must now be cleared away, and set up in the tops, and on the booms. By the time this is done, and you are looking out for a soft plank for a nap,—"Lay aft here, and square in the head yards!" and the studding-sails are all set again on the starboard side. So it goes until it is eight bells,—call the watch,—heave the log,—relieve the wheel, and go below the larboard watch.

Sunday, May 22d. Lat. 5° 14′ N., long. 106° 45′ W.[50] We were now a fortnight out, and within five degrees of the line, to which two days of good breeze would take us; but we had, for the most part, what the sailors call 'an Irishman's hurricane, right up and down.' This day it rained nearly all day, and being Sunday, and nothing to do, we stopped up the scuppers and filled the decks with rain water and bringing all our clothes on deck, had a grand wash, fore and aft. When this was through, we stripped to our drawers, and taking pieces of soap with strips of canvass for towels, we turned-to and soaped, washed, and scrubbed one another down, to get off, as we said, the *California dust;* for the common wash in salt water, which is all that Jack can get, being on an allowance of fresh, had little efficacy, and was more for taste than utility. The captain was below all the afternoon, and we had something nearer to a *Saturnalia* than anything we had yet

[50]In the 1840 edition and again in the 1869 edition, the longitude was printed at 166° 45′ W. In the manuscript it is quite clearly 106° 45′ W. Daniel V. Gallery in "Too far before the mast," *The Colophon* (New Series), vol. II, no. 1 (Autumn, 1936), pp. 60-64 suggests that in view of previous and subsequent longitudes given for this part of the voyage, it should probably read 116° 45′ W.

seen; for the mate came into the scuppers, with a couple of boys to scrub him, and got into a battle with them in heaving water. By unplugging the holes, we let the soap-suds off the decks, and in a short time had a new supply of rain water, in which we had a grand rinsing. It was surprising to see how much soap and fresh water did for the complexions of many of us; how much of what we supposed to be tan and sea-blacking, we got rid of. The next day, the sun rising clear, the ship was covered, fore and aft, with clothes of all sorts, hanging out to dry.

As we approached the line, the wind became more easterly, and the weather clearer, and in twenty days from San Diego,—

Saturday, May 28th, at about three P. M., with a fine breeze from the east-south-east, we crossed the equator. In twenty-four hours after crossing the line, which was very unusual, we took the regular southeast trades. These winds come a little from the eastward of south-east, and, with us, they blew directly from the east-south-east, which was fortunate for us, for our course was south-by-west, and we could thus go one point free. The yards were braced so that every sail drew, from the spanker to the flying-jib; and the upper yards being squared in a little, the fore and main top-gallant studding-sails were set, and just drew handsomely. For twelve days this breeze blew steadily, not varying a point, and just so fresh that we could carry our royals; and, during the whole time, we hardly started a brace. Such progress did we make, that at the end of seven days from the time we took the breeze, on

Sunday, June 5th, we were in lat. 19° 29′ S., and long. 118° 01′ W., having made twelve hundred miles in seven days, very nearly upon a taut bowline. Our good ship was getting to be herself again, had increased her rate of sailing more than one third since leaving San Diego. The crew ceased growling at her, and the officers hove the log every two hours with evident satisfaction. This was glorious sailing. A steady breeze; the light trade-wind clouds over our heads; the incomparable temperature of the Pacific,—neither hot nor cold; a clear sun every day, and clear moon and stars each night; and new constellations rising in the south, and the familiar ones sinking in the north, as we went on our course,—"nightly stemming toward the pole." Already we had sunk the north star and the Great Bear in the northern horizon, and all hands looked out sharp to the southward for the Magellan Clouds, which, each succeeding night, we expected to make. "The next time we see the north star," said one, "we shall be standing to the northward, the other side of the Horn." This was true enough, and no doubt it would be a welcome sight; for sailors say that in coming home from round Cape Horn, and the Cape of Good Hope, the north star is the first land you make.

These trades were the same that, in the passage out in the Pilgrim, lasted nearly all the way from Juan Fernandez to the line; blowing steadily on our starboard quarter for three weeks, without our starting a brace, or even brailing down the sky-sails. Though we had now the same wind, and were in the same latitude with the Pilgrim on her passage out, yet we were nearly twelve hundred miles to the westward of her course; for the captain, depending upon the strong south-west winds which prevail in high southern latitudes during the winter months, took the full advantage of the trades, and stood well to the westward, so far that we passed within two hundred miles of Ducie's Island.

It was this weather and sailing that brought to my mind a little incident that occurred on board the Pilgrim, while we were in the same latitude, and which from that time to this I never remember called to mind. We were going along at a great rate, dead before the wind, with studding-sails out on both sides, alow and aloft, on a dark night, just after midnight, and everything as still as the grave, except the washing of the water by the vessel's side; for, being before the wind, with a smooth sea, the little brig, covered with canvass, was doing great business, with very little noise. The other watch was below, and all our watch, except myself and the man at the wheel, were asleep under the lee of the boat. The second mate, who came out before the mast, and was always very *thick* with me, had been holding a yarn with me, and just gone aft to his place on the quarter-deck, and I had resumed my usual walk to and from the windlass-end, when, suddenly, we heard a loud scream coming from ahead, apparently directly from under the bows. The darkness, and complete stillness of the night, and the solitude of the ocean, gave to the sound a dreadful and almost supernatural effect. I stood perfectly still, and my heart beat a little quick. The sound woke up the rest of the watch, who stood looking at one another. "What, in the name of God, is that?" said the second mate, coming slowly forward. The first thought I had was, that it might be a boat, with the crew of some wrecked vessel, or perhaps the boat of some whale-ship, out over night, and we had run them down in the darkness. Another scream! but less loud than the first. This started us, and we ran forward, and looked over the bows, and over the sides, to leeward, but nothing was to be seen or heard. What was to be done? Call the captain, and heave the ship aback? Just at this moment, in crossing the forecastle, one of the men saw a light below, and looking down the scuttle, saw the watch all out of their berths, and afoul of one poor fellow, dragging him out of his berth, and shaking him, to wake him out of a nightmare. They had been waked out of their sleep, and as much alarmed at the scream as we were, and were hesitating whether to come on deck, when the second sound, coming directly from one of the berths, revealed the cause of the alarm. The fellow got a good shaking for the trouble he had given. We made a joke of the matter; and we could well laugh, for our minds were not a little relieved by its ricidulous termination.

We were now close upon the southern tropical line, and, with so fine a breeze, were daily leaving the sun behind us, and drawing nearer to Cape Horn, for which it behoved us to make every preparation. Our rigging was all examined and overhauled, and mended, or replaced with new, where it was necessary: new and strong bobstays fitted in the place of the chain ones, which were worn out; the sprit-sail yard and martingale guys and back-ropes set well taut; bran new fore and main braces rove; top-gallant sheets, and wheel-ropes, made of green hide, laid up in the form of rope, were stretched and fitted; and new top-sail clew-lines, &c., rove; new fore top-mast back-stays fitted; and other preparations made, in good season, that the ropes might have time to stretch and become limber before we got into cold weather.

Sunday, June 12th. Lat. 26° 04′ S., long. 116° 31′ W. We had now lost the regular trades, and had the winds variable, principally from the westward, and kept on, in a southerly course, sailing very nearly upon a meridian, and at the end of the week,—

Sunday, June 19, were in lat. 34° 15′ S., and long. 116° 38′ W.

CHAPTER THIRTY-ONE
*Bad Prospects . . . First Touch of
Cape Horn . . . Icebergs . . .
Temperance Ships . . . Lying-up . . .
Ice . . . Difficulty on Board . . .
Change of Course . . .
Straits of Magellan*

There began now to be a decided change in the appearance of things. The days became shorter and shorter; the sun running lower in its course each day, and giving less and less heat; and the nights so cold as to prevent our sleeping on deck; the Magellan Clouds in sight, of a clear night; the skies looking cold and angry; and, at times, a long, heavy, ugly sea, setting in from the southward, told us what we were coming to. Still, however, we had a fine, strong breeze, and kept on our way, under as much sail as our ship would bear. Toward the middle of the week, the wind hauled to the southward, which brought us upon a taut bowline, made the ship meet, nearly head-on, the heavy swell which rolled from that direction; and there was something not at all encouraging in the manner in which she met it. Being so deep and heavy, she wanted the buoyancy which should have carried her over the seas, and she dropped heavily into them, the water washing over the decks; and every now and then, when an unusually large sea met her fairly upon the bows, she struck it with a sound as dead and heavy as that with which a sledge-hammer falls upon the pile, and took the whole of it in upon the forecastle, and rising, carried it aft in the scuppers, washing the rigging off the pins, and carrying along with it everything which was loose on deck. She had been acting in this way all of our forenoon watch below; as we could tell by the washing of the water over our heads, and the heavy breaking of the seas against her bows, with a sound as though she were striking against a rock, only the thickness of the plank from our heads, as we lay in our berths, which are directly against the bows. At eight bells, the watch was called, and we came on deck, one hand going aft to take the wheel, and another going to the galley to get the *grub* for dinner. I stood on the forecastle, looking at the seas, which were rolling high, as far as the eye could reach, their tops white with foam, and the body of them of a deep indigo blue, reflecting the bright rays of the sun. Our ship rose slowly over a few of the largest of them, until one immense fellow came rolling on, threatening to cover her, and which I was sailor enough to know, by 'the feeling of her' under my feet, she would not rise over. I sprang upon the knight-heads, and seizing hold of the fore-stay with my hands, drew myself up upon it. My feet were just off the stanchion, when she struck fairly into the middle of the sea, and it washed her fore and aft, burying her in the water. As soon as she rose out of it, I looked aft, and everything forward of the main-mast, except the long-boat, which was griped and double-lashed down to the ring-bolts, was swept off clear. The galley, the pig-sty, the hen-coop, and a large sheep-pen which had been built upon the fore-hatch, were all gone, in the twinkling of an eye—leaving the deck as clean as a chin new-reaped—and not a stick left, to show where they had stood. In the scuppers floating about,—the wreck of the sheep-pen,—and half a dozen miserable sheep floating among them, wet through, and not a little frightened at the sudden change that had come upon them. As soon as the sea had washed by, all hands sprung up out of the forecastle to see what had become of the ship; and in a few moments the cook and Old Bill crawled out from under the galley, where they had been lying in the water, nearly smothered, with the galley over them. Fortunately, it rested against the bulwarks, or it would have broken some of their bones. When the water ran off, we picked the sheep up, and put them in the long-boat, got the galley back in its place, and set things a little to rights; but, had not our ship had uncommonly high bulwarks and rail, everything must have been washed overboard, not excepting Old Bill and the cook. Bill had been standing at the galley-door, with the kid of beef in his hand for the forecastle mess, when, away he went, kid, beef, and all. He held on to the kid till the last, like a good fellow, but the beef was gone, and when the water had run off, we saw it lying high and dry, like a rock at low tide—nothing could hurt *that*. We took the loss of our beef very easily, consoling ourselves with the recollection that the cabin had more to lose than we; and chuckled not a little at seeing the remains of the chicken-pie and pancakes floating in the scuppers. "This will never do!" was what some said, and every one felt. Here we were, not yet within a thousand miles of the latitude of Cape Horn, and our decks swept by a sea, not one half so high as we must expect to find there. Some blamed the captain for loading his ship so deep, when he knew what he must expect; while others said that the wind was always southwest, off the Cape, in the winter; and that running before it, we should not mind the seas so much. When we got down into the forecastle, Old Bill, who was somewhat of a croaker,—having met with a great many accidents at sea—said that if that was the way she was going to act, we might as well make our wills, and balance the books at once, and put on a clean shirt. "'Vast there, you bloody old owl! you're always hanging out blue lights! You're frightened by the ducking you got in the scuppers, and can't take a joke! What's the use in being always on the look-out for Davy Jones?"

"Stand by!" says another, "and we'll get an afternoon watch below, by this scrape;" but in this they were disappointed, for at two bells, all hands were called and set to work, getting lashings upon everything on deck; and the captain talked of sending down the long top-gallant masts; but, as the sea went down toward night, and the wind hauled abeam, we left them standing, and set the studding-sails.

The next day, all hands were turned-to upon unbending the old sails, and getting up the new ones; for a ship, unlike people on shore, puts on her best suit in bad weather. The old sails were sent down, and three new top-sails, and new fore and main courses, jib and fore topmast stay-sail, which were made on the coast, and never had been used, were bent, with a complete set of new earings, robands and reef-points; and reef-tackles were rove to the courses, and spilling-lines to the top-sails. These, with new braces and clewlines, fore and aft, gave us a good suit of running rigging.

The wind continued westerly, and the weather and sea less rough since the day on which we shipped the heavy sea, and we were making great progress under studding-sails, with our light sails all set, keeping a little to the eastward of south; for the captain, depending upon westerly winds off the Cape, had kept so far to the westward, that, though we were within about five hundred miles of the latitude of Cape Horn, we were westerly seventeen hundred miles (more than half the distance across the Atlantic) to the westward of it. Through the rest of the week, we continued on with a fair wind, gradually, as we got more to the southward, keeping a more easterly course, and bringing the wind on our larboard quarter, until—

Sunday, June 26th; when, having a fine, clear day, the captain got a lunar observation, as well his meridian altitude, which made us in lat. 47° 50′ S., long. 113° 49′ W.; Cape Horn bearing, according to my calculation, E. S. E. 1/2 E., and distant eighteen hundred miles.

Monday, June 27th. During the first part of this day, the wind continued fair, and, as we were going before it, did not feel very cold, so that we kept at work on deck, in our common clothes and round jackets. Our watch had an afternoon watch below, for the first time since leaving San Diego, and having inquired of the third mate what the latitude was at noon, and made our usual guesses as to the time she would need, to be up with the Horn, we turned-in, for a nap. We were sleeping away 'at the rate of knots,' when three knocks on the scuttle, and "All hands, ahoy!" started us from our berths. What could be the matter? It did not appear to be blowing hard, and looking up through the scuttle, we could see that it was a clear day, overhead; yet the watch were taking in sail. We thought there must be a sail in sight, and that we were about to heave-to and speak her; and were just congratulating ourselves upon it—for we had seen neither sail nor land since we left port—when we heard the mate's voice on deck, (he turned-in 'all standing', and was always on deck the moment he was called,) singing out to the men who were taking in the studding-sails, and asking where his watch were. We did not wait for a second call, but tumbled up the ladder; and there, on the starboard bow, was a bank of mist, covering sea and sky, and driving directly for us. I had seen the same before, in my passage round in the Pilgrim, and knew what it meant, and that there was no time to be lost. We had nothing on but thin clothes, yet there was not a moment to spare, and at it we went.

The boys of the other watch were in the tops, taking in the top-gallant studding-sails, and the lower and top-mast studding-sails were coming down by the run. For five or ten minutes it was nothing but "haul down the clew up," until we got all the studding-sails in, and the royals, flying-jib, and mizen top-gallant sail furled, and the ship kept off a little, to take the squall. The fore and main top-gallant sails were still on her, for the 'old man' did not mean to be frightened in in broad daylight, and was determined to carry sail till the last minute. We all stood waiting for its coming, when the first blast showed us that it was not to be trifled with. Rain, sleet, snow, and wind, enough to take our breath from us, and make the toughest turn his back to windward! The ship lay nearly over upon her beam-ends; the spars and rigging snapped and cracked; and her top-gallant masts bent like whip-sticks. "Clew up the fore and main top-gallant sails!" shouted the captain, and all hands sprang to the clewlines. The decks were standing nearly at an angle of forty-five degrees, and the ship going like a mad steed through the water, the whole forward part of her in a smother of foam. The halyards were let go and the yard clewed down, and the sheets started, and in a few minutes the sails smothered and kept in by clewlines and buntlines.—"Furl 'em, sir?" asked the mate. —"Let go the top-sail halyards, fore and aft!" shouted the captain, in answer, at the top of his voice. Down came the top-sail yards, the reef-tackles were manned and hauled out, and we climbed up to windward, and sprang into the weather rigging. The violence of the wind, and the hail and sleet, driving nearly horizontally across the ocean, seemed actually to pin us down to the rigging. It was hard work making head against them. One after another, we got out upon the yards; and here we had work to do; for our new sails, which had hardly been bent long enough to get the starch out of them, were as stiff as boards, and the new earings and reef-points, stiffened with the sleet, knotted like pieces of iron wire. Having only our round jackets and straw hats on, we were soon wet through, and it was every moment growing colder. Our hands were soon stiffened and numbed, which, added to the stiffness of everything else, kept us a good while on the yard. After we had got the sail hauled upon the yard, we had to wait a long time for the weather earing to be passed; but there was no fault to be found, for French John was at the earing, and a better sailor never laid out on a yard; so we leaned over the yard, and beat our hands upon the sail, to keep them from freezing. At length the word came—"Haul out to leeward,"—and we seized the reef-points and hauled the band taut for the lee earing. "Taut band—Knot away," and we got the first reef fast, and were just going to lay down, when—"Two reefs—two reefs!" shouted the mate, and we had a second reef to take, in the same way. When this was fast, we laid down on deck, manned the halyards to leeward, nearly up to our knees in water, set the top-sail, and then laid aloft on the main top-sail yard, and reefed that sail in the same manner; for by leaving two hands on the coast, and by the sickness of another, we were a good deal reduced in numbers, and, to make it worse, the carpenter, only two days before, cut his leg with an axe, so that he could not go aloft. This weakened us so that we could not well manage more than one top-sail at a time, in such weather as this, and, of course, our labor was doubled. From the main top-sail yard, we went upon the main yard, and took a reef in the main-sail. No sooner had we got on deck, than—"Lay aloft there, mizen-top-men, and close-reef the mizen top-sail!" This called me; and being nearest to the rigging, I got first aloft, and out to the weather earing. English Ben was on the yard just after me, and took the lee earing, and the rest of our gang were soon on the yard, and began to fist the sail, when the mate considerately sent up the cook and steward, to help us, but he never let an able seaman go upon the yard. I could now account for the long time it took to pass the other earings, for, to do my best, with a strong hand to help me at the dog's ear, I could not get it passed until I heard them beginning to complain in the bunt. One reef after another we took in, until the sail was close-reefed, when we lay down and hoisted away at the halyards. In the mean time, the jib had been furled and the stay-sail set, and the ship, under her reduced sail, had got more upright and was under management; but the two top-gallant sails were still hanging in the buntlines, and slatting and jerking as though they would take the masts out of her. We gave a look aloft, and knew that our work was not done yet; and sure enough, no sooner did the mate see that we were on deck, than—"Lay aloft there, four of you, and furl the top-gallant sails!" This called me again, and two of us went aloft, up the fore rigging, and two more up the main, upon the top-gallant yards. The shrouds were now iced over, the sleet having formed a crust or cake round all the standing rigging, and on the weather side of the masts and yards. When we got upon the yard, my hands were so numb that I could not have cast off the knot of the gasket to have saved my life. We both lay over the yard for a few seconds, beating our hands upon the sail, until we started the blood into our fingers' ends, and at the next moment our hands were in a burning heat. My companion on the yard was a lad, who came out in the ship a weak, puny boy, from one of the Boston schools,—'no larger than a sprit-sail sheet knot', nor 'heavier than a paper of lamp-black', and 'not strong enough to haul a shad off a gridiron', but who was now 'as long as a spare top-mast, strong enough to knock down an ox, and hearty enough to eat him'. We fisted the sail together, and after six or eight minutes of hard hauling and pulling and beating down the sail, which was as stiff as sheet iron, we managed to get it furled; and snugly furled it must be, for we knew the mate well enough to be certain that if it got adrift again, we should be called up from our watch below, at any hour of the night, to furl it.

I had been on the look-out for a moment to jump below and clap on a thick jacket and south-wester; but when we got on deck we found that eight bells had been struck, and the other watch gone below, so that there were two hours of dog watch for us, and a plenty of work to do. It had now set in for a steady gale from the south-west; but we were not yet far enough to the southward to make a fair wind of it, for we must give Terra del Fuego a wide berth. The decks were covered with snow, and there was a constant driving of sleet. In fact, Cape Horn had set in with good earnest. In the midst of all this, and before it became dark, we had all the studding-sails to make up and stow away, and then to lay aloft and rig in all the booms, fore and aft, and coil away the tacks, sheets, and halyards. This was pretty tough work for four or five hands, in the face of a gale which almost took us off the yards, and with ropes so stiff with ice that it was almost impossible to bend them. I was nearly half an hour out on the end of the fore yard, trying to coil away and stop down the top-mast studding-sail tack and lower halyards. It was after dark when we got through, and we were not a little pleased to hear four bells struck, which sent us below for two hours, and gave us each a pot of hot tea with our cold beef and bread, and, what was better yet, a suit of thick, dry clothing, fitted for the weather, in place of our thin clothes, which were wet through and now frozen stiff.

This sudden turn, for which we were so little prepared, was as unacceptable to me as to any of the rest; for I had been troubled for several days with a slight tooth-ache, and this cold weather, and wetting and freezing, were not the best things in the world for it. I soon found that it was getting strong hold, and running over all parts of my face; and before the watch was out I went aft to the mate, who had charge of the medicine-chest, to get something for it. But the chest showed

Drawing by Robert A. Weinstein

Wednesday, Nov. 5th—"Off Cape Horn, at night violent storm. Wind S.W."

like the end of a long voyage, for there was no oil of cloves or creo-
sote, and only a few drops of laudanum, which must be saved for any
sudden emergency; so I had only, as the saying is, to grin and bear it.

When we went on deck at eight bells, it had stopped snowing, and
there were a few stars out, but the clouds were still black, and it was
blowing a steady gale. Just before midnight, I went aloft and sent
down the mizen royal yard, and had the good luck to do it to the satisfaction of the mate, who said it was done "out of hand and ship-
shape." I set this down in my tables, for to send a royal yard down well
at sea, by night, and in a gale of wind, is somewhat of a feather in the
cap of a beginner. The next four hours below were but little relief to
me, for I lay awake in my berth, the whole time, from the pain in my
face, and heard every bell strike, and, at four o'clock, turned out with
the watch, feeling little spirit for the hard duties of the day. Bad
weather and hard work at sea can be borne up against very well, if one
only has spirit and health; but there is nothing brings a man down, at
such a time, like bodily pain and want of sleep. There was, however,
too much to do to allow time to think; for the gale of yesterday, and
the heavy seas we met with a few days before, while we had yet ten
degrees more southing to make, had convinced the captain that we
had something before us which was not to be trifled with, and orders
were given to send down the long top-gallant masts. The top-gallant
and royal yards were accordingly struck, the flying jib-boom rigged
in, and the top-gallant masts sent down on deck, and all lashed together by the side of the long-boat. The rigging was then sent down
and coiled away below, and everything made snug aloft. There was
not a sailor in the ship who was not rejoiced to see these sticks come
down; for, so long as the yards were aloft, on the least sign of a lull,
the top-gallant sails were loosed, and then we had to furl them again
in a snow-squall, and *shin* up and down single ropes caked with ice,
and send royal yards down in the teeth of a gale coming right from the
south pole. It was an interesting sight, too, to see our noble ship, dismantled of all her top-hamper of long tapering masts and yards, and
boom pointed with spear-head, which ornamented her in port; and
all that canvass, which a few days before had covered her like a cloud,
from the truck to the water's edge, spreading far out beyond her hull
on either side, now gone; and she, stripped and dismantled like a
strong wrestler for the fight. It corresponded, too, with the desolate
character of her situation;—alone, as she was, battling with storms,
wind, and ice, at this extremity of the globe, and in almost constant
night.

Friday, July 1st. We were now nearly up to the latitude of Cape
Horn, and having over forty degrees of easting to make, we squared

away the yards before a strong westerly gale, shook a reef out of the fore top-sail, and stood on our way, east-by-south, with the prospect of being up with the Cape in a week or ten days. As for myself, I had had no sleep for forty-eight hours; and the want of rest, together with constant wet and cold, had increased the swelling, so that my face was nearly as large as two, and I found it impossible to get my mouth open wide enough to eat. In this state, the steward applied to the captain for some rice to boil for me, but he only got a—"No! d— you! Tell him to eat salt junk and hard bread, like the rest of them." For this, of course, I was much obliged to him, and in truth it was just what I expected. However, I did not starve, for the mate, who was a man as well as a sailor, and had always been a good friend to me, smuggled a pan of rice into the galley, and told the cook to boil it for me, and not let the 'old man' see it. Had it been fine weather, or in port, I should have gone below and lain by until my face got well; but in such weather as this, and short-handed as we were, it was not for me to desert my post; so I kept on deck, and stood my watch and did my duty as well as I could.

Saturday, July 2d. This day the sun rose fair, but it ran too low in the heavens to give any heat, or thaw out our sails and rigging; yet the sight of it was pleasant; and we had a steady 'reef-top-sail breeze' from the westward. The atmosphere, which had previously been clear and cold, for the last few hours grew damp, and had a disagreeable, wet chilliness in it; and the man who came from the wheel said he heard the captain tell 'the passenger' that the thermometer had fallen several degrees since morning, which he could not account for in any other way than by supposing that there must be ice near us; though such a thing had never been heard of in this latitude, at this season of the year. At twelve o'clock we went below, and had just got through dinner, when the cook put his head down the scuttle and told us to come on deck and see the finest sight that we had ever seen. "Where away, cook?" asked the first man who was up. "On the larboard bow." And there lay, floating in the ocean, several miles off, an immense, irregular mass, its top and points covered with snow, and its centre of a deep indigo color. This was an iceberg, and of the largest size, as one of our men said who had been in the Northern ocean. As far as the eye could reach, the sea in every direction was of a deep blue color, the waves running high and fresh, and sparkling in the light, and in the midst lay this immense mountain-island, its cavities and valleys thrown into deep shade, and its points and pinnacles glittering in the sun. All hands were soon on deck, looking at it, and admiring in various ways its beauty and grandeur. But no description can give any idea of the strangeness, splendor, and, really, the sublimity, of the sight. Its immense size;—for it must have been from two to three miles in circumference, and several hundred feet in height;—its slow motion, as its base rose and sank in the water, and its high points nodded against the clouds; the dashing of the waves upon it, which, breaking high with foam, lined its base with a white crust; and the thundering sound of the cracking of the mass, and the breaking and tumbling down of huge pieces; together with its nearness and approach, which added a slight element of fear,—all combined to give to it the character of true sublimity. The main body of the mass was, as I have said, of an indigo color, its base crusted with frozen foam; and as it grew thin and transparent toward the edges and top, its color shaded off from a deep blue to the whiteness of snow. It seemed to be drifting slowly toward the north, so that we kept away and avoided it. It was in sight all the afternoon; and when we got to leeward of it, the wind died away, so that we lay-to quite near it for a greater part of the night. Unfortunately, there was no moon, but it was a clear night, and we could plainly mark the long, regular heaving of the stupendous mass, as its edges moved slowly against the stars. Several times in our watch loud cracks were heard, which sounded as though they must have run through the whole length of the iceberg, and several pieces fell down with a thundering crash, plunging heavily into the sea. Toward morning, a strong breeze sprang up, and we filled away, and left it astern, and at daylight it was out of sight. The next day, which was

Sunday, July 3d, the breeze continued strong, the air exceedingly chilly, and the thermometer low. In the course of the day we saw several icebergs, of different sizes, but none so near as the one which we saw the day before. Some of them, as well as we could judge, at the distance at which we were, must have been as large as that, if not larger. At noon we were in latitude 55° 12′ south, and supposed longitude 89° 5′ west. Toward night the wind hauled to the southward, and headed us off our course a little, and blew a tremendous gale; but this we did not mind, as there was no rain nor snow, and we were already under close sail.

Monday, July 4th. This was 'independent day' in Boston. What firing of guns, and ringing of bells, and rejoicing of all sorts, in every part of our country! The ladies (who have not gone down to Nahant, for a breath of cool air, and sight of the ocean) walking the streets with parasols over their heads, and the dandies in their white pantaloons and silk stockings! What quantities of ice-cream have been eaten, and what quantities of ice brought into the city from a distance, and sold out by the lump and the pound! The smallest of the islands which we saw to-day would have made the fortune of poor Jack, if he had had it in Boston; and I dare say he would have had no objection to being there with it. This, to be sure, was no place to keep the fourth of July. To keep ourselves warm, and the ship out of the ice, was as much as we could do. Yet no one forgot the day; and many were the wishes, and conjectures, and comparisons, both serious and ludicrous, which were made among all hands. The sun shone bright as long as it was up, only that a scud of black clouds was ever and anon driving across it. At noon we were in lat. 54° 27' S., and long. 85° 5' W., having made a good deal of easting, but having lost in our latitude by the heading of the wind. Between daylight and dark—that is, between nine o'clock and three—we saw thirty-four ice islands, of various sizes; some no bigger than the hull of our vessel, and others apparently nearly as large as the one that we first saw; though, as we went on, the islands became smaller and more numerous; and, at sundown of this day, a man at the mast-head saw large fields of floating ice, called 'field-ice,' at the south-east. This kind of ice is much more dangerous than the large islands, for those can be seen at a distance, and kept away from; but the field-ice, floating in great quantities, and covering the ocean for miles and miles, in pieces of every size—from small lumps to large, flat, and broken cakes, with here and there an island rising twenty and thirty feet, and as large as the ship's hull;—this, it is very difficult to shear clear of. A constant look-out was necessary; for any of these pieces, coming with the heave of the sea, were large enough to have knocked a hole in the ship, and that would have been the end of us; for no boat (even if we could have got one out) could have lived in such a sea; and no man could have lived in a boat in such weather. To make our condition still worse, the wind came out due east, just after sundown, and blew a gale dead ahead, with hail and sleet, and a thick fog, so that we could not see half the length of the ship. Our chief reliance, the prevailing westerly gales, was thus cut off; and here we were, nearly seven hundred miles to the westward of the Cape, with a gale dead from the eastward, and the weather so thick that we could not see the ice with which we were surrounded, until it was directly under our bows. At four P. M. (it was then quite dark) all hands were called, and sent aloft in a violent squall of hail and rain, to take in sail. We had now all got on our 'Cape Horn rig'—thick boots, sou'westers coming down over our necks and ears, thick trousers and jackets, and some with oil-cloth suits over all. Mittens, too, we wore on deck, but it would not do to go aloft with them on, for it was impossible to work with them, and, being wet and stiff, they might let a man slip overboard, for all the hold he could get upon a rope; so, we were obliged to work with bare hands, which, as well as our faces, were often cut with the hail-stones, which fell thick and large. Our ship was now all cased with ice,—hull, spars, and standing rigging;—and the running rigging so stiff that we could hardly bend it so as to belay it, or, still worse, take a knot with it; and the sails nearly as stiff as sheet iron. One at a time, (for it was a long piece of work and required many hands,) we furled the courses, mizen top-sail, and a fore top-mast stay-sail, and close-reefed the fore and main top-sails, and hove the ship to under the fore, with the main hauled up by the clewlines and buntlines, and ready to be sheeted home, if we found it necessary to make sail to get to windward of an island. A regular look-out was then set, and kept by each watch in turn, until the morning. It was a tedious and anxious night. It blew hard the whole time, and there was an almost constant driving of either rain, hail, or snow. In addition to this, it was 'as thick as muck', and the ice was all about us. The captain was on deck nearly the whole night, and kept the cook in the galley, with a roaring fire, to make coffee for him, which he took every few hours, and once or twice gave a little to his officers; but not a drop of anything was there for poor Jack. The captain, who sleeps all the daytime, and comes and goes at night as he chooses, can have his brandy and water in the cabin, and his hot coffee at the galley; while Jack, who has to stand through everything, and work in wet and cold, can have nothing to wet his lips or warm his stomach. This was a "temperance ship," and, like too many such ships, the temperance was all in the forecastle. The sailor, who only takes his one glass as it is dealt out to him, is in danger of being drunk; while the captain, who has all under his hand, and can drink as much as he chooses, and upon whose self-possession and cool judgment the lives of all depend, may be trusted with any amount, to drink at his will. Sailors will never be convinced that rum is a dangerous thing, by taking it away from them, and giving it to the officers; nor that, that temperance is their friend, which takes from them what they have always had, and gives them nothing in the place of it. By seeing it allowed to their officers, they will not be convinced that it is taken from them for their good; and by receiving nothing in its place, they will not believe that it is done in kindness. On the contrary, many of them look upon the change as a new instrument of tyranny. Not that they prefer rum. I never knew a sailor, in my life, who would not prefer a pot of hot coffee or chocolate, in a cold night, to all the rum afloat. They all say that rum only warms them for a time; yet, if they can get nothing better, they will miss what they have lost. The momentary warmth and glow from drinking it; the break and change which is made in a long, dreary watch by the mere calling all hands aft and serving of it out; and the merely having some event to look forward to, and to talk about; give it an importance and a use which no one can appreciate who has not stood his watch before the mast. On my passage round Cape Horn before, the vessel that I was in

Drawing by Robert A. Weinstein

we furled the courses, mizzen topsail . . .

and close reefed the fore and main topsails

was not under temperance articles, and grog was served out every middle and morning watch, and after every reefing of top-sails; and though I had never drank rum before, and never intend to again, I took my allowance then at the capstan, as the rest did, merely for the momentary warmth it gave the system, and the change in our feelings and aspect of our duties on the watch. At the same time, as I have stated, there was not a man on board who would not have pitched the rum to the dogs, (I have heard them say so, a dozen times) for a pot of coffee or chocolate; or even for our common beverage—'water bewitched, and tea begrudged', as it was.* The temperance reform is the best thing that ever was undertaken for the sailor; but when the grog is taken from him, he ought to have something in its place. As it is now, in most vessels, it is a mere saving to the owners; and this accounts for the sudden increase of temperance ships, which surprised even the best friends of the cause. If every merchant, when he struck grog from the list of the expenses of his ship, had been obliged to substitute as much coffee, or chocolate, as would give each man a pot-full when he came off the top-sail yard, on a stormy night;—I fear Jack might have gone to ruin on the old road.†

But this is not doubling Cape Horn. Eight hours of the night, our watch was on deck, and during the whole of that time we kept a bright look-out: one man on each bow, another in the bunt of the fore yard, the third mate on the scuttle, one on each quarter, and a man always standing by the wheel. The chief mate was everywhere, and commanded the ship when the captain was below. When a large piece of ice was seen in our way, or drifting near us, the word was passed along, and the ship's head turned one way and another; and sometimes the yards squared or braced up. There was little else to do than to look out; and we had the sharpest eyes in the ship on the forecastle. The only variety was the monotonous voice of the look-out forward—"An-

---

*The proportions of ingredients of the tea that was made for us, (and ours, as I have before stated, was a favorable specimen of American merchantmen) were, a pint of tea, and a pint and a half of molasses, to about three gallons of water. These are all boiled down together in the "coppers," and before serving it out, the mess is stirred up with a stick, so as to give each man his fair share of sweetening and tea-leaves. The tea for the cabin is, of course, made in the usual way, in a tea-pot, and drank with sugar.

†I do not wish these remarks, so far as they relate to the saving of expense in the outfit, to be applied to the owners of our ship, for she was supplied with an abundance of stores, of the best kind that are given to seamen; though the dispensing of them is necessarily left to the captain. Indeed, so high was the reputation of 'the employ' among men and officers, for the character and outfit of their vessels, and for their liberality in conducting their voyages, that when it was known that they had a ship fitting out for a long voyage, and that hands were to be shipped at a certain time,—a half hour before the time, as one of the crew told me, numbers of sailors were steering down the wharf, hopping over the barrels, like flocks of sheep.

The Ship ALERT *off Cape Horn*

other island!"—"Ice ahead!"—"Ice on the lee bow!"—"Hard up the helm!"—"Keep her off a little!"—"Stead-y!"

In the meantime, the wet and cold had brought my face into such a state that I could neither eat nor sleep; and though I stood it out all night, yet, when it became light, I was in such a state, that all hands told me I must go below, and lie-by for a day or two, or I should be laid up for a long time, and perhaps have the lock-jaw. When the watch was changed I went into the steerage, and took off my hat and comforter, and showed my face to the mate, who told me to go below at once, and stay in my berth until the swelling went down, and gave the cook orders to make a poultice for me, and said he would speak to the captain.

I went below and turned-in, covering myself over with blankets and jackets, and lay in my berth nearly twenty-four hours, half asleep and half awake, stupid, from the dull pain. I heard the watch called, and the men going up and down, and sometimes a noise on deck, and a cry of "ice," but I gave little attention to anything. At the end of twenty-four hours the pain went down, and I had a long sleep, which brought me back to my proper state; yet my face was so swollen and tender, that I was obliged to keep to my berth for two or three days longer. During the two days I had been below, the weather was much the same that it had been, head winds, and snow and rain; or, if the wind came fair, too foggy, and the ice too thick, to run. At the end of the third day the ice was very thick; a complete fog-bank covered the ship. It blew a tremendous gale from the eastward, with sleet and snow, and there was every promise of a dangerous and fatiguing night, At dark, the captain called all hands aft, and told them that not a man was to leave the deck that night; that the ship was in the greatest danger; any cake of ice might knock a hole in her, or she might run on an island and go to pieces. No one could tell whether she would be a ship the next morning. The look-outs were then set, and every man was put in his station. When I heard what was the state of things, I began to put on my clothes to stand it out with the rest of them, when the mate came below, and looking at my face, ordered me back to my berth, saying that if we went down, we should all go down together, but if I went on deck I might lay myself up for life. This was the first word I had heard from aft; for the captain had done nothing, nor inquired how I was, since I went below.

In obedience to the mate's orders, I went back to my berth; but a more miserable night I never wish to spend. I never felt the curse of sickness so keenly in my life. If I could only have been on deck with the rest, where something was to be done, and seen, and heard; where there were fellow-beings for companions in duty and danger—but to be cooped up alone in a black hole, in equal danger, but without the power to do, was the hardest trial. Several times, in the course of the night, I got up, determined to go on deck; but the silence which showed that there was nothing doing, and the consciousness that I might make myself seriously ill, for nothing, kept me back. It was not easy to sleep, lying, as I did, with my head directly against the bows, which might be dashed in by an island of ice, brought down by the very next sea that struck her. This was the only time I had been ill since I left Boston, and it was the worst time it could have happened. I felt almost willing to bear the plagues of Egypt for the rest of the voyage, if I could but be well and strong for that one night. Yet it was a dreadful night for those on deck. A watch of eighteen hours, with wet, and cold, and constant anxiety, nearly wore them out; and when they came below at nine o'clock for breakfast, they almost dropped asleep on their chests, and some of them were so stiff that they could with difficulty sit down. Not a drop of anything had been given them during the whole time, (though the captain, as on the night that I was on deck, had his coffee every four hours,) except that the mate stole a potfull, and gave it to the men to drink behind the galley, while he kept a look-out for the captain. Every man had his station, and was not allowed to leave it; and nothing happened to break the monotony of the night, except once setting the main top-sails to run clear of a large island to leeward, which they were drifting fast upon. Some of the boys got so sleepy and stupified, that they actually fell asleep at their posts; and the young third mate, whose station was the exposed one of standing on the fore scuttle, was so stiff, when he was relieved, that he could not bend his knees to get down. By a constant look-out, and a quick shifting of the helm, as the islands and pieces came in sight, the ship went clear of everything but a few small pieces, though daylight showed the ocean covered for miles. At daybreak it fell a dead calm, and with the sun, the fog cleared a little, and a breeze sprung up from the westward, which soon grew into a gale. They had now a fair wind, daylight, and comparatively clear weather; yet, to the surprise of every one, the ship continued hove-to. Why does not he run? What is the captain about? was asked by every one; and from questions, it soon grew into complaints and murmurings. When the daylight was so short, it was too bad to lose it, and a fair wind, too, which every one had been praying for. As hour followed hour, and the captain showed no sign of making sail, the crew became impatient, and there was a good deal of talking and consultation together, on the forecastle. They had been beaten out with the exposure and hardship, and impatient to get out of it, and this unaccountable delay was more than they could bear in quietness, in their excited and restless state. Some said that the captain was frightened,—completely cowed, by the dangers and difficulties that surrounded us, and was afraid to make sail; while others said that in his anxiety and suspense he had made a free use of brandy and opium, and was unfit for his duty. The carpenter, who was an intelligent man, and a thorough seaman, and had great influence with the crew, came down into the forecastle, and tried to induce the crew to go aft and ask the captain why he did not run, or request him, in the name of all hands, to make sail. This appeared to be a very reasonable request, and the crew agreed that if he did not make sail before noon, they would go aft. Noon came, and no sail was made. A consultation was held again, and it was proposed to take the ship from the captain and give the command of her to the mate, who had been heard to say that, if he could have his way, the ship would have been half the distance to the Cape before night,—ice or no ice. And so irritated and impatient had the crew become, that even this proposition, which was open mutiny, punishable with state prison, was entertained, and the carpenter went to his berth, leaving it tacitly understood that something serious would be done, if things remained as they were many hours longer. When the carpenter left, we talked it all over, and I gave my advice strongly against it. Another of the men, too, who had known something of the kind attempted in another ship by a crew who were dissatisfied with their captain, and which was followed with serious consequences, was opposed to it. Ben Stimson, who soon came down, joined us, and we determined to have nothing to do with it. By these means, they were soon induced to give it up, for the present, though they said they would not lie where they were much longer without knowing the reason.

The affair remained in this state until four o'clock, when orders came forward for all hands to come aft upon the quarter-deck. In about ten minutes they came forward again, and the whole affair had been blown. The carpenter, very prematurely, and without any authority from the crew, had sounded the mate as to whether he would take command of the ship, and intimated an intention to displace the captain; and the mate, as in duty bound, had told the whole to the captain, who immediately sent for all hands aft. Instead of violent measures, or, at least, an outbreak of quarter-deck bravado, threats, and abuse, which they had every reason to expect, a sense of common danger and common suffering seemed to have tamed his spirit, and begotten something like a humane fellow-feeling; for he received the crew in a manner quiet, and even almost kind. He told them what he had heard, and said that he did not believe that they would try to do any such thing as was intimated; that they had always been good men,—obedient, and knew their duty, and he had no fault to find with them; and asked them what they had to complain of—said that no one could say that he was slow to carry sail, (which was true enough;) and that, as soon as he thought it was safe and proper, he should make sail. He added a few words about their duty in their present situation, and sent them forward, saying that he should take no further notice of the matter; but, at the same time, told the carpenter to recollect whose power he was in, and that if he heard another word from him he would have cause to remember him to the day of his death.

This language of the captain had a very good effect upon the crew, and they returned quietly to their duty.

For two days more the wind blew from the southward and eastward; or in the short intervals when it was fair, the ice was too thick to run; yet the weather was not so dreadfully bad, and the crew had watch and watch. I still remained in my berth, fast recovering, yet still not well enough to go safely on deck. And I should have been perfectly useless; for, from having eaten nothing for nearly a week, except a little rice which I forced into my mouth the last day or two, I was as weak as an infant. To be sick in a forecastle is miserable business. It is the worst part of a dog's life; especially in bad weather. The forecastle, shut up tight to keep out the water and cold air;—the watch either on deck, or asleep in their berths;—no one to speak to;—the pale light of the single lamp, swinging to and fro from the beam, so dim that one can scarcely see, much less read by it;—the water dropping from the beams and carlines, and running down the sides; and the forecastle so wet, and dark, and cheerless, and so lumbered up with chests and wet clothes, that sitting up is worse than lying in the berth! These are some of the evils. Fortunately, I needed no help from any one, and no medicine; and if I had needed help, I don't know where I should have found it. Sailors are willing enough, but it is true, as is often said—No one ships for nurse on board a vessel. Our merchant ships are always under-manned, and if one man is lost by sickness, they cannot spare another to take care of him. A sailor is always presumed to be well, and if he's sick, he's a poor dog. One has to stand his wheel, and another his look-out, and the sooner he gets on deck again, the better.

Accordingly, as soon as I could possibly go back to my duty, I put on my thick clothes and boots and sou'wester, and made my appearance on deck. Though I had been but a few days below, yet everything looked strangely enough. The ship was cased in ice,—decks, sides, masts, yards, and rigging. Two close-reefed top-sails were all the sail she had on, and every sail and rope was frozen so stiff in its place, that it seemed as though it would be impossible to start anything. Reduced, too, to her top-masts, she had altogether a most forlorn and crippled appearance. The sun had come up brightly; the snow was swept off the decks, and ashes thrown upon them, so that we could walk, for they had been as slippery as glass. It was, of course, too cold to carry on any ship's work, and we had only to walk the deck and keep ourselves warm. The wind was still ahead, and the whole ocean, to the eastward, covered with islands and field-ice. At four bells the order was given to square away the yards; and the man who came from the helm said that the captain had kept her off to N. N. E. What could this mean? Some said that he was going to put into Valparaiso, and winter, and others that he was going to run out of the ice and cross the Pacific, and go home round the Cape of Good Hope. Soon, however, it leaked out, and we found that we were running for the straits of Magellan. The news soon spread through the ship, and all tongues were at work, talking about it. No one on board had been through the straits, but I had in my chest an account of the passage of the ship A. J. Donelson, of New York, through those straits, a few years before. The account was given by the captain, and the representation was as favorable as possible. It was soon read by every one on board, and various opinions pronounced. The determination of our captain had at least this good effect; it gave every one something to think and talk about, made a break in our life, and diverted our minds from the monotonous dreariness of the prospect before us. Having made a fair wind of it, we were going off at a good rate, and leaving the thickest of the ice behind us. This, at least, was something.

Having been long enough below to get my hands well warmed and softened, the first handling of the ropes was rather tough; but a few days hardened them, and as soon as I got my mouth open wide enough to take in a piece of salt beef and hard bread, I was all right again.

Sunday, July 10th. Lat. 54° 10', lon. 79° 07'. This was our position at noon. The sun was out bright; the ice was all left behind, and things had quite a cheering appearance. We brought our wet pea-jackets and trousers on deck, and hung them up in the rigging, that the breeze and the few hours of sun might dry them a little; and, by the permission of the cook, the galley was nearly filled with stockings and mittens, hung round to be dried. Boots, too, were brought up; and having got a little tar and slush from below, we gave them a thick coat. After dinner, all hands were turned-to, to get the anchors over the bows, bend on the chains, &c. The fish-tackle was got up, fish-davit rigged out, and after two or three hours of hard and cold work, both anchors were ready for instant use, a couple of kedges got up, a hawser coiled away upon the fore-hatch, and the deep-sea-lead-line overhauled and got ready. Our spirits returned with having something to do; and when the tackle was manned to bowse the anchor home, notwithstanding the desolation of the scene, we struck up "Cheerily ho!" in full chorus. This pleased the mate, who rubbed his hands and cried out—"That's right, my boys; never say die! That sounds like the old crew!" and the captain came up, on hearing the song, and said to the passenger, within hearing of the man at the wheel,—"That sounds like a lively crew. They'll have their song so long as there're enough left for a chorus!"

This preparation of the cable and anchors was for the passage of the straits; for, being very crooked, and with a variety of currents, it is necessary to come frequently to anchor. This was not, by any means, a pleasant prospect, for, of all the work that a sailor is called upon to do in cold weather, there is none so bad as working the ground-tackle. The heavy chain cables to be hauled and pulled about decks with bare hands; wet hawsers, slip-ropes, and buoy-ropes to be hauled aboard, dripping in water, which is running up your sleeves, and freezing; clearing hawse under the bows; getting under weigh and coming-to, at all hours of the night and day, and a constant look-out for rocks and sands and turns of tides;—these are some of the disagreeables of such a navigation to a common sailor. Fair or foul, he wants to have nothing to do with the ground-tackle between port and port. One of our hands, too, had unluckily fallen upon a half of an old newspaper which contained an account of the passage, through the straits, of a Boston brig, called, I think, the Peruvian, in which she lost every cable and anchor she had, got aground twice, and arrived at Valparaiso in distress. This was set off against the account of the A. J. Donelson, and led us to look forward with less confidence to the passage, especially as no one on board had ever been through, and the captain had no very perfect charts. However, we were spared any further experience on the point; for the next day, when we must have been near the Cape of Pillars, which is the south-west point of the mouth of the straits, a gale set in from the eastward, with a heavy fog, so that we could not see half of the ship's length ahead. This, of course, put an end to the project, for the present; for a thick fog and a gale blowing dead ahead are not the most favorable circumstances for the passage of difficult and dangerous straits. This weather, too, seemed likely to last for some time, and we could not think of beating about the mouth of the straits for a week or two, waiting for a favorable opportunity; so we braced up on the larboard tack, put the ship's head due south, and stuck her off for Cape Horn again.

CHAPTER THIRTY-TWO
*Ice Again . . . A beautiful afternoon
. . . Cape Horn . . . Land Ho!*

In our first attempt to double the Cape, when we came up to the latitude of it, we were nearly seventeen hundred miles to the westward, but, in running for the straits of Magellan, we stood so far to the eastward, that we made our second attempt at a distance of not more than four or five hundred miles; and we had great hopes, by this means, to run clear of the ice; thinking that the easterly gales, which had prevailed for a long time, would have driven it to the westward. With the wind about two points free, the yards braced in a little, and two close-reefed top-sails and a reefed foresail on the ship, we made great way toward the southward; and, almost every watch, when we came on deck, the air seemed to grow colder, and the sea to run higher. Still, we saw no ice, and had great hopes of going clear of it altogether, when, one afternoon, about three o'clock, while we were taking a *siesta* during our watch below, "All hands!" was called in a loud and fearful voice. "Tumble up here, men!—tumble up!—don't stop for your clothes—before we're upon it!" We sprang out of our berths and hurried upon deck. The loud, sharp voice of the captain was heard giving orders, as though for life or death, and we ran aft to the braces, not waiting to look ahead, for not a moment was to be lost. The helm was hard up, the after yards shaking, and the ship in the act of wearing. Slowly, with the stiff ropes and iced rigging, we swung the yards round, everything coming hard and with a creaking and rending sound, like pulling up a plank which has been frozen into the ice. The ship wore round fairly, the yards were steadied, and we stood off on the other tack, leaving behind us, directly under our larboard quarter, a large ice island, peering out of the mist, and reaching high above our tops, while astern, and on either side of the island, large tracts of field-ice were dimly seen, heaving and rolling in the sea. We were now safe, and standing to the northward; but, in a few minutes more, had it not been for the sharp look-out of the watch, we should have been fairly upon the ice, and left our ship's old bones adrift in the Southern ocean. After standing to the northward a few hours, we wore ship, and, the wind having hauled, we stood to the southward and eastward. All night long, a bright look-out was kept from every part of the deck; and whenever ice was seen on the one bow or the other, the helm was shifted and the yards braced, and by quick working of the ship she was kept clear. The accustomed cry of "Ice ahead!"—"Ice on the lee bow!"—"Another island!" in the same tones, and with the same orders following them, seemed to bring us directly back to our old position of the week before. During our watch on deck, which was from twelve to four, the wind came out ahead, with a pelting storm of hail and sleet, and we lay hove-to, under a close-reefed fore top-sail, the whole watch. During the next watch it fell calm, with a drenching rain, until daybreak, when the wind came out to the westward, and the weather cleared up, and showed us the whole ocean, in the course which we should have steered, had it not been for the head wind and calm, completely blocked up with ice. Here then our progress was stopped, and we wore ship, and once more stood to the northward and eastward; not for the straits of Magellan, but to make another attempt to double the Cape, still farther to the eastward; for the captain was determined to get round if perseverance could do it, and the third time, he said, never failed.

With a fair wind we soon ran clear of the field-ice, and by noon had only the stray islands floating far and near upon the ocean. The sun was out bright, the sea of a deep blue, fringed with the white foam of the waves which ran high before a strong sou'wester; our solitary ship tore on through the water as though glad to be out of her confinement; and the ice islands lay scattered upon the ocean far and near, of various sizes and shapes, reflecting the bright rays of the sun, and drifting slowly northward before the gale. It was a contrast to much that we had lately seen, and a spectacle not only of beauty, but of life; for it required but little fancy to imagine these islands to be animate masses which had broken loose from the "thrill regions of thick-ribbed ice," and were working their way, by wind and current, some alone, and some in fleets, to milder climes. It was a scene for a painter yet no pencil has ever yet given anything like the true effect of an iceberg. In a picture, they are huge, uncouth masses, stuck in the sea, while their chief beauty and grandeur,—their slow, stately motion; the whirling of the snow about their summits, and the fearful groaning and cracking of their parts,—the picture cannot give. This is the large iceberg; while the small and distant islands, floating on the smooth sea, in the light of a clear day, look like little floating fairy isles of sapphire.

From a north-east course we gradually hauled to the eastward, and after sailing about two hundred miles, which brought us as near to the western coast of Terra del Fuego as was safe, and having lost sight of the ice altogether,—for the third time we put the ship's head to the southward, to try the passage of the Cape. The weather continued clear and cold, with a strong gale from the westward, and we were fast getting up with the latitude of the Cape, with a prospect of soon being round. One fine afternoon, a man who had gone into the fore-top to shift the rolling tackles, sung out, at the top of his voice, and with evident glee,—"Sail ho!" Neither land nor sail had we seen since leaving San Diego; and any one who has traversed the length of a whole ocean alone, can imagine what an excitement such an announcement produced on board. "Sail ho!" shouted the cook, jumping out of his galley; "Sail ho!" shouted a man, throwing back the slide of the scuttle, to the watch below, who were soon out of their berths and on deck; and "Sail ho!" shouted the captain down the companionway to the passenger, who was below. Beside the pleasure of seeing a ship and human beings in so desolate a place, it was important for us to speak a vessel, to learn whether there was ice to the eastward, and to ascertain the longitude; for we had no chronometer, and had been drifting about so long that we had nearly lost our reckoning, and opportunities for lunar observations are not frequent or sure in such a place as Cape Horn. For these various reasons, the excitement in our little community was running high, and conjectures were made, and everything thought of for which the captain would hail, when the man aloft sung out—"Another sail, large on the weather bow!" This was a little odd, but so much the better, and did not shake our faith in their being sails. At length the man in the top hailed, and said he believed it was land, after all. "Land in your eye!" said the mate, who was looking through the telescope; "they are ice islands, if I can see a hole through a ladder!" and a few moments showed the mate to be right; and all our expectations fled; and instead of what we most wished to see, we had what we most dreaded, and what we hoped we had seen the last of. We soon, however, left these astern, having passed within about two miles of them; and at sundown the horizon was clear in all directions.

Having a fine wind, we were soon up with and passed the latitude of the Cape, and having stood far enough to the southward to give it a wide berth, we began to stand to the eastward, with a fine prospect of being round and steering to the northward on the other side, in a very few days. But evil luck seemed to have lighted upon us. Not four hours had we been standing on in this course, before it fell dead calm; and in half an hour it clouded up; a few straggling blasts, with spits of snow and sleet, came from the eastward; and in an hour more, we lay hove-to under a close-reefed main top-sail, drifting bodily off to leeward before the fiercest storm we had yet felt, blowing dead ahead, from the eastward. It seemed as though the genius of the place had been roused at finding that we had nearly slipped through his fingers, and had come down upon us with tenfold fury. The sailors said that every blast, as it shook the shrouds, and whistled through the rigging, said to the old ship, "No, you don't!"—"No, you don't!"

For eight days we lay drifting about in this manner. Sometimes,—generally towards noon,—it fell calm; once or twice a round copper ball showed itself for a few moments in the place where the sun ought to have been; and a few puffs came from the westward, giving some hope that a fair wind had come at last. For the first day or two we made sail for these puffs, shaking the reefs out of the top-sails and boarding the tacks of the courses; but finding that it only made work for us when the gale set in again, it was soon given up, and we lay-to under our close-reefs. We had less snow and hail than when we were farther to the westward, but we had an abundance of what is worse to a sailor in cold weather—drenching rain. Snow is blinding, and very bad when coming upon a coast, but, for genuine discomfort, give me rain with freezing weather. A snow-storm is exciting, and it does not wet through the clothes (which is important to a sailor); but a constant rain there is no escaping from. It wets to the skin, and makes all protection vain. We had long ago run through all our dry clothes, and as sailors have nothing to dry their clothes by but the sun, we had nothing to do but to put on those which were the least wet. At the end of each watch, when we came below, we took off our clothes and wrung them out; two taking hold of a pair of trousers,—one at each end,—and jackets in the same way. Stockings, mittens, and all, were wrung out also, and then hung up to drain and chafe dry against the bulk-heads. Then, feeling of all our clothes, we picked out those which were the least wet, and put them on, so as to be ready for a call, and turned-in, covered ourselves up with blankets, and slept until three knocks on the scuttle and the dismal sound of "All starbowlines ahoy! Eight bells, there below! Do you hear the news?" drawled out from on deck, and the sulky answer of "Aye, aye!" from below, sent us up again.

On deck, all was as dark as a pocket, and either a dead calm, with the rain pouring steadily down, or, more generally, a violent gale dead ahead, with rain pelting horizontally, and occasional variations of hail and sleet;—decks afloat with water swashing from side to side, and constant wet feet; for boots could not be wrung out like drawers, and no composition could stand such a constant soaking. In fact, wet and cold feet are inevitable in such weather, and are not the least of those little items which go to make up the grand total of the discomforts of a winter passage round the Cape. Few words were spoken between the watches as they shifted, the wheel was relieved, the mate took his place on the quarter-deck, the look-outs in the bows; and each man had his narrow space to walk fore and aft in, or, rather, to swing himself forward and back in, from one belaying pin to another,—for the decks were too slippery with ice and water to allow of much walking. To make a walk, which is absolutely necessary to pass away the time, one of us hit upon the expedient of sanding the deck; and afterwards, whenever the rain was not so violent as to wash it off, the weather-side of the quarter-deck, and a part of the waist and forecastle were sprinkled with the sand which we had on board for holystoning; and thus we had a good promenade, where we walked fore and aft, two and two, hour after hour, in our long, dull, and comfortless watches. The bells seemed to be an hour or two apart, instead of half an hour, and an age elapse before the welcome sound of eight bells. The sole object was to make the time pass on. Any change was sought for, which would break the monotony of the watch; and even the two hours' trick at the wheel, which came round to each of us, in turn, once in every other watch, was looked upon as a relief. Even the never-failing resource of long yarns, which eke out many a watch, seemed to have failed us now; for we had been so long together that we had heard each other's stories told over and over again, till we knew them by heart; each one knew the whole history of each of the others, and we were fairly and literally talked out. Singing and joking, we were in no humor for, and, in fact, any sound of mirth or laughter would have struck strangely upon our ears, and would not have been tolerated, any more than whistling, or a wind instrument. Even the last resort of speculating upon the future, seemed now to fail us, for our discouraging situation, and the danger we were really in, (for we expected every day to find oureslves drifted back among the ice) 'clapped a stopper' upon all that. From saying—"*when* we get home"—we began insensibly to alter it to—"*if* we get home"—and at last the subject was dropped by a tacit consent.

In this state of things, a new light was struck out, and a new field opened, by a change in the watch. One of our watch was laid up for two or three days by a bad hand, (for in cold weather the least cut or bruise ripens into a sore,) and his place was supplied by the carpenter. This was a windfall, and there was quite a contest, who should have the carpenter to walk with him. As 'Chips' was a man of some little education, and he and I had had a good deal of intercourse with each other, he fell in with me in my walk. He was a Fin, but spoke English very well, and gave me long accounts of his country;—the customs, the trade, the towns, what little he knew of the government, (I found he was no friend of Russia,) his voyages, his first arrival in America, his marriage and courtship;—he had married a countrywoman of his, a dress-maker, whom he met with in Boston. I had very little to tell him of my quiet, sedentary life at home; and in spite of our best efforts, which had protracted these yarns through five or six watches, we fairly talked one another out, and I turned him over to another man in the watch, and put myself upon my own resources.

I commenced a deliberate system of time-killing, which united some profit with a cheering up of the heavy hours. As soon as I came on deck, and took my place and regular work, I began with repeating over to myself a string of matters which I had in my memory, in regular order. First, the multiplication table and the tables of weights and measures; then the states of the Union, with their capitals; the counties of England, with their shire towns; the kings of England in their order; and a large part of the peerage, which I committed from an almanac that we had on board; and then the Kanaka numerals. This carried me through my facts, and being repeated deliberately, with long intervals, often eked out the two first bells. Then came the ten commandments; the thirty-ninth chapter of Job, beginning with, 'Who hath sent out the wild ass free?', and the well known verses from the 12th chapter of Ecclesiastes: which was the end of my biblical literature. The next in the order, which I never varied from, came my greatest favorite Cowper's Castaway; the solemn measure and gloomy character of which, as well as the incident upon which it was founded, made it well suited to a lonely watch at sea. Then his lines to Mary, his address to the jackdaw, and a short extract from Table Talk; (I abounded in Cowper, for I happened to have a volume of his poems in my chest;) "Ille et nefasto" from Horace, and Goethe's Erl King.[51] After I had got through these, I allowed myself a more general range among everything that I could remember, both in prose and verse. In this way, with an occasional break by relieving the wheel, heaving the log, and going to the scuttle-butt for a drink of water, the longest watch was passed away; and I was so regular in my silent recitations, that if there was no interruption by ship's duty, I could tell very nearly the number of bells by my progress.

Our watches below were no more varied than the watch on deck. All washing, sewing, and reading was given up; and we did nothing but eat, sleep, and stand our watch, leading what might be called a Cape Horn life. The forecastle was too uncomfortable to sit up in; and whenever we were below, we were in our berths. To prevent the rain, and the sea-water which broke over the bows, from washing down, we were obliged to keep the scuttle closed, so that the forecastle was nearly air-tight. In this little, wet, leaky hole, we were all quartered, in an atmosphere so bad that our lamp, which swung in the

---

[51]In the process of setting type for the 1840 edition, a good many alterations and corrections were introduced which are not indicated in the manuscript. At this point, for instance, he wrote: "'Quam pere furvae' from Horace, and Schiller's Erl King."

middle from the beams, sometimes actually burned blue, with a large circle of foul air about it. Still, I was never in better health than after three weeks of this life. I gained a great deal of flesh, and we all ate like horses. At every watch, when we came below, before turning-in, the bread barge and beef kid were overhauled. Each man drank his quart of hot tea night and morning; and glad enough we were to get it, for no nectar and ambrosia were sweeter to the lazy immortals, than was a pot of hot tea, a hard biscuit, and a slice of cold salt beef, to us after a watch on deck. To be sure, we were mere animals, and had this life lasted a year instead of a month, we should have been little better than the ropes in the ship. Not a razor, nor a brush, nor a drop of water, except the rain and the spray, had come near us all the time; for we were on an allowance of fresh water; and who would strip and wash himself in salt water on deck, in the snow and ice, with the thermometer at zero?

After about eight days of constant easterly gales, the wind hauled occasionally a little to the southward, and blew hard, which, as we were well to the southward, allowed us to brace in a little and stand on, under all the sail we could carry. These turns lasted but a short while, and sooner or later it set in again from the old quarter; yet at each time we made something, and were gradually edging along to the eastward. One night, after one of these shifts of the wind, and when all hands had been up a great part of the time, our watch was left on deck, with the main-sail hanging in the buntlines, ready to be set if necessary. It came on to blow worse and worse, with hail and snow beating like so many furies upon the ship, it being as dark and thick as night could make it. The main-sail was blowing and slatting with a noise like thunder, when the captain came on deck, and ordered it to be furled. The mate was about to call all hands, when the captain stopped him, and said that the men would be beaten out if they were called up so often; that as our watch must stay on deck, it might as well be doing that as anything else. Accordingly, we went upon the yard; and never shall I forget that piece of work. Our watch had been so reduced by sickness, and by some having been left in California, that, with one man at the wheel, we had only the third mate and three beside myself to go aloft; so that, at most, we could only attempt to furl one yard-arm at a time. We manned the weather yard-arm, and set to work to make a furl of it. Our lower masts being short, and our yards very square, the sail had a head of nearly fifty feet, and a short leach, made still shorter by the deep reef which was in it, which brought the clue away out on the quarters of the yard, and made a bunt nearly as square as the mizen royal-yard. Beside this difficulty, the yard over which we lay was cased with ice, the gaskets and rope of

Iconographic Encyclopedia, J. G. Heck, 1851

We had to fist the sail with bare hands . . .

the foot and leach of the sail as stiff and hard as a piece of suction-hose, and the sail itself about as pliable as though it had been made of sheets of sheathing copper nailed together. It blew a perfect hurricane, with alternate blasts of snow, hail, and rain. We had to *fist* the sail with bare hands. No one could trust himself to mittens, for if he slipped, he was a gone man. All the boats were hoisted in on deck, and there was nothing to be lowered for him. We had need of every finger God had given us. Several times we got the sail upon the yard, but it blew away again before we could secure it. It required men to lie over the yard to pass each turn of the gaskets, and when they were passed, it was almost impossible to knot them so that they would hold. Frequently we were obliged to leave off altogether and take to beating our hands upon the sail, to keep them from freezing. After some time,—which seemed forever,—we got the weather side stowed after a fashion, and went over to leeward for another trial. This was still worse, for the body of the sail had been blown over to leeward, and as the yard was a-cock-bill by the lying over of the vessel, we had to light it all up to windward. When the yard-arms were furled, the bunt was all adrift again, which made more work for us. We got all secure at last, but we had been nearly an hour and a half upon the yard, and it seemed an age. It had just struck five bells when we went up, and eight were struck soon after we came down. This may seem slow work; but considering the state of everything, and that we had only five men to a sail with just half as many square yards of canvass in it as the main-sail of the Independence, sixty-gun ship which musters seven hundred men at her quarters, it is not wonderful that we were no quicker about it. We were glad enough to get on deck, and still more, to go below. The oldest sailor in the watch said, as he went down,—"I shall never forget that main yard;—it beats all my going a fishing. Fun is fun, but furling one yard-arm of a course, at a time, off Cape Horn, is no better than bloody murder."

During the greater part of the next two days, the wind was pretty steady from the southward. We had evidently made great progress, and had good hope of being soon up with the Cape, if we were not there already. We could put but little confidence in our reckoning, as there had been no opportunities for an observation, and we had drifted too much to allow of our dead reckoning being anywhere near the mark. If it would clear off enough to give a chance for an observation, or if we could make land, we should know where we were; and upon these, and the chances of falling in with a sail from the eastward, we depended almost entirely.

Friday, July 22d. This day we had a steady gale from the southward, and stood on under close sail, with the yards eased a little by the weather braces, the clouds lifting a little, and showing signs of breaking away. In the afternoon, I was below with Mr. Hatch, the third mate, and two others, filling the bread locker in the steerage from the casks, when a bright gleam of sunshine broke out and shined down the companion-way and through the sky-light, lighting up everything below, and sending a warm glow through the heart of every one. It was a sight we had not seen for weeks,—an omen, a god-send. Even the roughest and hardiest face acknowledged its influence. Just at that moment we heard a loud shout from all parts of the deck, and the mate called out down the companion-way to the captain, who was sitting in the cabin. What he said, we could not distinguish, but the captain kicked over his chair, and was on deck at one jump. What it was we could not tell; and, anxious as we were to know, the discipline of the ship would not allow of our leaving our places. Yet, as we were not called, we knew there was no danger. We hurried to get through with our job, when, seeing the steward's black face peering out of the pantry, Mr. Hatch hailed him, to know what was the matter. "Lan' o, to be sure, sir! No you hear 'em sing out, 'Lan' o?' De cap'em say 'im Cape Horn!'"

This gave us a new start, and we were soon through our work, and on deck; and there lay the land, fair upon the larboard beam, and slowly edging away upon the quarter. All hands were busy looking at it,—the captain and mates from the quarter-deck, the cook from his galley, and the sailors from the forecastle; and even Mr. Nuttall, the passenger, who had kept in his shell for nearly a month, and hardly been seen by anybody, and whom we had almost forgotten was on board, came out like a butterfly, and was hopping round as bright as a bird.

The land was the island of Staten Land, just to the eastward of Cape Horn; and a more desolate-looking spot I never wish to put eyes upon; —bare, broken, and girt with rocks and ice, and here and there, between the rocks and broken hillocks, a little stunted vegetation of shrubs. It was a place well suited to stand at the junction of the two oceans, beyond the reach of human cultivation, and encounter the blasts and snows of a perpetual winter. Yet, dismal as it was, it was a pleasant sight to us; not only as being the first land we had seen, but because it told us that we had passed the Cape,—were in the Atlantic, —and that, with twenty-four hours of this breeze, might bid defiance to the Southern ocean. It told us, too, our latitude and longitude better than any observation; and the captain now knew where we were, as well as if we were off the end of Long wharf.[52]

In the general joy, Mr. Nuttall said he should like to go ashore upon

[52]Long Wharf, Boston.

the island and examine a spot which probably no human being had ever set foot upon; but the captain intimated that he would see the island—specimens and all,—in—another place, before he would get out a boat or delay the ship one moment for him.

We left the land gradually astern; and at sundown had the Atlantic ocean clear before us.

Drawing by Robert A. Weinstein

and the water poured over . . . as it would over a dam

CHAPTER THIRTY-THREE
*Heading for home . . . Cracking on
. . . Progress homeward . . .
A pleasant Sunday . . . A fine sight
. . . By-play*

It is usual, in voyages round the Cape from the Pacific, to keep to the eastward of the Falkland Islands; but as it had now set in a strong, steady, and clear sou'wester, with every prospect of its lasting, and we had had enough of high latitudes, the captain determined to stand immediately to the northward, running inside the Falkland Islands. Accordingly, when the wheel was relieved at eight o'clock, the order was given to keep her due north, and all hands were turned up to square away the yards and make sail. In a moment, the news ran through the ship that the captain was keeping her off, with her nose straight for Boston, and Cape Horn over her taffrail. It was a moment of enthusiasm. Every one was on the alert, and even the two sick men turned out to lend a hand at the halyards. The wind was now due south-west, and blowing a gale to which a vessel close hauled could have shown no more than a single close-reefed sail; but as we were going before it, we could carry on. Accordingly, hands were sent aloft, and a reef shaken out of the top-sails, and the reefed fore-sail set. When we came to mast-head the top-sail yards, with all hands at the halyards, we struck up "Cheerily, men," with a chorus which might have been heard half way to Staten Land. Under her increased sail, the ship tore on through the water at a prodigious rate. Yet she could bear it well; and the captain sang out from the quarter-deck—"Another reef out of that fore top-sail, and give it to her!" Two hands sprang aloft; the frozen reef-points and earings were cast adrift, the halyards manned, and the sail gave out her increased canvass to the gale. All hands were kept on deck to watch the effect of the change. It was much as she could well carry, and with a heavy sea astern, it took two men at the wheel to steer her. She flung the foam from her bows; the spray breaking aft as far as the gangway. She was tearing on like a fast steed. Still, everything held. Preventer braces were rove and hauled taut; tackles got upon the backstays; and each thing done to keep all taut and strong. The captain walked the deck at a rapid stride, looked aloft at the sails, and then to windward; the mate stood in the gangway, rubbing his hands, and talking aloud to the ship—"Hurrah, old bucket! the Boston girls have got hold of the tow-rope!" and the like; and we were on the forecastle, looking to see how the spars stood it, and guessing the rate at which she was going,—

"Mr. Brown, get up the top-mast studding-sail! What she can't carry she may drag!" The mate looked a moment; but he would let no one be before him in daring. He sprang forward,—"Hurrah, men! rig out the top-mast studding-sail boom! Lay aloft, and I'll send the rigging up to you!"—We sprang aloft into the top; lowered a girt-line down, by which we hauled up the rigging; rove the tacks and halyards; ran out the boom and lashed it fast, and sent down the lower halyards, as a preventer. It was a clear starlight night, cold and blowing; but everybody worked with a will. Some, indeed, looked as though they thought the 'old man' was mad, but no one said a word. We had had a new topmast studding-sail made with a reef in it,—a thing hardly ever heard of, and which the sailors had ridiculed a good deal, saying that when it was time to reef a studding-sail, it was time to take it in. But we found a use for it now; for, there being a reef in the top-sail, the studding-sail could not be set without a reef in it. To be sure, a studding-sail with reefed top-sails was rather a new thing; yet there was some reason in it, for if we carried that away, we should lose only a sail and a boom; but a whole top-sail might have carried away the mast and all.

While we were aloft, the sail had been got out, bent to the yard, reefed, and ready for hoisting. Waiting for a good opportunity, the halyards were manned and the yard hoisted fairly up to the block; but when the mate came to shake the catspaw out of the downhaul, and we began to boom-end the sail, it shook the ship to her centre. The boom buckled up and bent like a whip-stick, and we looked every moment to see something go; but, being of the short, tough upland spruce, it bent like a whale bone, and nothing could break it. The carpenter said it was the best stick he had ever seen. The strength of all hands soon brought the tack to the boom-end, and the sheet was trimmed down, and the preventer and the weather brace hauled taut to take off the strain. Every rope-yarn seemed strained to the utmost, and every thread of canvass; and with this sail added to her, the ship sprang through the water like a thing possessed. The sail being nearly all forward, it lifted her out of the water, and she seemed actually to jump from sea to sea. From the time her keel was laid, she had never been so driven; and had it been life or death with every one of us, she could not have borne another stitch of canvass.

Finding that she would bear the sail, the hands were sent below, and our watch remained on deck. Two men at the wheel had as much as they could do to keep her within three points of her course, for she steered as wild as a young colt. The mate walked the deck, looking at the sails, and then over the side to see the foam fly by her,—slapping his hands upon his thighs and talking to the ship—"Hurrah, you jade, you've got the scent!—you know where you're going!" And when she leaped over the seas, and almost out of the water, and trembled to her very keel, the spars and masts snapping and creaking,—"There she goes!—There she goes,—handsomely!—As long as she cracks she holds!" —while we stood with the rigging laid down fair for letting go, and ready to take in sail and clear away, if anything went. At four bells the log was hove, and she was going eleven knots fairly; and had it not been for the sea from aft which sent the chip home, and threw her continually off her course, the log would have shown her to have been going much faster. I went to the wheel with a young fellow from the Kennebec, who was a good helmsman; and for two hours we had our hands full. A few minutes showed us that our monkey-jackets must come off; and cold as it was, we stood in our shirt-sleeves, in a perspiration; and were glad enough to have it eight bells, and the wheel relieved. We turned-in and slept as well as we could, though the sea made a constant roar under her bows, and washed over the forecastle like a small cataract.

At four o'clock, we were called again. The same sail was on the vessel, and the gale, if anything, appeared to have increased a little. No attempt was made to take the studding-sail in; and, indeed, it was too late now. If we had started anything toward taking it in, either tack or halyards, it would have blown to pieces, and carried something away with it. The only way now was to let everything stand, and if the gale went down, well and good; if not, something must go—the weakest stick or rope first—and then we could get it in. For more than an hour she was driven on at such a rate that she seemed actually to crowd the sea into a heap before her; and the water poured over the sprit-sail yard as it would over a dam. Toward daybreak the gale abated a little, and she was just beginning to go more easily along, relieved of the pressure, when Mr. Brown, determined to give her no respite, and depending upon the gale's abating with the sun, ordered us to get along the lower studding-sail. This was an immense sail, and held wind enough to last a Dutchman a week,—hove-to. It was soon ready, the boom topped up, preventer guys rove, and the idlers called up to man the halyards; yet such was still the force of the gale, that we were nearly an hour setting the sail; carried away the outhaul in doing it, and came very near snapping off the swinging boom. No sooner was it set than the ship tore on again like one that was mad, and began to steer as wild as a hawk. The men at the wheel were puffing and blowing at their work, and the helm was going hard up and hard down, constantly. Add to this, the gale did not lessen as the day came on, but the sun rose in clouds. A sudden lurch threw the man from the weather wheel across the deck and against the side. The mate sprang to the wheel, and the man, regaining his feet, seized the spokes, and the wheel was hove up just in time to save her from broaching to; though nearly half the studding-sail went under water; and as she came to, the boom stood up at an angle of forty-five degrees. She had evidently more on her than she could bear; yet it was in vain to try to take it in—the clewline was not strong enough; and they were thinking of cutting away, when another wide yaw and a come-to, snapped the guys, and the swinging boom came in, with a crash, against the lower rigging. The outhaul block gave way, and the top-mast studding-sail boom bent in a manner which I never before supposed a stick could bend. I had my eye on it when the guys parted, and it gave one spring and buckled up so as to form nearly a half circle, and sprang out again to its shape. The clewline gave way at the first pull; the cleat to which the halyards were belayed was wrenched off, and the sail blew round the sprit-sail yard and head guys, which gave us a bad job to get it in. A half hour served to clear all away, and she was suffered to drive on under the top-mast studding-sail, being now as much as she could stagger under.

During all this day and the next night, we went on under the same sail, the gale blowing with undiminished force; two men at the wheel all the time; watch and watch, and nothing to do but to steer and look out for the ship, and be blown along;—until the noon of the next day—

Sunday, July 24th, when we were in latitude 50° 27′ S., longitude 62° 13′ W., having made four degrees of latitude in the last twenty-four hours. Being now to the northward of the Falkland Islands, the ship was kept off, north-east, for the equator; and with her head for the equator, and Cape Horn over her taffrail, she went gloriously on; every heave of the sea leaving Cape Horn astern; and every hour bringing us nearer to home, and to warm weather. Many a time, when blocked up in the ice, with everything dismal and discouraging about us, had we said,—if we were only fairly round, and standing north on the other side, we should ask for no more:—and now we had it all, with a clear sea, and as much wind as a sailor could pray for. If the best part of a voyage is the last part, surely we had all now that we could wish. Every one was in the highest spirits, and the ship seemed as glad as any of us at getting out of her confinement. At each change of the watch, those coming on deck asked those going below—"How does she go along?" and got for answer, the rate, and the customary addition—"Aye! and the Boston girls have had hold of the tow-rope all the watch, and can't haul half the slack in!" Each day the sun rose higher in the horizon and the nights grew shorter; and at coming on deck each morning, there was a sensible change in the temperature. The ice, too, began to melt from off the rigging and spars, and, except a little which remained in the tops and round the hounds of the lower masts, was soon gone. As we left the gale behind us, the reefs were shaken out of the top-sails, and sail made as fast as she could bear it; and every time all hands were sent to the halyards, a song was called for, and we hoisted away with a will.

Sail after sail was added, as we drew into fine weather; and in one week after leaving Cape Horn, the long top-gallant masts were got up, top-gallant and royal yards crossed, and the ship restored to her fair proportions.

The Southern Cross we saw no more after the first night; the Magellan Clouds settled lower and lower in the horizon; and so great was our change of latitude each succeeding night, that we sank some constellation in the south, and raised another in the northern horizon.

Sunday, July 31st. At noon we were in lat. 36° 41' S., long. 38° 08' W.; having traversed the distance of two thousand miles, allowing for changes of course, in nine days. A thousand miles in four days and a half!—This is equal to steam.

Soon after eight o'clock, the appearance of the ship gave evidence that this was the first Sunday we had yet had in fine weather. As the sun came up clear, giving promise of a fair, warm day, and, as usual on Sunday, there was no work going on, all hands turned-to upon clearing out the forecastle. The wet and soiled clothes which had accumulated there during the past month, were brought up on deck; chests moved; brooms, buckets of water, swabs, scrubbing-brushes, and scrapers carried down, and applied, until the forecastle floor was as white as chalk, and everything neat and in order. The bedding from the berths was then spread on deck, and dried, and aired; the deck-tub filled with water; and a grand washing begun of all the clothes which were brought up. Shirts, frocks, drawers, trousers, jackets, stockings, of every shape and color, wet and dirty—many of them mouldy from having been lying a long time wet in a dirty corner—these were all washed and scrubbed out, and finally towed overboard for half an hour; and then made fast in the rigging to dry. Wet boots and shoes were spread out to dry in sunny places on deck; and the whole ship looked like a back yard on a washing day. After we had done with our clothes, we began upon our own persons. A little fresh water, which we had saved from our allowance, was put in buckets, and, with soap and towels, we had what sailors call a fresh-water wash. The same bucket, to be sure, had to go through several hands, and was spoken for by one after another, but as we rinsed off in salt water, pure from the ocean, and the fresh was used only to start the accumulated grime and blackness of five weeks, it was held of little consequence. We soaped down and scrubbed one another with towels and pieces of canvass, stripping to it; and then, getting into the head, threw buckets of water upon each other. After this, came shaving, and combing, and brushing; and when, having spent the first part of the day in this way, we sat down on the forecastle, in the afternoon, with clean duck trousers, and shirts on, washed, shaved, and combed, and looking a dozen shades lighter for it, reading, sewing, and talking at our ease, with a clear sky and warm sun over our heads, a steady breeze over the larboard quarter, studding-sails out alow and aloft, and all the flying kites abroad;—we felt that we had got back into the pleasantest part of a sailor's life. At sundown the clothes were all taken down from the rigging—clean and dry—and stowed neatly away in our chests; and our sou'westers, thick boots, guernsey frocks, and other accompaniments to bad weather, put out of the way, we hoped, for the rest of the voyage, as we expected to come upon the coast early in the autumn.

Notwithstanding all that has been said about the beauty of a ship under full sail, there are very few who have ever seen a ship, literally, under all her sail. A ship coming in or going out of port, with her ordinary sails, and perhaps two or three studding-sails, is commonly said to be under full sail; but a ship never has all her sail upon her, except when she has a light, steady breeze, very nearly, but not quite, dead aft, and so regular that it can be trusted, and is likely to last for some time. Then, with all her sails, light and heavy, and studding-sails, on each side, alow and aloft, she is the most glorious moving object in the world. Such a sight, very few, even some who have been at sea a good deal, have ever beheld; for from the deck of your own vessel you cannot see her, as you would a separate object.

One night, while we were in these tropics, I went out to the end of the flying-jib-boom, upon some duty, and, having finished it, turned round, and lay over the boom for a half an hour, admiring the beauty of the sight before me. Being so far out from the deck, I could look at the ship, as at a separate vessel;—and, there, rose up from the water, supported only by the small black hull, a pyramid of canvass, spreading out far beyond the hull, and towering up almost, as it seemed in the indistinct night air, to the clouds. The sea was as still as an inland lake; the light trade-wind was gently and steadily breathing from astern; the dark blue sky was studded with the tropical stars; there was not a sound but the rippling of the water under the stem; and the sails were spread out, wide and high;—the two lower studding-sails stretching out on each side, twenty or thirty feet beyond the deck; the topmast studding-sails, like wings to the top-sails; the top-gallant studding-sails spreading fearlessly out above them; still higher, the two royal studding-sails, looking like two kites flying from the same string; and, highest of all, the little sky-sail, the apex of the pyramid, seeming actually to touch the stars, and to be out of reach of human hand. So quiet, too, was the sea, and so steady the breeze, that if these sails had been sculptured marble, they could not have been more motionless. Not a ripple upon the surface of the canvass; not even a quivering of the extreme edges of the sail—so perfectly were they distended by the breeze. I was so lost in the sight, that I forgot the presence of the man who came out with me, until he said, (for he, too, rough old man-of-war's-man as he was, had been gazing at the show,) half to himself, still looking at the marble sails—"How quietly they do their work!"

The fine weather brought work with it, as the ship was to be put in order for coming into port. This may give a landsman some notion of what is done on board ship.—All the first part of a passage is spent in getting a ship ready for sea, and the last part in getting her ready for port. She is, as sailors say, like a lady's watch, always out of repair. The new, strong sails, which we had up off Cape Horn, were to be sent down, and the old set, which were still serviceable in fine weather, to be bent in their place; all the rigging to be set up, fore and aft; the masts stayed; the standing rigging to be tarred down; lower and top-mast rigging rattled down, fore and aft; the ship scraped, inside and out, and painted; decks varnished; new and neat knots, seizings and coverings to be put on; and every part put in order, to look well to the owner's eye, on coming into Boston. This, of course, was a long matter; and all hands were kept on deck at work for the whole of each day, during the rest of the voyage. Sailors call this hard usage; but the ship must be in crack order, and "we're homeward bound" was the answer to everything.

Employed in this way, we went on for several days, nothing remarkable occurring; and, at the latter part of the week, fell in with the south-east trades, blowing about east-south-east, which brought them about two points abaft our beam. These blew strong and steady, so that we hardly started a rope, until we were beyond their latitude. The first day of "all hands," one of those little incidents occurred, which are nothing in themselves, but are great matters in the eyes of a ship's company, as they serve to break the monotony of a voyage, and afford conversation to the crew for days afterwards. These small matters, too, are often interesting, as they show the customs and state of feeling on shipboard.

In merchant vessels, the captain gives his orders, as to the ship's work, to the mate, in a general way, and leaves the execution of them, with the particular ordering, to him. This has become so fixed a custom, that it is like a law, and is never infringed upon by a wise master, unless his mate is no seaman; in which case, the captain must often oversee things for himself. This, however, could not be said of our chief mate; and he was very jealous of any encroachment upon the borders of his authority.

On Monday morning, the captain told him to stay the fore top-mast plumb. He accordingly came forward, turned all hands to, with tackles on the stays and backstays, coming up with the seizings, hauling here, belaying there, and full of business, standing between the knight-heads to sight the mast,—when the captain came forward, and also began to give orders. This made confusion, and the mate, finding that he was all aback, left his place and went aft, saying to the captain—

"If you come forward, sir, I'll go aft. One is enough on the fore-castle."

This produced a reply, and another fierce answer; and the words flew, fists were doubled up, and things looked threatening.

"I'm master of this ship!"

"Yes, sir, and I'm mate of her, and know my place! My place is forward, and yours is aft!"

"My place is where I choose! I command the *whole* ship; and you are mate only so long as I choose!"

"Say the word, Capt. T[hompson], and I'm done! I can do a man's work aboard! I didn't come through the cabin windows! If I'm not mate, I can be man," &c., &c.

This was all fun for us, who stood by, winking at each other, and enjoying the contest between the higher powers. The captain took the mate aft; and they had a long talk, which ended in the mate's returning to his duty. The captain had broken through a custom, which is a part of the common-law of a ship, and without reason; for he knew that his mate was a sailor, and needed no help from him; and the mate was excusable for being angry. Yet he was wrong, and the captain right. Whatever the captain does is right, ipso facto, and any opposition to it is wrong, on board ship; and every officer and man knows that, when he signs the ship's articles. It is a part of the contract. Yet there has grown up in merchant vessels a series of customs, which have become a well understood system, and have almost the force of prescriptive law. To be sure, all power is in the captain, and the officers hold their authority only during his will; and the men are liable to be called upon for any service; yet, by breaking in upon these usages, many difficulties have occurred on board ship, and even come into courts of justice, which are perfectly unintelligible to any one not acquainted with the universal nature and force of these customs. Many a provocation has been offered, and a system of petty oppression pursued upon men, the force and meaning of which would appear to be nothing to strangers, and doubtless do appear so to many "'long-shore" juries and judges.

The next little diversion, was a battle on the forecastle, one afternoon, between the mate and the steward. They had been on bad terms the whole voyage; and had threatened a rupture several times.

This afternoon, the mate asked him for a tumbler of water, and he refused to get it for him, saying that he waited upon nobody but the captain: and here he had the custom on his side. But in answering, he left off 'the handle to the mate's name'. This enraged the mate, who called him a "black soger;" and at it they went, clenching, striking, and rolling over and over; while we stood by, looking on, and enjoying the fun. The darkey tried to butt him, but the mate got him down, and held him, the steward singing out, "Let me go, Mr. Brown, or there'll be blood spilt!" In the midst of this, the captain came on deck, separated them, took the steward aft, and gave him a half a dozen with a rope's end. The steward tried to justify himself; but the captain had heard him talk of spilling blood, and that was enough to earn him his flogging; and the captain did not choose to inquire any further.

CHAPTER THIRTY-FOUR
Sail ho! . . . Tropical squalls . . .
Thunder storm

The same day was my birth day, which I remember from a little incident which befel me. one of those narrow escapes, which are so often happening in a sailor's life and which from the coincidence of its happening on my birthday I remember well. I had been aloft nearly all the afternoon, at work, standing for as much as an hour on the fore top-gallant yard, which was hoisted up, and hung only by the tie; when, having got through my work, I balled up my yarns, took my serving-board in my hand, laid hold deliberately of the top-gallant rigging, took one foot from the yard, and was just lifting the other, when the tie parted, and down fell the yard. I was safe, by my hold upon the rigging, but it made my heart beat quick. Had the tie parted one instant sooner, or had I stood an instant longer on the yard, I should inevitably have been thrown violently from the height of ninety or an hundred feet, overboard; or, what is worse, upon the deck. However, "a miss is as good as a mile;" and this is a saying which sailors very often have occasion to use. An escape is always a joke on board ship. A man would be ridiculed who should make a serious matter of it. A sailor knows too well that his life hangs upon a thread, to wish to be always reminded of it; so, if a man has an escape, he keeps it to himself, or makes a joke of it. I have often known a man's life to be saved by an instant of time, or by the merest chance, —the swinging of a rope,—and no notice taken of it. One of our boys, when off Cape Horn, reefing top-sails of a dark night, and when there were no boats to be lowered away, and where, if a man fell overboard, he must be left behind,—lost his hold of the reef-point, slipped from the foot-rope, and would have been in the water in a moment, when the man who was next to him on the yard hauled him by the collar of his jacket, and hauled him up upon the yard, with—"Hold on, another time, you young monkey, and be d——d to you!"—and that was all that was heard about it.

Sunday, August 7th. Lat. 25° 59′ S., long. 27° 0′ W. Spoke the English bark Mary-Catherine, from Bahia, bound to Calcutta. This was the first sail we had fallen in with, and the first time we had seen a human form or heard the human voice, except of our own number, for nearly an hundred days. The very yo-ho-ing of the sailors at the ropes sounded hospitably upon the ear. She was an old, damaged-looking craft, with a high poop and top-gallant forecastle, and sawed off square, stem and stern, like a true English "tea-wagon," and with a run like a sugar-box. She had studding-sails out alow and aloft with a light but steady breeze, and her captain said he could not get more than four knots out of her; and thought he should have a long passage. We were going six on an easy bowline.

The next day, about three P. M., passed a large corvette-built ship, close upon the wind, with royals and sky-sails set fore and aft, under English colors. She was standing south-by-east, probably bound round Cape Horn. She had men in her tops, and black mast-heads; heavily sparred, sails cut to a *t*, and with other marks of a man-of-war. She sailed well, and presented a fine appearance; the proud, aristocratic-looking banner of St. George, the cross in a blood-red field, waving from the mizen. We probably were as fine a sight, with our studding-sails spread far out beyond the ship on either side, and rising in a pyramid to royal studding-sails and sky-sails, burying the hull in canvass and looking like what the whalemen on the Banks, under their stump top-gallant masts, call "a Cape Horn-er under a cloud of sail."

Friday, August 12th. At daylight made the island of Trinidad, situated in lat. 20° 28′ S., long. 29° 08′ W. At twelve, M., it bore N. W. ½ N., distant twenty-seven miles. It was a beautiful day, the sea hardly ruffled by the light trades, and the island looking like a small blue mound rising from a field of glass. Such a beautiful, peaceful-looking spot is said to have been, for a long time, the resort of a band of pirates, who ravaged the tropical seas.

Thursday, August 18th. At three, P. M., made the island of Fernando Naronha, lying in lat. 3° 55′ S., long. 32° 35′ W.; and between twelve o'clock Friday night and one o'clock Saturday morning, crossed the equator, for the fourth time since leaving Boston, in long. 35° W.; having been twenty-seven days from Staten Land—a distance, by the courses we had made, of more than four thousand miles.

We were now to the northward of the line, and every day added to our latitude. The Magellan Clouds, the last sign of south latitude, were sunk in the horizon, and the north star, the Great Bear, and the familiar signs of northern latitudes, were rising in the heavens. Next to seeing land, there is no sight which makes one realize more that he is drawing near home, than to see the same heavens, under which he was born, shining at night over his head. The weather was extremely hot, with the usual tropical alternations of a scorching sun and squalls of rain; yet not a mouth was opened to complain of the heat, for we all remembered that only three or four weeks before we would have given nearly our all to have been where we now were. We had plenty of water, too, which we caught by spreading an awning, with shot thrown in to make hollows. These rain squalls came up in the usual manner between the tropics.—A clear sky; burning, vertical sun; work going lazily on, and men about decks with nothing but duck trousers, checked shirts, and straw hats; the ship moving as lazily through the water; the man at the helm resting against the wheel, with his hat drawn over his eyes; the captain below, taking an afternoon nap; the passenger leaning over the taffrail, watching a dolphin following slowly in our wake and glittering as the light of the vertical sun strikes through the water like a rainbow; the sailmaker mending an old top-sail on the lee side of the quarter-deck; the carpenter at work at his bench, in the waist; the boys making sinnet; the spun-yarn winch whizzing round and round with its lazy sound, and the men walking slowly fore and aft with the yarns.—A cloud rises to windward, looking a little black; the sky-sails are brailed down; the captain puts his head out of the companion-way, looks at the cloud, comes up, and begins to walk the deck.—The cloud spreads and comes on;—the tub of yarns, the sail, and other matters, are thrown below, and the sky-light and booby-hatch put on, and the slide drawn over the forecastle.—"Stand by the royal halyards;"—the man at the wheel keeps a good weather helm, so as not to be taken aback.—The squall strikes her. If it is light, the royal yards are clewed down, and the ship keeps on her way; but if the squall takes strong hold, the royals are clewed up, fore and aft; light hands lay aloft and furl them; top-gallant yards clewed down, flying-jib hauled down, and the ship kept off before it,—the man at the helm laying out his strength to heave the wheel up to windward. At the same time a drenching rain, which soaks one through in an instant. Yet no one puts on a jacket or cap; for if it is only warm, a sailor does not mind a ducking; and the sun will soon be out again. As soon as the force of the squall has passed, though to a common eye the ship would seem to be in the midst of it,—"Keep her up to her course, again!"—"Keep her up, sir," (answer);—"Hoist away the top-gallant yards!"—"Run up the flying-jib!"—"Lay aloft, you boys, and loose the royals!"—and all sail is on her again before she is fairly out of the squall; and she is going on in her course. The sun comes out once more, hotter than ever, dries up the decks and the sailors' clothes; the hatches are taken off; the sail got up and spread on the quarter-deck; spun-yarn winch set a going again; rigging coiled up; captain goes below; and every sign of an interruption is removed.

These scenes, with occasional dead calms, lasting for hours, and sometimes for days, are fair specimens of the Atlantic tropics. The nights were fine; and as we had all hands all day, the watch were allowed to sleep on deck at night, except the man at the wheel, and one look-out on the forecastle. This was not so much expressly allowed, as winked at. We could do it if we did not ask leave. If the look-out was caught napping, the whole watch was kept awake. We made the most of this permission, and stowed ourselves away upon the rigging, under the weather rail, on the spars, under the windlass, and in all the snug corners; and frequently slept out the watch, unless we had a wheel or a look-out. And we were glad enough to get this rest; for under the "all hands" system, every other day, out of every other thirty-six hours, we had only four below; and even an hour's sleep was a gain not to be neglected. One would have thought so, to have seen our watch, some nights, sleeping through a heavy rain. And often have we come on deck, and finding a dead calm and a light, steady rain, and determined not to lose our sleep, have laid a coil of rigging down so as to keep us out of the water which was washing about decks, and stowed ourselves away upon it, covering a jacket over us, and slept as soundly as a Dutchman between two feather beds.

For a week or ten days after crossing the line, we had the usual variety of calms, squalls, head winds, and fair winds;—at one time braced sharp upon the wind, with a taut bowline, and in an hour after, slipping quietly along, with a light breeze over the taffrail, and studding-sails out on both sides;—until we fell in with the north-east trade-winds; which we did on the afternoon of

Sunday, August 28th, in lat. 12° N. The trade wind clouds had been in sight for a day or two previously, and we expected to take them every hour. The light southerly breeze, which had been blowing languidly during the first part of the day, died away toward noon, and in its place came puffs from the north-east, which caused us to take our studding-sails in and brace up; and, in a couple of hours more, we were bowling gloriously along, dashing the spray from the bows far to leeward, with the cool, steady north-cast trades, freshening up the sea, and giving us as much as we could carry our royals to with the halyards sent over to windward, breast backstays rigged out, and everything hauled taut. These winds blew strong and steady, keeping us generally upon a bowline, as our course was about north-north-west; and sometimes, as they veered a little to the eastward, giving us a chance at a main top-gallant studding-sail; and sending us well to the northward, until—

Sunday, Sept. 4th, when they left us, in lat. 22° N., long. 51° W., directly under the tropic of Cancer.

For several days we lay 'humbugging about' in the Horse latitudes, with all sorts of winds and weather, and occasionally, as we were in the latitude of the West Indies,—a thunder storm. It was hurricane month, too, and we were just in the track of the tremendous hurricane of 1830, which swept the North Atlantic, destroying almost everything before it. The first night after the trade-winds left us, while we were in the latitude of the island of Cuba, we had a specimen of a true tropical thunder storm. A light breeze had been blowing directly from aft during the first part of the night, which gradually died away, and before midnight it was dead calm, and an immense black cloud had shrouded the whole sky. When our watch came on deck at twelve o'clock, it was as black as Erebus; the studding-sails were all taken in, and the royals furled; not a breath was stirring; the sails hung heavy and motionless from the yards; and the perfect stillness, and the darkness, which was almost palpable, were truly appalling. Not a word was spoken, but every one stood as though expecting something to happen. In a few minutes the mate came forward, and in a low tone, which was almost a whisper, told us to haul down the jib. The fore and mizen top-gallant sails were taken in, in the same silent manner; and we lay motionless upon the water, with an expectation of something, which, from the long suspense, became actually painful. We could hear the captain walking the deck, but it was too dark to see anything more than one's hand before the face. Soon the mate came forward again, and gave an order, in a low tone, to clew up the main top-gallant sail; and so infectious was the awe and silence, that the clewlines and buntlines were hauled up without any of the customary singing out at the ropes. An English lad and myself went up to furl it; and we had just got the bunt up, when the mate called out to us, something, we did not hear what,—but supposing it to be an order to bear-a-hand, we hurried, and made all fast, and came down, feeling our way among the rigging. When we got down we found all hands looking aloft, and there, directly over where we had been standing, upon the main top-gallant-mast-head, was a ball of light, which the sailors call a corposant (corpus sancti), and which the mate had called out to us to look at. They were all watching it carefully, for sailors have a notion that if the corposant rises in the rigging, it is a sign of fair weather, but if it comes lower down, there will be a storm. Unfortunately, as an omen, it came down, and showed itself on the top-gallant yard-arm. We came off the yard in good season, for it is held a fatal sign to have the pale light of the corpus sancti thrown upon one's face. As it was, the English lad did not feel comfortably at having had it so near him, and directly over his head. In a few minutes it disappeared, and showed itself again on the fore top-gallant yard; and after playing about for some time, disappeared again; when the man on the forecastle pointed to it upon the flying-jib-boom-end. But our attention was drawn from watching this, by the falling of some drops of rain, and by a perceptible increase of the darkness, which seemed suddenly to add a new shade of blackness to the night. In a few minutes, low, grumbling thunder was heard,

From a watercolor by William Meyers, U.S.N., 1843. Courtesy The Bancroft Library

Angel Island, San Francisco, California

and some random flashes of lightning came from the south-west. Every sail was taken in but the top-sails; still, no squall appeared to be coming. A few puffs lifted the top-sails, but they fell again to the mast, and all was as still as ever. A moment more, and a terrific peal and flash came simultaneously upon us, and a cloud appeared to open directly over our heads and let down the water in one body, like a falling ocean. We stood motionless, and almost stupefied; yet nothing had been struck. Peal after peal rattled over our heads, with a sound which seemed actually to stop the breath in the body, and the "speedy gleams" kept the whole ocean in a glare of light. The violent fall of rain lasted but a few minutes, and was succeeded by occasional drops and showers; but the lightning continued incessant for several hours, breaking the midnight darkness with irregular and blinding flashes. During all which time there was not a breath stirring, and we lay motionless, like a mark to be shot at, probably the only object on the surface of the ocean for miles and miles. Hour after hour we stood until our watch was out, and we were relieved, at four o'clock. During all this time, hardly a word was spoken; no bells were struck, and the wheel was silently relieved. The rain fell at intervals in heavy showers, and we stood drenched through and blinded by the flashes, which broke the Egyptian darkness with a brightness which seemed almost malignant; while the thunder rolled in peals, the concussion of which appeared to shake the very ocean. A ship is not often injured by lightning, for the electricity is separated by the great number of points she presents, and the quantity of iron which she has scattered in various parts. The electric fluid ran over our anchors, top-sail sheets and ties; yet no harm was done to us. We went below at four o'clock, leaving things in the same state. It is not easy to sleep, when the very next flash may tear the ship in two, or set her on fire; or where the deathlike calm may be broken by the blast of a hurricane, taking the masts out of the ship. But a man is no sailor if he cannot sleep when he turns-in, and turn out when he's called. And when, at seven bells, the customary "All the larboard watch, ahoy!" brought us on deck, it was a fine, clear, sunny morning, the ship going leisurely along, with a good breeze and all sail set.

CHAPTER THIRTY-FIVE
A reef-top-sail breeze . . . Scurvy . . .
Preparing for Port . . . Gulf stream

From the latitude of the West Indies, until we got inside the Bermudas, where we took the westerly and south-westerly winds, which blow steadily off the coast of the United States early in the autumn, we had every variety of weather, and two or three moderate gales, or, as sailors call them, double-reef-top-sail breezes, which came on in the usual manner, and of which one is a specimen of all.—A fine afternoon; all hands at work, some in the rigging, and others on deck; a stiff breeze, and ship close upon the wind, and sky-sails brailed down.—Latter part of the afternoon, breeze increases, ship lies over it, and clouds look windy. Spray begins to fly over the forecastle, and wets the yarns the boys are knotting;—ball them up and put them below.—Mate knocks off work and clears up decks earlier than usual, and orders a man who has been employed aloft to send the royal halyards over to windward, as he comes down. Breast backstays hauled taut, and tackle got upon the martingale back-rope.—One of the boys furls the mizen royal.—Cook thinks there is going to be 'nasty work', and has supper ready early.—Mate gives orders to get supper by the watch, instead of all hands, as usual.—While eating supper, hear the watch on deck taking in the royals.—Coming on deck, find it is blowing harder, and an ugly head sea is running.—Instead of having all hands on the forecastle in the dog watch, smoking, singing, and telling yarns, one watch goes below and turns-in, saying that it's going to be an ugly night, and two hours' sleep is not to be lost. Clouds look black and wild; wind rising, and ship working hard against a heavy head sea, which breaks over the forecastle, and washes aft through the scuppers. Still, no more sail is taken in, for the captain is a driver, and, like all drivers, very partial to his top-gallant sails. A top-gallant sail, too, makes the difference between a breeze and a gale. When a top-gallant sail is on a ship, it is only a breeze, though I have seen ours set over a reefed top-sail, when half the bowsprit was under water, and it was up to a man's knees in the lee scuppers. At eight bells, nothing is said about reefing the top-sails, and the watch go below, with orders to 'stand by for a call'. Watch go below growling at the 'old man' for not reefing the top-sails when the watch was changed, but putting it off so as to call all hands, and break up a whole watch below. Turn-in 'all standing,' and keep ourselves awake by saying there is no use in going to sleep to be waked up again.—Wind whistles on deck, and ship works hard, groaning and creaking, and pitching into a heavy head sea, which strikes against the bows, with a noise like knocking upon a rock.—The dim lamp in the forecastle swings to and fro, and things 'fetch away' and go over to leeward.—"Doesn't that booby of a second mate ever mean to take in his top-gallant sails?—He'll have the sticks out of her soon," says old Bill, who was always growling, and, like most old sailors, did not like to see a ship abused.—Bye and bye, an order is given;—"Aye, aye, sir!" from the forecastle;—rigging is hove down on deck;—the noise of a sail is heard fluttering aloft, and the short, quick cry which sailors make when hauling upon clewlines.—"Here comes his fore top-gallant sail in!"—We are wide awake, and know all that's going on as well as if we were on deck.—A well-known voice is heard from the mast-head singing out to the officer of the watch to haul taut the weather brace.—"Hallo! There's Ben aloft to furl the sail!"—Next thing, rigging is hove down directly over our heads, and a long-drawn cry and a rattling of hanks announces that the flying-jib has come in.—The second mate holds on to the main top-gallant sail until a heavy sea is shipped, and washes over the forecastle as though the whole ocean had come aboard; when a noise further aft shows that that is taking in also. After this, the ship is more easy for a time; two bells are struck, and we try to get a little sleep. By-and-by,—bang, bang, bang, on the scuttle—"All ha-a-ands, a ho o y!"—We spring out of our berths, clap on a monkey-jacket and sou'wester, and tumble up the ladder.—Mate up before us, and on the forecastle, singing out like a roaring bull; the captain singing out on the quarter-deck, and the second mate yelling, like a hyena, in the waist. The ship lying over half upon her beam-ends; lee scuppers under water, and forecastle all in a smother of foam.—Rigging all let go, and washing about decks; top-sail yards down upon the caps, and sails flapping and beating against the masts; and starboard watch hauling out the reef-tackles of the main top-sail. Our watch haul out the fore, and lay aloft and put two reefs into it, and reef the fore-sail, and race with the star-board watch, to see which will mast-head its top-sail first. All hands tally-on to the main tack, and while some are furling the jib, and hoisting the stay-sail, we mizen-top-men (English Ben and I at the ear-rings) double-reef the mizen top-sail and hoist it up. All being made fast—"Go below, the watch!" and we turn-in to sleep out the rest of the watch, which is perhaps an hour and a half. During all the middle, and for the first part of the morning watch, it blows as hard as ever, but toward daybreak it moderates considerably, and we shake a reef out of each top-sail, and set the top-gallant sails over them; and when the watch come up, at seven bells, for breakfast, shake the other reefs out, turn all hands to upon the halyards, get the watch-tackle upon the top-gallant sheets and halyards, set the flying-jib, and crack on to her again.

Our captain had been married only a few weeks before he left Boston; and, after an absence of over two years, it may be supposed he was not slow in carrying sail. The mate, too, was not to be beaten by anybody; and the second mate, though he was afraid to carry sail, was afraid as death of the captain, and being between two fears, sometimes carried on longer than any of them. We carried away three flying-jib booms in twenty-four hours, as fast as they could be fitted and rigged out; sprung the sprit-sail yard; and made nothing of studding-sail booms. Beside the natural desire to get home, we had another reason for urging the ship on. The scurvy had begun to show itself on board. One man had it so badly as to be disabled and off duty, and the English lad, Ben, was in a dreadful state, and was daily growing worse. His legs swelled and pained him so that he could not walk; his flesh lost its elasticity, so that if it was pressed in, it would not return to its shape; and his gums swelled until he could not open his mouth. His breath, too, became very offensive; he lost all strength and spirit; could eat nothing; grew worse every day; and, in fact, unless something was done for him, would be a dead man in a week, at the rate at which he was sinking. The medicines were all, or nearly all, gone; and if we had had a chest-full, they would have been of no use; for nothing but fresh provisions and terra firma has any effect upon the scurvy. This disease is not so common now as formerly; and is attributed generally to salt provisions, want of cleanliness, the free use of grease and fat (which is the reason for its prevalence among whale-men,) and, last of all, to laziness. It never could have been from the latter cause on board our ship; nor from the second, for we were a very cleanly crew, kept our forecastle in neat order, and were more particular about washing and changing clothes than many better-dressed people on shore. It was probably from having none but salt provisions, and possibly from our having run very rapidly into hot weather, after having been so long in the extremest cold.

Depending upon the westerly winds, which prevail off the coast in the autumn, the captain stood well to the westward, to run inside of the Bermudas, and in the hope of falling in with some vessel bound to the West Indies or the Southern States. The scurvy had spread no farther among the crew, but there was danger that it might; and these cases were bad ones.

Sunday, Sept. 11th. Lat. 30° 04' N., long. 63° 23' W.; Bermuda bearing north-north-west, distant one hundred and fifty miles. The next morning, about ten o'clock, "Sail ho" was cried on deck; and all hands turned up to see the stranger. As she drew nearer, she proved to be an ordinary-looking hermaphrodite brig, standing south-south-east; and probably bound out, from the Northern States, to the West Indies; and was just the thing we wished to see. She hove-to for us, seeing that we wished to speak her; and we ran down to her; boom-ended our studding-sails; backed our main top-sail, and hailed her—"Brig, ahoy!" —"Hallo!"—"Where are you from, pray?"—"From New York, bound to Curaçoa."—"Have you any fresh provisions to spare?"—"Aye, aye! plenty of them!" We lowered away the quarter-boat, instantly; and the captain and four hands sprang in, and were soon dancing over the water, and alongside the brig. In about half an hour, they returned with half a boat-load of potatoes and onions, and each vessel filled away, and kept on her course. She proved to be the brig Solon, of Plymouth, from the Connecticut river, and last from New York, bound to the Spanish Main, with a cargo of fresh provisions, mules, tin bake-pans, white oak, watermelon seeds, and other *notions.* The onions however there was no mistake about; and the mate of the brig told the men in the boat, as he passed the bunches over the side, that the Wethersfield girls had strung them on purpose for us the day he sailed. We had a notion, on board, that a new president had been chosen, the last winter, and, just as we filled away, the captain hailed and asked who was president of the United States. They answered, Andrew Jackson; but thinking that the old General could not have been elected for a third time, we hailed again, and they answered—Jack Downing; and left us to correct the mistake at our leisure.[53]

It was just dinner-time when we filled away; and the steward, taking a few bunches of onions for the cabin, gave the rest to us, with a bottle of vinegar. We carried them forward, stowed them away in the forecastle, refusing to have them cooked, and ate them raw, with our beef and bread. And a glorious treat they were. The freshness and crispness of the raw onion, with the earthy taste, give it a great relish to one who has been a long time on salt provisions. We were perfectly ravenous after them. It was like a scent of blood to a hound. We ate them at every meal, by the dozen; and filled our pockets with them, to eat in our watch on deck; and the beautiful bunches, rising in the form of a cone, from the largest at the bottom, to the smallest, no larger than a strawberry, at the top, soon disappeared. The chief use, however, of the fresh provisions, was for the men with the scurvy. One of them was able to eat, and he soon brought himself to, by gnawing

[53]This is a puzzling statement. The election of 1836 did not take place until 7 December. Martin Van Buren was then elected over William Henry Harrison, Hugh L. White, and Daniel Webster. Andrew Jackson remained President until March 1837. Possibly Captain Thompson had forgotten that 1836 rather than 1835 was an election year. Who Jack Downing was is not clear.

upon raw potatoes; but the other, by this time, was hardly able to open his mouth; and the cook took the potatoes raw, pounded them in a mortar, and gave him the juice to drink. This he swallowed, by the tea-spoonful at a time, and rinsed it about his gums and throat. The strong earthy taste and smell of this extract of the raw potato at first produced a shuddering through his whole frame, and after drinking it, an acute pain, which ran through all parts of his body; but knowing, by this, that it was taking strong hold, he persevered, drinking a spoonful every hour or so, and holding it a long time in his mouth; until, by the effect of this drink, and of his own restored hope, (for he had nearly given up, in despair) he became so well as to be able to move about, and open his mouth enough to eat the raw potatoes and onions pounded into a soft pulp. This course soon restored his appetite and strength; and in ten days after we spoke the Solon, so rapid was his recovery, that, from lying helpless and almost hopeless in his berth, he was at the mast-head, furling a royal.

With a fine south-west wind, we passed inside of the Bermudas; and notwithstanding the old couplet, which was quoted again and again by those who thought we should have one more touch of a storm before our voyage was up,—

> "If the Bermudas let you pass,
> You must beware of Hatteras—"

we were to the northward of Hatteras, with fine weather, and beginning to count, not the days, but hours, to the time when we should be at anchor in Boston harbor.

Our ship was in fine order, all hands having been hard at work upon her from daylight to dark, every day but Sunday, from the time we got into warm weather on this side the Cape.

It is a common notion with landsmen that a ship is in her finest trim when she leaves port to enter upon her voyage; and that she comes home, after a long absence,

> "With over-weathered ribs and ragged sails;
> Lean, rent and beggared by the strumpet wind."

But so far from that, unless a ship meets with some accident, or comes upon the coast in the dead of winter, when work cannot be done upon the rigging, she is in her finest order at the end of the voyage. When she sails from port, her rigging is generally slack; the masts need staying; the decks and sides are black and dirty from taking in cargo; riggers' seizings and overhand knots in place of nice seamanlike work; and everything, to a sailor's eye, adrift. But on the passage home, the fine weather between the tropics is spent in putting the ship into the neatest order. No merchant vessel looks better than an Indiaman, or a Cape Horn-er, after a long voyage; and many captains and mates will stake their reputation for seamanship upon the appearance of their ship when she hauls into the dock. All our standing rigging, fore and aft, was set up and tarred; the masts stayed; the lower and top-mast rigging rattled down, (or, up, as the fashion now is;) and so careful were our officers to keep the rattlins taut and straight, that we were obliged to go aloft upon the ropes and shearpoles with which the rigging was swifted in; and these were used as jury rattlins until we got close upon the coast. After this, the ship was scraped, inside and out, decks, masts, booms and all; a stage being rigged outside, upon which we scraped her down to the water-line; pounding the rust off the chains, bolts, and fastenings. Then, taking two days of calm under the line, we painted her on the outside, giving her open ports in her streak, and finishing off the nice work upon the stern, where sat Neptune in his car, holding his trident, drawn by sea horses; and re-touched the gilding and coloring of the cornucopia which ornamented her billet-head. The inside was then painted, from the sky-sail truck to the waterways—the yards black; mast-heads and tops, white; monkey-rail, black, white, and yellow; bulwarks, green; plank-shear, white, waterways, lead color, &c. &c. The anchors and ring-bolts, and other iron work, were blackened with coal-tar; and the steward kept at work, polishing the brass of the wheel, bell, capstan, &c. The cabin, too, is scraped, varnished, and painted; and the forecastle scraped and scrubbed; there being no need of paint and varnish for Jack's quarters. The decks are then scraped and varnished, and everything useless thrown overboard; among which, the empty tar barrels were set on fire and thrown overboard the first dark night, and left blazing astern, lighting up the ocean for miles. Add to all this labor, the neat work upon the rigging;—the knots, flemish-eyes, splices, seizings, coverings, pointings, and graffings, which show a ship in crack order. The last preparation, and which looked still more like coming into port, was getting the anchors over the bows, bending the cables, rowsing the hawsers up from between decks, and overhauling the deep-sea-lead-line.

Thursday, Sept. 15th. This morning the temperature and peculiar appearance of the water, the quantities of gulf-weed floating about, and a bank of clouds lying directly before us, showed that we were on the border of the Gulf Stream. This remarkable current, running north-east, nearly across the ocean, is almost constantly shrouded in clouds, and is the region of storms and heavy seas. Vessels frequently run from a clear sky and fair light wind, at once into a heavy sea, dark cloudy sky, and double-reefed top-sails. A sailor told me that on a passage from Gibraltar to Boston, his vessel neared the Gulf Stream with a light breeze, clear sky, and studding-sails out, alow and aloft; while, before it, was a long line of heavy, black clouds, lying like a bank upon the water, and a vessel coming out of it, under double-reefed top-sails, and with royal yards sent down. As they drew near, they began to take in sail after sail, until they were reduced to the same condition; and, after twelve or fourteen hours of rolling and pitching in a heavy sea, before a smart gale, they ran out of the bank on the other side, and were in fine weather again, and under their royals and skysails. As we drew into it, the sky became cloudy, the sea high, and everything had the appearance of the going off, or the coming on, of a storm. It was blowing no more than a stiff breeze; yet the wind, being north-east, which is directly against the course of the current, made an ugly, chopping sea, which heaved and pitched the vessel about, so that we were obliged to send down the royal yards, and to take in our light sails. At noon, the thermometer, which had been repeatedly lowered into the water, showed the temperature to be seventy; which was considerably above that of the air,—as is always the case in the centre of the Stream. A lad who had been at work at the royal mast-head, came down upon deck, and took a turn round the long-boat; and looking very pale, said he was so sick that he could stay aloft no longer, but was ashamed to acknowledge it to the officer. He went up again, but soon gave out and came down, and leaned over the rail, 'as sick as a lady passenger.' He had been to sea several years, and had, he said, never been sick before. It was caused by the irregular, pitching motion of the vessel, increased by the height to which he had been above the hull, which is like the fulcrum of the lever. An old sailor, who was at work on the top-gallant yard, said he felt disagreeably all the time, and was glad, when his job was done, to get down into the top, or upon deck. Another hand was sent to the royal masthead, who staid nearly an hour, but gave up. The work must be done, and the mate sent me. I did very well for some time, but the pitching over came me, though I had never been sick since the first two days from Boston, and had been in all sorts of weather and situations. Still, I kept my place, and did not come down, until I had got through my work, which was more than two hours. The ship certainly never acted so badly before. The current and wind running against one another, made such an ugly chopping sea that the vessel was pitched and jerked about in all manner of ways; the sails seeming to have no steadying power over her. The tapering points of the masts made various curves and angles against the sky overhead, and sometimes, in one sweep of an instant, described an arc of more than forty-five degrees, bringing up with a sudden jerk which made it necessary to hold on with both hands, and then sweeping off, in another long, irregular curve. I was not positively sick, and came down with a look of indifference, yet was not unwilling to get upon the comparative terra firma of the deck. A few hours more carried us through it, and when we saw the sun go down, upon our larboard beam, in the direction of the continent of North America, we had left the bank of dark, stormy clouds astern, in the twilight.

CHAPTER THIRTY-SIX
*Soundings . . . Lights about
home . . . Anchor down . . . Boston
Harbor . . . Leaving the ship*

Friday, Sept. 16th. Lat. 38° N., long.
69° oo′ W. A fine south-west wind; every hour carrying us nearer in
toward the land. All hands on deck at the dog watch, and nothing
talked about, but our getting in; where we should make the land;
whether we should arrive before Sunday; going to church; how Boston would look; friends; wages paid;—and the like. Every one was in
the best spirits; and, the voyage being nearly at an end, the strictness
of discipline was relaxed; for it was not necessary to order in a cross
tone, what every one was ready to do with a will. The little differences
and quarrels which a long voyage breeds on board a ship, were forgotten, and every one was friendly; and two men, who had been on the
eve of a battle half the voyage, were laying out a plan together for a
cruise on shore. When the mate came forward, he talked to the men,
and said we should be on George's Bank before tomorrow noon; and
joked with the boys, promising to go and see them, and to take them
down to Marblehead in a coach.

Saturday, 17th. The wind was light all day, which kept us back
somewhat; but a fine breeze springing up toward night, we were running fast in toward the land. At six o'clock we expected to have the
ship hove-to for soundings, as a thick fog, coming up, showed we were
near them; but no order was given, and we kept on our way. Eight
o'clock came, and the watch went below, and, for the whole of the first
hour, the ship was tearing on, with studding-sails out, alow and aloft,
and the night as dark as a pocket. At two bells the captain came on
deck, and said a word to the mate, when the studding-sails were hauled
into the tops, or boom-ended, the after yards backed, the deep-sea-lead
carried forward, and everything got ready for sounding. A man on the
sprit-sail yard with the lead, another on the cat-head with a handful
of the line coiled up, another in the fore chains, another in the waist,
and another in the main chains, each with a quantity of the line coiled
away in his hand. "All ready there, forward?"—"Aye, aye, sir'"—
"He-e-ave"—"Watch! ho! watch!" sings out the man on the sprit-sail
yard, and the heavy lead drops into the water. "Watch! ho! watch!"
bawls the man on the cat-head, as the last fake of the coil drops from
his hand, and "Watch! ho! watch!" is shouted by each one as the line

falls from his hand; until it comes to the mate, who tends the lead, and has the line in coils on the quarter-deck. Eighty fathoms, and no bottom! A depth as great as the height of St. Peters! The line is snatched in a block upon the swifter, and three or four men haul it in and coil it away. The after yards are filled away, the studding -sails hauled out again, and in a few minutes more the ship had her whole way upon her. At four bells, backed again, hove the lead, and—soundings! at sixty fathoms! Hurrah for Yankee land! Hand over hand, we hauled the lead in, and the captain, taking it to the light, found the black mud on the bottom. Studding-sails taken in; after yards filled, and ship kept on under easy sail all night; the wind dying away.

The soundings on the American coast are so regular that a navigator knows as well where he has made land, by the soundings, as he would by seeing the land. Black mud is the soundings of Block Island. As you go toward Nantucket, it changes to a dark sand; then, sand and white shells; and on George's Banks, white sand; and so on. Being off Block Island, our course was due east, to Nantucket Shoals, and the South Channel; but the wind died away and left us becalmed in a thick fog, in which we lay the whole of Sunday. At noon of

Sunday, 18th, Block Island bore, by calculation, N. W. ¼ W. fifteen miles; but the fog was so thick all day that we could see nothing.

Having got through the ship's duty, and washed and shaved, we went below, and had a grand time overhauling our chests, laying aside the clothes we meant to go ashore in, and throwing overboard all that were worn out and good for nothing. Away went the woollen caps in which we had carried hides upon our heads, for sixteen months, on the coast of California; the duck frocks, for tarring down rigging; and the worn-out and darned mittens and patched woollen trousers which had stood the tug of Cape Horn. We hove them overboard with a good will; for there is nothing like being quit of the very last appendages and remnants of our evil fortune. We got our chests all ready for going ashore; ate the last 'duff' we expected to have on board the ship Alert; and talked as confidently about matters on shore as though our anchor were on the bottom.

"Who'll go to church and hear Father Taylor with me a week from to-day?"

"I will," says Jack; who said aye to everything.

"Go away, salt water!" says Tom. "As soon as I get both legs ashore, I'm going to shoe my heels, and button my ears behind me, and start off into the bush, a straight course, and not stop till I'm out of the sight of salt water!"

"Oh! belay that! Spin that yarn where nobody knows your filling! If you get once moored, stem and stern, in old B——'s grog-shop, with a coal fire ahead and the bar under your lee, you won't see daylight for three weeks!"

"No!" says Tom, "I'm going to knock off grog, and go and board at the Home, and see if they won't ship me for a deacon!"

"And I," says Bill, "am going to buy a quadrant and ship for navigator of a Hingham packet!"

These and the like jokes served to pass the time while we were lying waiting for a breeze to clear up the fog and send us on our way.

Toward night a moderate breeze sprang up; the fog however continuing as thick as before; and we kept on to the eastward. About the middle of the first watch, a man on the forecastle sang out, in a tone which showed that there was not a moment to be lost,—"Hard up the helm!" and a great ship loomed up out of the fog, coming directly down upon us. She luffed at the same moment, and we just passed one another; our spanker boom grazing over her quarter. The officer of the deck had only time to hail, and she answered, as she went into the fog again, something about Bristol—probably a whaleman from Bristol, Rhode Island, bound out. The fog continued through the night, with a very light breeze, before which we ran to the eastward, literally feeling our way along. The lead was hove every two hours and the gradual change from black mud to sand, showed that we were approaching Nantucket South Shoals. On Monday morning, the increased depth and deep blue color of the water, and the mixture of shells and white sand which we brought up, upon sounding, showed that we were in the channel, and nearing George's; accordingly, the ship's head was put directly to the northward, and we stood on, with perfect confidence in the soundings, though we had not taken an observation for two days, nor seen land; and the difference of an eighth of a mile out of the way might put us ashore. Throughout the day a provokingly light wind prevailed, and at eight o'clock, a small fishing schooner, which we passed, told us we were nearly abreast of Chatham lights. Just before midnight, a light land-breeze sprang up, which carried us well along; and at four o'clock, thinking ourselves to the northward of Race Point, we hauled upon the wind and stood into the bay, north-north-west, for Boston light, and commenced firing guns for a pilot. Our watch went below at four o'clock, but could not sleep, for the watch on deck were banging away at the guns every few minutes. And, indeed, we cared very little about it, for we were in Boston Bay; and if fortune favored us, we could all 'sleep in' the next night, with nobody to call the watch every four hours, and have what sailors call 'a blow out on sleep.'

We turned out, of our own will, at daybreak, to get a sight of land. In the grey of the morning, one or two small fishing smacks peered out of the mist; and when the broad day broke upon us, there lay the low sand-hills of Cape Cod, over our larboard quarter, and before us, the wide waters of Massachusetts Bay, with here and there a sail gliding over its smooth surface. As we drew in toward the mouth of the harbor, as toward a focus, the vessels began to multiply, until the bay seemed actually alive with sails gliding about in every direction; some on the wind, and others before it, as they were bound to or from the emporium of trade and centre of the bay. It was a lively sight for us, who had been months on the ocean without seeing anything but two solitary sails; and over two years without seeing more than the three or four traders on the coast of California. There were the little coasters, bound to and from the various towns along the south shore, down in the bight of the bay, and to the eastward; here and there a square-rigged vessel standing out to seaward; and, far in the distance, beyond Cape Ann, was the smoke of a steamer, stretching along in a narrow, black cloud upon the water. Every sight was full of beauty and interest. We were coming back to our homes; and the signs of civilization, and prosperity, and happiness, from which we had been so long banished, were multiplying about us. The high land of Cape Ann and the rocks and shore of Cohasset were full in sight, the light-houses, standing like sentries in white before the harbors, and even the smoke from the chimneys on the plains of Hingham was seen rising slowly in the morning air. One of our boys was the son of a bucket-maker; and his face lighted up as he saw the tops of the well-known hills which surround his native place. About ten o'clock a little boat came bobbing over the water, and put a pilot on board, and sheered off in pursuit of other vessels bound in. Being now within the scope of the telegraph stations, our signals were run up at the fore, and in half an hour afterwards, the owner on 'change, or in his counting-room, knew that his ship was below; and the landlords, runners, and sharks in Ann street learned that there was a rich prize for them down in the bay: a ship from round the Horn, with a crew to be paid off with two years' wages.

The wind continuing very light, with nothing to do all hands were sent aloft to strip off the chafing gear; and battens, parcellings, roundings, hoops, mats, and leathers, came flying from aloft, and left the rigging neat and clean, stripped of all its sea bandaging. The last touch was to put to the vessel by painting the sky-sail poles; and I was sent up to the fore, with a bucket of white paint and a brush, and touched her off, from the truck to the eyes of the royal rigging. At noon, we lay becalmed off the lower light-house; and it being about slack water, we made little progress. A firing was heard in the direction of Hingham, and the pilot said there was a review there. The Hingham boy got wind of this, and said if the ship had been twelve hours sooner, he should have been down among the soldiers, and in the booths, and having a grand time. As it was, we had little prospect of getting in before night. About two o'clock a breeze sprang up ahead, from the westward, and we began beating up against it. A full-rigged brig was beating in at the same time, and we passed one another, in our tacks, sometimes one and sometimes the other, working to windward, as the wind and tide favored or opposed. It was my trick at the wheel from two till four; and I stood my last helm, making between nine hundred and a thousand hours which I had spent at the helms of our two vessels since the last time we were on Boston bay. The tide beginning to set against us, we made slow work; and the afternoon was nearly spent, before we got abreast of the inner light. In the mean time, several vessels were coming down, outward bound; among which, a fine, large ship, with yards squared, fair wind and fair tide, passed us like a race-horse, the men running out upon her yards to rig out the studding-sail booms. Toward sundown the wind came off in flaws, sometimes blowing very stiff, so that the pilot took in the royals, and then dying away, when, anxious to get us in before the tide became too strong, the royals were set again. This keeping us running up and down the rigging all the time, one hand was sent aloft at each mast-head, to stand-by to loose and furl the sails, at the moment of the order. I took my place at the fore, and loosed and furled the royal five times between Rainsford Island and the Castle. At one tack we ran so near to Rainsford Island, that, looking down from the royal yard, the island, with its hospital buildings, nice gravelled walks, and green plats, seemed to lie directly under our yard-arms. So close is the channel to some of these islands, that we ran the end of our flying-jib-boom over some of the out-works of the fortifications on George's Island; and had an opportunity of seeing the advantages of that point as a fortified place; for, in working up the channel, we presented a fair stem and stern, for raking, from the batteries, three or four times. One gun might have knocked us to pieces.

All hands had all set their hearts upon getting up to town before night and going ashore, but the tide beginning to set strong against us, and the wind, what there was of it, being ahead, we made but little by weather-bowing the tide, and the pilot gave orders to cock-bill the anchor and overhaul the chain; and making two long stretches, which brought us into the roads, under the lee of the castle, clewed up the top-sails, and let go the anchor; and for the first time since leaving San Diego,—one hundred and thirty-five days—our anchor was upon bottom. In half an hour more, we were lying snugly, with all sails furled, safe in Boston harbor, our long voyage ended; the well-known scene about us; the dome of the State House fading in the western sky; the lights of the city starting into sight, as the darkness came on; and at nine o'clock the clangor of the bells, ringing their accustomed peals; among which the Boston boys tried to distinguish the well-known tone of the Old South. Let no one talk of the sights and sounds of home who has not seen and heard them for the first time after a long, long absence at sea and in strange and half savage lands where the sound of the church going bell is never heard.

We had just done furling the sails, when a beautiful little pleasure-boat luffed up into the wind, under our quarter, and the junior partner of the firm to which our ship belonged, jumped on board.[54] I saw him from the mizen top-sail yard, and knew him well. He shook the captain by the hand, and went down into the cabin, and in a few moments came up and inquired of the mate for me. The last time I had seen him, I was in the uniform of an under-graduate of Harvard College, tight dress coat and kid gloves, and now, to his astonishment, there came down from aloft a 'rough alley' looking fellow, with duck trousers and red shirt, long hair, and face burnt as black as an Indian's. He shook me by the hand, congratulated me upon my return and my appearance of health and strength, and said my friends were all well. I thanked him for telling me what I should not have dared to ask; and if—

> ——— "the first bringer of unwelcome news
> Hath but a losing office; and his tongue
> Sounds ever after like a sullen bell—"

certainly I shall ever remember this man and his words with pleasure.

The captain went up to town in the boat with Mr. H[ooper], and left us to pass another night on board ship, and come up with the morning's tide under command of the pilot.

So much did we feel ourselves to be already at home, by anticipation, that our plain supper of hard bread and salt beef was barely touched; and many on board, to whom this was the first voyage, could scarcely sleep. As for myself, by one of those anomalous changes of feeling of which we are all the subjects, I found myself in a state of indifference, for which I could by no means account. A year before, while carrying hides on the coast of California, the assurance that in a twelve-month we should see Boston, made me half wild; but now that I was actually there, and in sight of home, the emotions which I had so long anticipated feeling, I did not find, and in their place was a state of very nearly entire antipathy. Something of the same experience was related to me by a sailor whose first voyage was one of five years upon the North-west Coast. He had left home, a lad, and after several years of

[54]Samuel Hooper.

very hard and trying experience, found himself homeward bound; and such was the excitement of his feelings that, during the whole passage, he could talk and think of nothing else but his arrival, and how and when he should jump from the vessel and take his way directly home. Yet when the vessel was made fast to the wharf and the crew dismissed, he seemed suddenly to lose all feeling about the matter. He told me that he went below and changed his clothes; took some water from the scuttle-butt and washed himself leisurely; overhauled his chest, and put his clothes all in order; took his pipe down from its place, filled it, and sitting down upon his chest, smoked it slowly for the last time— looked round upon the forecastle in which he had spent so many years, and being alone and his shipmates scattered, he began to feel actually unhappy. Home became almost a dream; and it was not until his brother (who had heard of the ship's arrival) came down into the forecastle and told him of things at home, and who were waiting there to see him, that he could realize where he was, and feel interest enough to put him in motion toward that place for which he had longed, and of which he had dreamed, for years. There is probably so much of excitement in prolonged expectation, that the quiet realizing of it produces a momentary stagnation of feeling as well as of effort. It was a good deal so with me. The activity of preparation, the rapid progress of the ship, the first making land, the coming up the harbor, and old scenes breaking upon the view, produced a mental as well as bodily activity, from which the change to a perfect stillness, when both expectation and the necessity of labor failed, left a calmness, almost of indifference, from which I must be roused by some new excitement. And the next morning, when all hands were called, and we were busily at work, clearing the decks, and getting everything in readiness for going up to the wharves,—loading the guns for a salute, loosing the sails, and manning the windlass—mind and body seemed to wake together.

About ten o'clock, a sea-breeze sprang up, and the pilot gave orders to get the ship under weigh. All hands manned the windlass, and the long-drawn "Yo, heave ho!" which we had last heard dying away among the desolate hills of San Diego, soon brought the anchor to the bows; and, with a fair wind and tide, a bright sunny morning, royals and skysails set, ensign, streamer, signals, and pennant, flying, and banging away at our guns, we came swiftly and handsomely up to the city. Off the end of the wharf, we rounded-to and let go our anchor; and no sooner was it on the bottom, than the decks were filled with people: custom-house officers; Topliff's agent, to inquire for news; others, inquiring for friends on board, or left upon the coast; dealers in grease, besieging the galley to make a bargain with the cook for his slush; 'loafers' in general; and last and chief, boarding-house runners, to se-

Bowen's Picture of Boston. Courtesy Huntington Library

Map of Boston, 1834

cure their prey.[55] Nothing can exceed the obliging disposition of these last, and the interest they take in a sailor returned from a long voyage with a plenty of money. Two or three of them, at different times, took me by the hand; remembered me perfectly; were quite sure I had boarded with them before I sailed; were delighted to see me back; gave me their cards; had a hand-cart waiting on the wharf, on purpose to take my things up; would lend me a hand to get my chest ashore; bring a bottle of grog on board if we did not haul in immediately,— and the like. In fact, we could hardly get clear of them, to go aloft and furl the sails. Sail after sail, for the hundredth time, in fair weather and in foul, we furled now for the last time together, and came down and took the warp ashore, manned the capstan, and with a chorus which waked up half the North End, and rang among the buildings in the dock, we hauled her in to the wharf. Here, too, the landlords and runners were active and ready, taking a bar to the capstan, lending a hand at the ropes, laughing and talking and telling the news. The city bells were just ringing one when the last turn was made fast, and the crew dismissed, and in five minutes more, not a soul was left on board the good ship Alert, but the old ship-keeper, who had come down from the counting-house to take charge of her.

[55]Samuel Topliff (1789-1864) was a news dealer and author who operated the Merchants' Reading Room in Boston from 1814 until 1842. He sold foreign news from his correspondents and from his agents who boarded incoming ships to newspapers in Boston, New York, and Philadelphia. He has been called the forerunner of the Associated Press.

CONCLUDING CHAPTER

I trust that they who have followed me to the end of my narrative, will not refuse to carry their attention a little farther, to the concluding remarks which I here present to them.

This chapter is written after the lapse of a considerable time since the end of my voyage, and after a return to my former pursuits; and in it I design to offer those views of what may be done for seamen, and of what is already doing, which I have deduced from my experiences, and from not a little subsequent reflection.

The romantic interest which many take in the sea, and in those who live upon it, may be of use in exciting their attention to this subject, though I cannot but feel sure that all who have followed me in my narrative must be convinced that the sailor has no romance in his every-day life to sustain him, but that it is very much the same plain, matter-of-fact drudgery and hardship, which would be experienced on shore. If I have not produced this conviction, I have failed in persuading others of what my own experience has most fully impressed upon myself.

There is a witchery in the sea, its songs and stories, and in the mere sight of a ship, and the sailor's dress, especially to a young mind, which has done more to man navies, and fill merchantmen, than all the press-gangs of Europe. I have known a young man with such a passion for the sea, that the very creaking of a block stirred up his imagination so that he could hardly keep his feet on dry ground; and many are the boys, in every seaport, who are drawn away, as by an almost irresistible attraction, from their work and schools, and hang about the decks and yards of vessels, with a fondness which, it is plain, will not be broken or resisted. No sooner, however, has the young sailor begun his new life in earnest, than all this fine drapery falls off, and he learns that it is but work and hardship, after all. This is the true light in which a sailor's life is to be viewed; and if in our books, and in the speeches made at Seamen's Friend Societies' anniversaries, we could leave out all the parade about 'blue water,' 'blue jackets,' 'open hearts,' going down to the sea in ships, seeing God's hand on the deep, and the like; and take it up like any other practical subject, I am quite sure we should do full as much for those we wish to benefit. The question is, what can be done for the sailor, as he is,—a being to be fed, and clothed, and lodged, for whom laws must be made and executed, and who is to be instructed in useful knowledge, and, above all, to be brought under religious influence and restraint? It is upon these topics that I propose to make a few observations.

In the first place, I have no fancies about equality on board ship. It is a thing out of the question, and certainly, in the present state of mankind, not to be desired. I cannot conceive of any rational man's troubling his head about it. I never knew a sailor who found fault with the orders and ranks of the service; and if I expected to pass the rest of my life before the mast, I would not wish to have the power of the captain diminished an iota. It is absolutely necessary that there should be one head and one voice to control everything, and be responsible for everything. There are emergencies which require the instant exercise of extreme power. These emergencies do not allow of consultation; and they who would be the captain's constituted advisers might be the very men over whom he would be called upon to exert his authority. It has been found necessary to vest in every government, even the most democratic, some extraordinary, and, at first sight, alarming powers; trusting in public opinion, and subsequent accountability, to restrain the exercise of them. These are provided to meet exigencies, which all hope may never occur, but which yet by possibility may occur, and if they should, and there were no power to meet them instantly, there would be an end put to the government at once. So it is with the authority of the shipmaster. It will not answer to say that he shall never do this and that thing, because it does not seem always necessary and advisable that it should be done. He has great cares and responsibilties; is answerable for everything; and is subject to emergencies which perhaps no other man exercising authority among civilized people is subject to. Let him, then, have powers commensurate with his utmost possible need; only let him be held strictly responsible for the exercise of them. Any other course would be in justice, as well as bad policy.

In the treatment of those under his authority, the captain is amenable to the common law, like any other person. He is liable at common law for murder, assault and battery, and other offenses; and in addition to this, there is a special statute of the United States which makes a captain or other officer liable to imprisonment for a term not exceeding five years, and to a fine not exceeding a thousand dollars, for inflicting any cruel punishment upon, withholding food from, or in any other way maltreating a seaman. This is the state of the law on the subject; and the relation in which the parties stand, and the peculiar necessities, excuses, and provocations arising from that relation, are merely circumstances to be considered in each case. As to the restraints upon the master's exercise of power, the laws themselves seem, on the whole, to be sufficient. I do not see that we are in need, at present, of more legislation on the subject. The difficulty seems to lie rather in the administration of the laws; and this is certainly a matter that deserves great consideration, and one which presents no little difficulty.

In the first place, the courts have said that public policy requires the power of the master and officers should be sustained. Many lives and a great amount of property are constantly in their hands, for which they are strictly responsible. To preserve these, and to deal justly by the captain, and not lay upon him a really fearful responsibility, and then tie up his hands, it is essential that discipline should be supported. And if every time a seaman may think himself ill used, the captain is to be vexed with a suit and damages, it will discourage and bring discredit upon the whole class. In the second place, there is always great allowance to be made for false swearing and exaggeration by seamen, and for combinations among them against their officers; and it is to be remembered that the latter have often no one to testify on their side. These are weighty and true statements, and should not be lost sight of by the friends of seamen. On the other hand, sailors make many complaints, some of which are well founded.

On the subject of testimony, seamen labor under a difficulty full as great as that of the captain. It is a well-known fact, that they are usually much better treated when there are passengers on board. The presence of passengers is a restraint upon the captain, not only from his regard to their feelings and to the estimation in which they may hold him, but because he knows they will be influential witnesses against him if he is brought to trial. Though officers may sometimes be inclined to show themselves off before passengers, by freaks of office and authority, yet cruelty they would hardly dare to be guilty of. It is on long and distant voyages, where there is no restraint upon the captain, and none but the crew to testify against him, that sailors need most the protection of the law. On such voyages as these, there are many cases of outrageous cruelty on record, enough to make one heart-sick, and almost disgusted with the sight of man; and many, many more, which have never come to light, and never will be known, until the sea shall give up its dead. Many of these have led to mutiny and piracy,—stripe for stripe, and blood for blood. If on voyages of this description the testimony of seamen is not to be received in favor of one another, or too great a deduction is made on account of their being seamen, their case is without remedy; and the captain, knowing this, will be strengthened in that disposition to tyrannize which the possession of absolute power, without the restraints of friends and public opinion, is too apt to engender.

It is to be considered, also, that the sailor comes into court under very different circumstances from the master. He is thrown among landlords, and sharks of all descriptions; is often led to drink freely; and comes upon the stand unaided, and under a certain cloud of suspicion as to his character and veracity. The captain, on the other hand, is backed by the owners and insurers, and has an air of greater respectability; though, after all, he may have but a little better education than the sailor, and sometimes, (especially among those engaged in certain voyages that I could mention) a very hackneyed conscience.

These are the considerations most commonly brought up on the subject of seamen's evidence; and I think it cannot but be obvious to every one that here, positive legislation would be of no manner of use. There can be no rule of law regulating the weight to be given to seamen's evidence. It must rest in the mind of the judge and jury; and no enactment or positive rule of court could vary the result a hair, in any one case. The effect of a sailor's testimony in deciding a case must depend altogether upon the reputation of the class to which he belongs, and upon the impression he himself produces in court by his deportment, and by those infallible marks of character which always tell upon a jury. In fine, after all the well-meant and specious projects that have been brought forward, we seem driven back to the belief, that the best means of securing fair administration of the laws made for the protection of seamen, and certainly the only means which can create any important change for the better is the gradual one of raising the intellectual and religious character of the sailor, so that as an individual, and as one of a class, he may, in the first instance, command the respect of his officers, and if any difficulty should happen, may upon the stand carry that weight which an intelligent and respectable man of the lower class almost always does with a jury. I know there are many men who, when a few cases of great hardship occur, and it is evident that there is an evil somewhere, think that some arrangement must be made, some law passed, or some society got up, to set all right at once. On this subject there can be no call for any such movement, on the contrary, I fully believe that any public and strong action would do harm, and that we must be satisfied to labor silently in the less easy and less exciting task of gradual improvement, and abide the issue of things working slowly together for good.

Equally injudicious would be any interference with the economy of the ship. The lodging, food, hours of sleep, &c., are all matters which, though capable of many changes for the better, must yet be left to regulate themselves. And I am confident that there will be, and is now going on a gradual improvement in all such particulars. The forecastles of most of our ships are small, black, and wet holes, which few landsmen would believe held a crew of ten or twelve men on a voyage of months or years. and often, indeed in most cases, the provisions are not good enough to make a meal anything more than a necessary part of a day's duty;* and on the score of sleep, I fully believe that the lives of merchant seamen are shortened by the want of it. I do not refer to those occasions when it is necessarily broken in upon; but, for months, during fine weather, in many merchantmen, all hands are kept, throughout the day, and, then, there are eight hours on deck for one watch each night. Thus it is usually the case that at the end of a voyage, where there has been the finest weather, and no disaster, the crew have a wearied and worn-out appearance. They never sleep longer than four hours at a time, and are seldom called without being really in need of more rest. There is no one thing that a sailor thinks more of as a luxury of life on shore, than a whole night's sleep. Still, all these things must be left to be gradually modified by circumstances. Whenever hard cases occur, they should be made known, and masters and owners should be held answerable, and will, no doubt, in time, be influenced in their arrangements and discipline by the increased consideration in which sailors are held by the public. It is perfectly proper that the men should live in a different part of the vessel from the officers; and if the forecastle is made large and comfortable, there is no reason why the crew should not live there as well as in any other part. In fact, sailors prefer the forecastle. It is their accustomed place, and in it they are out of the sight and hearing of their officers.

As to their food and sleep, there are laws, with heavy penalties, requiring a certain amount of stores to be on board, and safely stowed; and, for depriving the crew unnecessarily of food or sleep, the captain is liable at common law, as well as under the statute before referred to. Farther than this, it would not be safe to go. The captain must be the judge when it is necessary to keep his crew from their sleep; and

---

*I am not sure that I have stated, in the course of my narrative, the manner in which sailors eat, on board ship. There is no table, and no knives, forks, and plates, in a forecastle; but the kid (a wooden tub, with iron hoops) is placed on the floor, and the crew sit round it, and each man cuts for himself with the common jack-knife or sheath-knife, that he carries about him. They drink their tea out of tin pots, holding little less than a quart each.

These particulars are not looked upon as hardships, and, indeed, may be considered matters of choice. Sailors, in our merchantmen, furnish their own eating utensils, as they do many of the instruments which they use in the ship''s work, such as knives, palms and needles, marline-spikes, rubbers, &c. And considering their mode of life in other respects, the little time they would have for laying and clearing away a table with its apparatus and the room it would take up in a forecastle, as well as the simple character of their meals, consisting generally of only one piece of meat—it is certainly a convenient method, and, as the kid and pans are usually kept perfectly clean, a neat and single one. I had supposed these things to be generally known, until I heard, a few months ago, a lawyer of repute, who has had a good deal to do with marine cases, ask a sailor upon the stand whether the crew had "got up from table" when a certain thing happened.

sometimes a retrenching, not of the necessaries, but of some of the little niceties of their meals, as, for instance, *duff* on Sunday, may be a mode of punishment, though I think generally an injudicious one.

I could not do justice to this subject without noticing one part of the discipline of a ship, which has been very much discussed of late, and has brought out strong expression of indignation from many,— I mean the infliction of corporal punishment. Those who have followed me in my narrative will remember that I was witness to a scene of terrible cruelty inflicted upon my own shipmates; and indeed I can sincerely say that the simple mention of the word flogging, brings up in me feelings which I can hardly control. Yet, when the proposition is made to abolish it entirely and at once; to prohibit the captain from ever, under any circumstances, inflicting corporal punishment; I am obliged to pause, and, I must say, to doubt exceedingly the propriety of making any positive enactment which shall have that effect. If the design of those who are writing on this subject is merely to draw public attention to it, and to discourage the practice of flogging, and bring it into disrepute, it is well; and, indeed, whatever may be the end they have in view, the mere agitation of the question will have that effect, and, so far, must do good. Yet I should not wish to take the command of a ship to-morrow, running my chance of a crew, as most masters must, and know, and have my crew know, that I could not, under any circumstances, inflict even moderate chastisement. I should trust that I might never have to resort to it; and, indeed, I scarcely know what risk I would not run, and to what inconveniences I would not subject myself, rather than do so. Yet not to have the power of holding it up *in terrorem*, and indeed of protecting myself, and all under my charge, by it, if some extreme case should arise, would be a situation I should not wish to be placed in myself, or to take the responsibility of placing another in.

Indeed, the difficulties into which masters and officers are liable to be thrown, are not sufficiently considered by many whose sympathies are easily excited by stories, frequent enough, and true enough, of outrageous abuse of this power. It is to be remembered that more than three fourths of the seamen in our merchant vessels are foreigners. They are from all parts of the world. A great many from the north of Europe, beside Frenchmen, Spaniards, Portuguese, Italians, men from all parts of the Mediterranean, together with Lascars, Negroes, and, perhaps worst of all, the off-casts of British men-of-war, and men from our own country who have gone to sea because they have made the land too hot to hold them.

As things now are, many masters are obliged to sail without knowing anything of their crews, until they get out at sea. There may be pirates or mutineers among them; and one bad man will often infect all the rest; and it is almost certain that some of them will be ignorant foreigners, hardly understanding a word of our language, accustomed all their lives to no influence but force, and perhaps understanding the use of the knife quite as well as of the marline-spike. No prudent master, however peaceably inclined, would go to sea without his pistols and handcuffs were he the most peaceable man alive. Even with such a crew as I have supposed, kindness and moderation would be the best policy, and the duty of every conscientious man; and the administering of corporal punishment might be dangerous, and of doubtful use. But the question is not, what a captain ought or had better do, but whether it shall be put out of the power of every captain, under any circumstances, to make use of, even moderate, chastisement. As the law now stands, a parent may correct moderately his child, and the master his apprentice; and the case of the shipmaster has been placed upon the same principle. The statutes, and the common law as expounded in the decisions of courts, and in the books of commentators, are distinct and unanimous upon this head, that the captain may inflict moderate corporal chastisement, for a reasonable cause. If the punishment is excessive, or the cause not sufficient to justify it, he is answerable; and the jury are to determine, by their verdict in each case, whether, under all the circumstances, the punishment was moderate, and for a justifiable cause.

This seems to be to be as good a position as the whole subject can be left in. I mean to say, that no positive enactment, going beyond this, is needed, or would be a benefit either to masters or men, in the present state of things. This again would seem to be a case which should be left to the gradual working of its own cure. As the character of seamen improve, punishment will become less necessary; and as the character of officers is raised, they will be less ready to inflict it; and, still more, the infliction of it upon intelligent and respectable men, will be an enormity which will not be tolerated by public opinion, and by juries, who are the pulse of the body politic. No one can have a greater abhorrence of the infliction of such punishment than I have, and a stronger conviction that severity is bad policy with a crew; yet I would ask every reasonable man whether he had not better trust to the practice becoming unnecessary and disreputable; to the measure of moderate chastisement and a justifiable cause being better understood, and thus, the act becoming dangerous, and in course of time to be regarded as an unheard-of barbarity—than to take the responsibility of prohibiting it, at once, in all cases, and in whatever degree, by positive enactment?

There is, however, one point connected with the administration of justice to seamen, to which I wish seriously to call the attention of those interested in their behalf, and, if possible, also of some of those concerned in that administration. This is, the practice which prevails of making strong appeals to the jury in mitigation of damages, or to the judge, after a verdict has been rendered against a captain or officer, for a lenient sentence, on the grounds of their previous good character, and of their being poor, and having friends and families depending upon them for support. These appeals have been allowed a weight which is almost incredible, and which, I think, works a greater hardship upon seamen than any one other thing in the laws, or the execution of them. Notwithstanding every advantage the captain has over the seaman in point of evidence, friends, money, and able counsel, it becomes apparent that he must fail in his defence. An appeal is then made to the jury, if it is a civil action, or to the judge for a mitigated sentence, if it is a criminal prosecution, on the two grounds I have mentioned. The same form is usually gone through in every case. In the first place, as to the previous good character of the party. Witnesses are brought from the town in which he resides, to testify to his good character, and to his unexceptionable conduct when on shore. They say that he is a good father, or husband, or son, or neighbor, and that they never saw in him any signs of a cruel or tyrannical disposition. I have even known evidence admitted to show the character he bore when a boy at school. The owners of the vessel, and other merchants, and perhaps the president of the insurance company, are then introduced; and they testify to his correct deportment, express their confidence in his honesty and say that they have never seen anything in his conduct to justify a suspicion of his being capable of cruelty or tyranny. This evidence is then put together, and great stress is laid upon the extreme respectability of those who give it. They are the companions and neighbors of the captain, it is said,—men who know him in his business and domestic relations, and who knew him in his early youth. They are also men of the highest standing in the community, and who, as the captain's employers, must be supposed to know his character. This testimony is then contrasted with that of some half dozen obscure sailors, who, the counsel will not forget to add, are exasperated against the captain because he has found it necessary to punish them moderately, and who have combined against him, and if they have not fabricated a story entirely, have at least exaggerated it, so that little confidence can be placed in it.

The next thing to be done is to show to the court and jury that the captain is a poor man, and has a wife and family, or other friends, depending upon him for support; that if he is fined, it will only be taking bread from the mouths of the innocent and helpless, and laying a burden upon them which their whole lives will not be able to work off; and that if he is imprisoned, the confinement, to be sure, he will have to bear, but the distress consequent upon the cutting him off from his labor and means of his earning wages, will fall upon a poor wife and helpless children, or upon an infirm parent. These two topics, well put, and urged home earnestly, seldom fail of their effect.

In deprecation of this mode of proceeding, and in behalf of men who I believe are every day wronged by it, I would urge a few considerations which seem to me to be conclusive.

First, as to the evidence of the good character the captain sustains on shore. It is to be remembered that masters of vessels have usually been brought up in a forecastle; and upon all men, and especially upon those taken from lower situations, the conferring of absolute power is too apt to work a great change. There are many captains whom I know to be cruel and tyrannical men at sea, who yet, among their friends, and in their families, have never lost the reputation they bore in childhood. In fact, the sea-captain is seldom at home, and when he is, his stay is short, and during the continuance of it he is surrounded by friends who treat him with kindness and consideration, and he has everything to please, and at the same time to restrain him. He would be a brute indeed, if, after an absence of months or years, during his short stay, so short that the novelty and excitement of it has hardly time to wear off, and the attentions he receives as a visitor and stranger hardly time to slacken,—if, under such circumstances, he could justify a townsman or neighbor in testifying against his correct and peaceable deportment. With the owners of the vessel, also, to which he is attached, and among merchants and insurers generally, he is a very different man from what he may be at sea, when his own master, and the master of everybody and everything about him. He knows that upon such men, and their good opinion of him, he depends for his bread. So far from their testimony being of any value in determining what his conduct would be at sea, one would expect that the master who would abuse and impose upon a man under his power, would be the most compliant and deferential to his employers at home.

As to the appeal made in the captain's behalf on the ground of his being poor and having persons depending upon his labor for support, the main and fatal objection to it is, that it will cover every case of the kind, and exempt nearly the whole body of masters and officers from the punishment the law has provided for them. There are very few, if any, masters or other officers of merchantmen in our country, who are not poor men, and having either parents, wives, children or other relatives, depending mainly or wholly upon their exertions for support in life. Few others follow the sea for subsistence. Now if this appeal is to have weight with courts in diminishing the penalty the law would otherwise inflict, is not the whole class under a privilege which will, in a degree, protect it in wrong-doing? It is not a thing that happens now and then. It is the invariable appeal, the last resort, of counsel, when everything else has failed. I have known cases of the most flagrant nature, where, after every effort has been made for the captain, and yet a verdict rendered against him, and all other hope failed, this appeal has been urged, and with such success that the punishment has been reduced to something little more than nominal; the court not seeming to consider that it might be made in almost every such case that could come before them. It is a little singular, too, that it seems to be confined to cases of shipmasters and officers. No one ever heard of a sentence, for an offence committed on shore, being reduced by the court on the ground of the prisoner's poverty, and the relation in which he may stand to third persons. On the contrary, it has been thought that the certainty that disgrace and suffering will be brought upon others as well as himself, is one of the chief restraints upon the criminally disposed. Besides, this course works a peculiar hardship in the case of the sailor. For if poverty is the point in question, the sailor is the poorer of the two; and if there is a man on earth who depends upon whole limbs and an unbroken spirit for support, it is the sailor. He, too, has friends to whom his hard earnings may be a relief, and whose hearts will bleed at any cruelty or indignity practised upon him. Yet I never knew this side of the case to be once adverted to in these arguments addressed to the leniency of the court, which are now so much in vogue; and certainly they are never allowed a moment's consideration when a sailor is on trial for revolt, or for an injury done to an officer. Notwithstanding the many difficulties which lie in a seaman's way in a court of justice, there would be little to complain of, presuming that they will be modified in time, were it not for these two appeals. A case occurred a few years ago in Boston of a captain who was indicted under the statute for cruel treatment of his mate. The crew told a consistent story, and after a searching cross examination in which no flaw was detected in their testimony, his counsel, who was a gentleman distinguished for his success in getting off criminals, abandoned the defense, and a verdict of guilty was brought in. The case was an extreme one, and the counsel admitted it to be so, but as a last resort, made an appeal to the leniency of the court, on the two grounds I have mentioned. The president of the office at which the vessel had been insured, the owners, and one or two other merchants, some of whom were relatives of the captain, were brought upon the stand, and said that they should not hesitate to employ him again, and had never seen anything at all exceptionable in his conduct. And this was set off against the testimony of the crew, which, it must be remembered, was the only testimony the mate could properly have had in his favor. An eloquent appeal was then made for the captain's wife and family; and upon these two considerations only, the case was submitted to the judge, who, after a preface in which he alluded to the very great respectability of the witnesses for the prisoner, and the extreme hardship of his case, pronounced a sentence which made the conviction hardly worth proving. Another case of perhaps a still stronger character occurred more recently; where, after a verdict of guilty, the court pronounced a sentence which surprised every body for its lenity, and created a good deal of excitement; and to which the court was led by this, in connection with other reasons,—the weight to be given to the testimony of respected merchants and other townsmen of the captain, in opposition to the facts sworn to by the crew; though here, as in the previous case, as there were no passengers on board, all the testimony had been brought that could possibly have been brought, and no discrepancy was pretended to have been discovered in it.

It is no cause of complaint that the testimony of seamen against their officers is viewed with suspicion, and that great allowance is made for combinations and exaggeration. On the contrary, it is the judge's duty to charge the jury on these points, strongly. But there is reason for objection, when, after a strict cross examination of witnesses, after the arguments of counsel, and the judge's charge, a verdict is found against the master, that the court should allow the practice of hearing appeals to its lenity, supported solely by evidence of the captain's good conduct when on shore, (especially where the case is one in which no evidence but that of sailors could have been brought against the accused,) and then, on this ground, and on the invariable claims of the wife and family, be induced to cut down essentially the penalty imposed by a statute made expressly for masters and officers of merchantmen, and for no one else.

There are many particulars connected with the manning of vessels, the provisions given to crews, and the treatment of them while at sea, upon which I could find a good deal to say; but as I have, for the most part, remarked upon them as they came up in the course of my narrative, I will offer nothing further now, except on the single point of the manner of shipping men. This, it is well known, is usually left entirely to shipping-masters, the owners and masters usually knowing nothing about their crews. This is a cause of a great deal of difficulty, which might be remedied by the captain, or owner, if he has any knowledge of seamen, attending to it personally. The active member of the firm to which our ship belonged, Mr. S[turgis], had been himself a master of a vessel, and generally selected the crew from a number sent down to him from the shipping-office. In this way he almost always had healthy, serviceable, and respectable men; for any one who has seen much of sailors can tell pretty well at first sight, by a man's dress, countenance, and deportment, what he would be on board ship. This same gentleman was also in the habit of seeing the crew together, and speaking to them previously to their sailing. On the day before our ship sailed, while the crew were getting their chests and clothes on board, he went down into the forecastle and spoke to them about the voyage, the clothing they would need, the provision he had made for them, and saw that they had a lamp and a few other conveniences. If owners or masters would more generally take the same pains, they would often save their crews a good deal of inconvenience beside creating a sense of satisfaction and gratitude, which makes a voyage begin under good auspices, and goes far toward keeping up a better state of feeling throughout its continuance.

It only remains for me now to speak of the associated public efforts which have been making of late years for the good of seamen: a far more agreeable task than that of finding fault even where fault there is. The exertions of the general association, called the American Seamen's Friend Society, and of the other smaller societies throughout the Union, have been a true blessing to the seaman; and bid fair, in course of time to change the whole nature of the circumstances in which he is placed, and give him a new name, as well as a new character. These associations have taken hold in the right way, and aimed both at making the sailor's life more comfortable and creditable, and at giving him spiritual instruction. Connected with these efforts, the spread of temperance among seamen, by means of societies, called, in their own nautical language, Windward-Anchor Societies, and the distribution of books; the establishment of Sailors' Homes, where they can be comfortably and cheaply boarded, live quietly and decently, and be in the way of religious services, reading and conversation; also the institution of Savings Banks for Seamen; the distribution of tracts and Bibles;—are all means which are silently doing a great work for this class of men. I am glad that they make the religious instruction of seamen their prominent object. If this is gained, there is no fear but that all other things necessary will be added unto them. A sailor never becomes interested in religion, without immediately learning to read, if he did not know how before; and regular habits, forehandedness (if I may use the word) in worldly affairs, and hours reclaimed from indolence and vice, which follow in the wake of the converted man, make it sure that he will instruct himself in the knowledge necessary and suitable to his calling. The religious change is the great object.

If this is secured, there is no fear but that knowledge of things of the world will come in fast enough. With the sailor, as with all other men in fact, the cultivation of the intellect, and the spread of what is commonly called useful knowledge, while religious instruction is neglected, is little else than changing an ignorant sinner into an intelligent and powerful one. That sailor upon whom, of all others, the preaching of the Cross is least likely to have effect, is the one whose understanding has been cultivated, while his heart has been left to its own devices. I fully believe that those efforts which have their end in the intellectual cultivation of the sailor; in giving him scientific knowledge; putting it in his power to read everything, without securing, first of all, a right heart which shall guide him in judgment; in giving him political information, and interesting him in newspapers;—an end in the furtherance of which he is exhibited at ladies' fairs and public meetings, and complimented for his gallantry and generosity,—are all doing a harm which the labors of many faithful men cannot undo. I trust that I shall not be understood as being opposed to the education of seamen in any useful knowledge, or as thinking their piety is to be secured by their ignorance. I am only expressing my conviction that we are doing them no good by reversing the gospel rule, which says, "see *first* the Kingdom of Heaven."

The establishment of Bethels in most of our own seaports, and in many foreign ports frequented by our vessels, where the gospel is regularly preached; and the opening of 'Sailors' Homes', which I have before mentioned, where there are usually religious services and other good influences, are doing a vast deal in this cause. But it is to be remembered that the sailor's home is on the deep. Nearly all his life must be spent on board ship; and to secure a religious influence there, should be the great object. The distribution of Bibles and tracts into cabins and forecastles, will do much toward this. There is nothing which will gain a sailor's attention sooner, and interest him more deeply, than a tract, especially one which contains a story. It is difficult to engage their attention in mere essays and arguments, but the simplest and shortest story, in which home is spoken of, kind friends, a praying mother or sister, a sudden death, and the like, often touch the hearts of the roughest and most abandoned. The Bible is to the sailor a sacred book. It may lie in the bottom of his chest voyage after voyage; but he never treats it with positive disrespect. I never knew but one sailor who doubted its being the inspired word of God; and he was one who had otherwise received an uncommonly good education, from mistaken parents, who had brought him up without any early religious influence. The most abandoned man of our crew, one Sunday morning, asked one of the boys to lend him his Bible. The boy said he would, but was afraid he would make sport of it. "No!" said the man, "I don't make sport of God Almighty." This is a feeling general among sailors, and is a good foundation for religious influence.

A still greater gain is made whenever, by means of a captain who is interested in the eternal welfare of those under his command, there can be secured the performance of regular religious exercises, and the exertion of that mighty influence which a captain possesses for good, or for evil, on the side of religion. There are occurrences at sea which he may turn to great account,—a sudden death, the apprehension of danger, or the escape from it, and the like; and all the calls for gratitude and faith. Besides, this state of things alters the whole current of feeling between the crew and their commander. His authority assumes more of the parental character; and kinder feelings exist. Godwin, though an infidel, in one of his novels, describing the relation in which a tutor stood to his pupil, says that the conviction the tutor was under, that he and his ward were both alike awaiting a state of eternal happiness or misery, and that they must appear together before the same judgment-seat, operated so upon his naturally morose disposition, as to produce a feeling of kindness and tenderness toward his ward, which nothing else could have caused. Such must be the effect upon the relation of master and common seaman.

There are now many vessels sailing under such auspices, in which great good is done. Yet I never happened to fall in with one of them. There was not a man, captain, officer, or common seaman, in any of the vessels that I was in, who pretended to being a religious man. In our ship we had a crew of swearers, from the captain to the smallest boy, who swore the worst of them all. I did not hear a prayer made, a chapter read in public, nor see anything approaching to a religious service, for two years and a quarter. There were, in the course of the voyage, many incidents which made, for the time, serious impressions upon our minds, and which might have been turned to our good; but there being no one to use the opportunity, and no exercises, the regular return of which might have kept something of the feeling alive in us, the advantage of them was lost, to some, perhaps, forever.

The good which a single religious captain may do can hardly be calculated. In the first place, as I have said, a kinder state of feeling exists on board the ship. There is no profanity allowed; and the men are not called by any opprobrious names, which is a great thing with sailors. The Sabbath is observed. This gives the men a day of rest, even if they pass it in no other way. Such a captain, too, will not allow a sailor on board his ship to remain unable to read his Bible and the books given to him; but will usually instruct those who need it, in writing, arithmetic, and navigation; for he has a good deal of time on his hands, which he can easily employ in such a manner. He will also have regular religious exercises; and, in fact, by the power of his example, and, where it can judiciously be done, by the exercise of his authority, he gives a character to the ship, and all on board. In foreign ports, a ship is known by her captain; for, there being no general rules in the merchant service, each captain may adopt a plan of his own. It is to be remembered, too, that there are, in most ships, boys of a tender age, whose characters for life are forming, as well as old men, whose lives must be drawing toward a close. The greater part of sailors die at sea; and when they find their end approaching, if it does not, as is often the case, come without warning, they cannot, as on shore, send for a clergyman, or some religious friend, to speak to them of that hope in a Saviour, which they have neglected, if not despised, through life; but if the little hull does not contain such an one within its compass, they must be left without human aid in their great extremity. When such commanders and such ships, as I have last described, shall become more numerous, the hope of the friends of seamen will be greatly strengthened; and it is encouraging to remember that the efforts among common sailors will soon raise up such a class; for those of them who are brought under such influences will inevitably be the ones to succeed to the places of trust and authority. If there is on earth an instance where a little leaven may leaven the whole lump, it is that of the religious shipmaster.

It is to the progress of this work among seamen that we must look with the greatest confidence for the remedying of those numerous minor evils and abuses that we so often hear of. It will raise the character of seamen, both as individuals and as a class. It will give weight to their testimony in courts of justice, secure better usage to them on board ship, and add comforts to their lives on shore and at sea. There are some laws that can be passed to remove temptation from their way and to help them in their progress; and some changes in the jurisdiction of the lower courts, to prevent delays, may, and probably will be made. But generally speaking, more especially in things which concerns the discipline of ships, we had better labor in this great work, and view with caution the proposal of new laws and arbitrary regulations, remembering that most of those concerned in the making of them must necessarily be little qualified to judge of their operation.

These views of the religious bearing of my subject have for the most part been impressed upon my mind since the occurence of the events recorded in my narrative. In filling out and revising my narrative, I have studiously avoided incorporating into it any impressions which were not made upon me at the time of the happening of the events there related, or altering the character of any which I had expressed;

and it is mainly for the purpose of now speaking more fully upon the religious bearing of my subject, in addition to a few other topics which I have briefly treated of, that I offer this chapter to my readers.

Without any formal dedication of my narrative to that class of men, of whom common life it is intended to be a picture, I have yet borne them constantly in mind during its preparation. I cannot but trust that those of them, into whose hands it may chance to fall, will find in it that which shall render any profession of sympathy and good wishes on my part unnecessary. And I will take the liberty, on parting with my reader, who has gone down with us to the ocean, and "laid his hand upon its mane," to commend to his kind wishes, and to the benefit of his efforts, that class of men with whom, for a time, my lot was cast. I wish the rather to do this, since I feel that whatever attention this book may gain, and whatever favor it may find, I shall owe almost entirely to that interest in the sea, and those who follow it, which is so easily excited in us all.

JOURNALS, LETTERS AND DOCUMENTS
Relative to Dana's Voyages to California
in 1834-1836 and 1859-1860

From a photograph. Courtesy Craigie House, Cambridge, Mass.

Richard Henry Dana, Jr., 1859

JOURNAL OF A
VOYAGE FROM BOSTON
TO THE COAST OF
CALIFORNIA

[*The journal which Dana kept on his voyage to California in 1834-1836 is contained in eight and a quarter pages of manuscript in an unbound, sewn pamphlet of eight sheets, folded to form 16 pages. In addition to the journal itself, there is a table of dimensions, page of positions of the* Alert *on the homeward voyage, a title on the cover, and four blank leaves. With the journal at the Massachusetts Historical Society are two lists, largely duplicating one another, which apparently detail Dana's outfit for the voyage, clothing purchased, and cash advanced to him. These are included here. At a number of points in the journal, Dana wrote in, apparently later, words and phrases which were apparently memoranda useful in the writing of* Two Years before the Mast. *These have been included in footnotes.*

This journal was first published in The American Neptune, *vol. XII, no. 3 (July 1952), pp. 177-185 as edited by James Allison. This edition has been useful in the preparation of the text and notes presented here although the present editor does not agree with Mr. Allison's readings at every point.*]

Thursday Aug. 14th 1834. Went on board brig "Pilgrim," lying at Central Wharf. Towards night, being nearly ready for sea, the vessel hauled out into the stream, and came to anchor.

Friday Aug. 15th—34. Took on board gunpowder—had a fine breeze but did not set sail.

Saturday Aug. 16th—34. At 10 A.M. Wind E.N.E. took a pilot on board, weighed anchor, and set sail; but the wind coming round dead East, came to anchor in the Roads. At 10 P. M. a light breeze springing up from the Southard and Westward, got under weigh and stood out to sea.

Sunday Aug. 17th—34. Here out of sight of land. At night all hands called aft, and the sea watch set. The Crew consists of Fr. A. Thompson, Captain; Andrew B. Amerzene, chief mate; Geo. Forster 2nd Mate; 5 able seamen; 4 green hands, Steward, Cook, and Carpenter. This vessel is about two hundred tons burthen, and owned by Messrs. Bryant, Sturgis, and Co. Boston.

Tuesday Aug. 19th. Came into the Gulf Stream. In the evening—wind, rain, and a heavy sea. Double reefed the topsails.

Wednesday Aug. 20th. Fine weather returned with the morning. About two o'clock P. M. two sails hove in sight; they passed to leeward, out of reach of hail. They were the Ship "Helen Mar" of New York, and the Brig "Mermaid" of Boston; both homeward bound.

Thursday Aug. 21st—Spoke the French Ship "La Carolina" from Havre to New York. Desired her to report Brig "Pilgrim" from Boston to the Coast of California.

Friday Sept 5th. Spoke an English Brig, 49 days from Buenos Ayres for Liverpool. In the afternoon a small Brazilian Hermaphrodite Brig, passed astern; probably bound to Portugal.

Sunday Sept 7th—Fell in with the trade winds.

Monday Sept 22nd. At 7 A.M. a small Hermaphrodite Brig, filled with men, stood down for us. Not liking her appearance made sail, and ran before the wind. The vessel continued in chase all day; at night was nearly out of sight. It coming on dark, we changed our course, covered the binnacle, and cabin lights, and at daylight were out of sight.

Wednesday Oct 1st. Crossed the Equator at longitude 24°24' W.

Friday Oct 3rd. Broke the 2nd Mate for negligence and other misconduct. James Hall, one of the crew, made 2nd Mate, with consent of all hands.

Sunday Oct 5th. Saw land at daybreak. At 12 M. off Pernambuco; could distinguish the tower of Olinda, Church, Houses etc. At sunset, land out of sight.

Tuesday Nov 4th. Saw the Falkland Islands. Left them on the larboard Quarter. At Sunset saw land from mast-head on the starboard bow.

Wednesday Nov. 5th. Off Cape Horn. At night violent storm. Wind S. W.

Thursday 6th. Stormy.

Friday. Calm. At night a strong gale.

Saturday. Do. Ditto.

Monday 10th. High sea and violent wind.

Tuesday 11th. Rain, Hail, and Snow, with high winds.

Wednesday 12th. Ditto.

Friday 14th. Morning. Passed the Cape with Fine weather. At 2 P. M. Spoke the whale-ship "New England," 120 days from New York. (Albatrosses)

Saturday 15th. The "New England" being still in sight, backed our main-top-sail, and the Captain (Terry) came on board and spent the day.

Monday Nov 17th. At 7 A.M. Geo. Ballmer, one of the crew, fell overboard from the main rigging and was lost. Lowered away the whale-boat and manned her; but the man being heavily dressed, and ignorant of swimming, was never seen more.

Tuesday Nov 25th. At day-break saw Juan Fernandes. Came to anchor in the harbour, same night. Spoke, going in, a Chilian brig of war, bound to Valparaiso.

Wednesday Nov 26th. Went ashore, and brought off six casks of water. The Governor of the Island, the commander of the soldiers, and the priest, came on board to dinner. The same afternoon got under weigh; saw the whale-ship "Cortes" of New Bedford, lying off and on the Island.

Friday December 19th. Crossed the Equator.

Tuesday Jan. 13th—35. Made the land of Point Conception, Lat. 34°32′ N. Long. 120°6′ W.

Wednesday Jan 14th—35. Arrived at Santa Barbara. One hundred and fifty days from Boston.

Found at Santa Barbara, the Brig "Ayacoucha" Capt Wilson, under English colours.

Thursday Jan. 15—35. Arrived the Hermaphrodite Brig "Loriotte" Capt Nye, from the Sandwich Islands; and the Genoese Ship "La Rosa" from St Diego, bound up to windward. Same night got under weigh in a gale from the South East.

Sunday Jan 18th—35. Returned to our anchorage. From Santa Barbara sailed to Monterey. There, entered our cargo at the Custom House and commenced trading. Lay at Monterey 12 days; then returned to Santa Barbara. Thence to St Pedro. Lying at St Pedro, the Mexican Hermaphrodite Brig "Fazio." Sailed from St Pedro, and arrived at St Diego, *March 14th.* Found there the Ship "Lagoda" Capt Bradshaw, of Boston, and the Brig "Ayacoucha," loading for home. The Ship "California" Capt Arthur, belonging to Messrs. Bryant, Sturgis, and Co. had sailed thence for Boston during the last of February.

Discharged our hides, salt etc, and left a gang on shore at the Hide House. Geo. Forster, sometime 2nd Mate, here ran away, and went home in the "Lagoda," which sailed for Boston early in April. The "Ayacoucha" Capt. Wilson, sailed for Callao, *Sunday March 22nd.*

Friday March 27th 1835. Sailed from St Diego.

Wednesday April 1st Arrived at St Pedro. Found there the Hermaphrodite Brig "Loriotte," bound to St Blas. From St Pedro, sailed to Santa Barbara.[1] Found there the Genoese Ship "La Rosa," bound to St Diego, and the Brig "Catalina" just arrived from Valparaiso and Callao. From Santa Barbara, sailed to St Pedro; thence to St Juan's;

[1]Pencilled notation "kelp" in the ms.

↩ 367

Permanent — No. 393. Three hundred ninety three

IN PURSUANCE *of an* ACT
OF THE CONGRESS *of the* **United States of America,** *entitled "An act concerning the registering and recording of* SHIPS *or* VESSELS," *Samuel Hooper, of Boston, in the State of Massachusetts*

having taken or subscribed the oath *required by the said Act; and having* sworn *that* he together with John Bryant, William Sturgis & John Bryant Jr. all of Boston, aforesaid, are the ____

only owners of the Ship or Vessel called the Alert ____ *of* Boston ____ *whereof* Edward H. Faucon *is at present Master, and a* CITIZEN *of the* **United States,** as he hath sworn ____

and that the said Ship or Vessel was built at Boston in Year 1828, as appears by Reg. No. 114. issued at this office April 6th 1832, now cancelled, property partially transferred ____

And Said Register having certified that the said Ship or Vessel has two *Decks and* three Masts *and that her length is* One hundred thirteen feet, four inches *her breadth* Twenty eight feet, ____ *her depth* Fourteen feet ____ *and that she measures* Three hundred Ninety eight $\frac{18}{95}$ ____ *tons; that she is a* Ship ____ *has a* Square Stern, No galleries *and a* Billet *head; And the said* Samuel Hooper ____ *having agreed to the description and admeasurement above specified, and sufficient security having been given, according to the said Act, the said* Ship ____ *has been duly registered at the Port of* Boston and Charlestown

Given *under* our *hand and seal at the Port of* Boston ____ *this* 25th ____ *day of* November ____ *in the year one thousand eight hundred and* thirty four ____

A.B.

S. M. J.

Register of the Ship, ALERT, *1834*

thence to St Diego. Arr. *Friday May 8th—35*. Discharged hides. Was left ashore to join the gang at the Hide House.[2]

Tuesday May 12th—35. Arr. the Ship "Rosa" and the Brig "Catalina," and set sail, after discharging hides, for the Windward.

Thursday May 14th—35. Sailed the Brig "Pilgrim" for the windward. Same day arr. the Mexican Hermaphrodite Brig "Fazio" to take in Hides and tallow for Callao.

Wednesday July 8th—35. Arr. the Brig "Pilgrim" from the Windward. Reported at Santa Barbara, the Ship "Alert" from Boston, owned by Messrs. Bryant, Sturgis and Co. Capt Thompson of the "Pilgrim," transferred to the "Alert"; and Capt Faucon of the Alert to the Pilgrim.

Saturday July 11th. The "Pilgrim" set sail for the Windward.

Saturday July 18th—35. Sailed the "Fazio" for St Blas, Callao, etc.

Tuesday Aug. 25th Arrived Ship "Alert" from the windward, with seven thousand hides; also horns and tallow. Discharged cargo and took in ballast.

Saturday Aug. 29th. Arrived Brig "Catalina" from the windward.

Monday Sept 7th. Went on board the Ship "Alert."

Tuesday Sept 8th. Sailed from St Diego. Friday 11th. Arrived at St Pedro; found there the Brig "Pilgrim." Sailed from St Pedro in company with the Brig "Catalina." Arrived at Santa Barbara Sun. Oct. 4th. Sailed Sun 11th; arr. at St Diego Oct. 15th. Discharged hides and sailed Sun. 18th. Arrived at St Juan's on the 20th and sailed on the 21st. Arrived at St Pedro Thursday Oct. 22nd.[3]

Sailed from St Pedro, Sunday Nov. 1st. Arr. at Santa Barbara on the 5th. Found there the Brig "Ayacucho" from Callao[4] and the "Avon" Capt. Hinckley from Oahu. Nov 10th arr. the Whale Ship "Wilmington and Liverpool Packet" of New Bedford, from the Coast of Japan. 1900 barrels of oil. On the 12th slipped our cables for a South East gale; returned to our anchorage the next day. Saturday the 14th Nov. set sail for Monterey. Tuesday evening took a gale of wind from the N. W. Split our three topsails, foresail, jib, and foretopmast staysail. Continued under reefed topsails for eight days. Arrived at St Francisco on Friday the 4th of December. Lying at St. Francisco a Russian Brig from the N. W. Coast of America. Sailed on Sunday the 27th. Tuesday 29th arr. at Monterey. Spoke, going in, the Brig "Diana" of the Sandwich Islands, from the N. W. Coast, bound in.

---

[2]Pencilled notation "superstit. Cook, Sailmaker" in the ms.

[3]Pencilled notation "funeral, game cocks, George" above this entry in the ms.

[4]Notation in ink by Dana, "War with France."

42

Juan Fernandez

The mountains were high, but not so overhanging as they appeared to be by star light. They seemed to bear off towards the centre of the island; & were green & well wooded, with some large &, I am told, exceedingly fertile valleys, & with mule tracks leading to different parts of the islands. I cannot here forget how my friend Stimson & myself got the laugh of the crew upon us by our eagerness to get on shore. The captain having ordered the quarter boat to be lowered, we both sprang down into the forecastle, filled our jacket pockets with tobacco to barter with the people a'shore, & when the officer called for "four hands in the boat", nearly broke our necks in our haste to be first over the side, & had the pleasure of pulling ahead of the brig with a tow line for a half an hour, & coming on board again to be laughed at by the crew who had seen our maneuvre; as we they say—— "flogged altogether": ——

After breakfast, the 2nd mate was ordered ashore with five hands to fill the water casks, & to my joy, I was among the number. We pulled ashore with the empty casks; & here again fortune favoured me, for the water was too thick & muddy to put into the casks, & the Governor had sent men up to the head of the stream to clear it out for us, wh. gave us nearly two hours of leisure. This leisure I employed in wandering about among the houses, & eating a little fruit wh. was offered to us. The country. Ground apples, melons, grapes, strawberries of an enormous size, & cherries, abound. The latter are said to have been planted by Lord Anson. The soldiers were miserably clad, & asked with some interest whether we had shoes to sell on board. I doubt very much if they had the means of buying them. They were very eager to get tobacco, & for wh. they gave shells, fruits &c. Knives also were in demand, but we were forbidden by the Governor to let any one have them, as he told, that all the people there, except the soldiers, & a few officers, were convicts sent fr. Valparaiso, & that it was necessary to keep all weapons fr. their hands. The island it seems belongs to Chili & had been used by the government as a sort of Botany Bay for nearly

Facsimile Page from Dana's original manuscript of 1840

Sailed[5] from Monterey Wednesday 6th for Santa Barbara. (Found at Monterey the Russian Company's Barque "Sitka" from the N. W. coast. Sailed on Friday the 1st for St Blas etc.) Sailed in company with us the Brig "Diana" for Oahu. Spoke off Point Conception the Brig "Convoy" of the Sandwich Islands; hunting for otter. Arrived at Santa Barbara[6] Sun. Jan. 10th. Wedn. 13th slipped our cable and went to sea for a South East gale. Returned to our anchorage the following day. Sailed for St Pedro Feb. 1st. Arrived there on the following day. Found there the Brigs "Ayacucho" and "Pilgrim." Took from the latter three thousand hides. Thursday the 4th got under weigh. Arr. at St Diego on the 6th. The Italian ship "La Rosa" and the Brig "Catalina" had sailed thence for Callao. Discharged hides and sailed Wed. 10th for San Pedro; arrived at San Pedro on the 14th. Passed on the Brig "Ayacucho." On the 23rd received news of the arrival of the Ship "California," Arthur, from Boston, at Santa Barbara on the 20th. Received letters from home. Thursday 25th Feb. Set sail for Santa Barbara. (While lying at St Pedro, slipped our cables on Sat 19th for a gale of wind at the N. E. On Monday morning, returned to our anchorage.) Arr. at Santa Barbara Sunday the 28th. On the[7] following Saturday set sail for the leeward; having taken in our water, and left one of the crew, Geo. Marsh, (who shipped on the coast) for 2nd officer of the "Ayacucho." Arr. at St Pedro, on Monday the 7th of March and left on the following Wednesday. Thursday, March 10th St Diego. Landed[8] our hides and tallow, unbent the sails, housed the top-gallant-masts, and commenced discharging ballast. April 15th arr. the Brig "Pilgrim" for the windward.[9] Sunday, the 24th arr. the Ship "California," Arthur, from the windward. Sailed on the 29th Sailed the Brig "Pilgrim" for San Pedro. "Reefer" Sun. May the 8th sailed from St Diego homeward bound. Same day, sailed the Ship "California" for the windward.

Stood out to sea with a fine breeze from the N.W. which continued until we came to the N. E. trades, which we fell[10] in with in Lat 29° N. These trade winds continued to blow fresh until we were in Lat. 10°N. when we had more variable winds, with some rain. As we approached the line, the winds hauled to the Southward and Eastward. Crossed the Equinoctial line on the afternoon of Saturday the 28th day of May, in Long 110°W. being twenty days out from St. Diego.

[5]Notation in ink, "fight" in the ms.

[6]Notation in ink "wedding" in the ms.

[7]Notation in ink "papers" in the ms.

[8]Notation in ink "Hope" in the ms.

[9]Notation in ink "Fresh Provisions" in the ms.

[10]Notation in ink "Mr. Nutall" in the ms.

From a photograph of a watercolor painting by F. Roux. Courtesy Musée de la Marine

Ship BAZAAR, *Boston 1834. A vessel*
similar to the ship ALERT

Immediately[11] after crossing the line we had the trade winds steadily from the E. S. E. and on Sunday the 5th of June were in Lat. 29°30' S. Supposed Long. 119° W.

Were in the Lat of Cape Horn during the last week in June, and commenced running to the Eastward. On Saturday July 2nd at 1 o'clock P.M. fell in with three large ice islands. On July 4th saw 34 islands. Being unable to proceed any farther on account of the ice, wore ship and stood to the Northward. Being free from ice, attempted again the passage of the Cape; but were again driven back by the ice. The Capt. then determined to run for the Straits of Magellan. Having reached the Lat. 53° and having continual easterly winds and thick, foggy weather, and no prospect of finding the mouth of the Straits; we again stood for Cape Horn. This time we saw but little ice, but had continual head winds with snow and rain. On Friday the 22nd of July made the Island of Staten Land, and on Saturday the 23rd stood to the Northward with a strong wind from the S. W. This breeze continued with little variation, and on Sunday July 31st we were in Lat. 36°37S. Long 40° W. Sunday Aug. 7th spoke the English barque "Mary and Catherine" from Bahia bound to Calcutta. Lat 25°59' N. Long. 27° W. On Monday 8th passed a large Ship under English colours standing S. by E. Friday Aug. 12th at daylight, made the Island of Trinidad situated in Lat 20°28' S. Long 29°8' W. At 12 M. it bore N. W. ½ N. Dist 27 miles. Sunday the 14th at noon. Lat 16° 30' S. Thursday 18th at 3 P. M. made the island of Fernando Noronha Lat 3°55 S. Long 32°35' W. Between 12 o'clock on Friday night, and 1 o'clock on Saturday morning Crossed the Equator in Long 33° W. Having been 29 days from Staten Land, a distance of upwards of 4000 miles. Sunday, Aug 28th.[12] N. E. trades. Lat. 12° 58' Long. [38°00' W.]

Sunday Sept. 4th. Lat. 22°01' N. Long.[13] 52°01'15' W.

Sunday Sept 11th Lat 30° N. Monday 12th[14] Lat 31° N. Long 65° W. Spoke brig "Solon" of Plymouth, from New York for Curaçoa. Saturday[15] 17th at 10 o'clock P. M. got soundings in 60 fathoms water, black mud bottom. Supposed Block Island Channel. Kept under easy sail throughout Saturday night. Sunday 18th—a dead calm and heavy fog throughout the day. Toward evening a light breeze—Kept away for Nantucket South Shoals—At sun-down on Monday the 19th were off Chatham Lights. Were in Boston Bay on Tuesday morning at daylight. At eight A.M. took on board a pilot. Throughout the day, light and baffling winds, at 7 P.M. came to anchor just below the Castle.

11Notation in ink "Sounds at sea" in the ms.
12Notation in pencil "top gall. yard" in the ms.
13Pencilled notation "thunder storm" in the ms.
14Pencilled notation "scurvy" in the ms.
15Pencilled notation "Gulf stream" in the ms.

On Wednesday the 21st day of September 1836, The Ship "Alert" was made fast to the wharf and the crew discharged.[16]

Sailed Sunday May 8th.

Tuesday, May 10th Lat. 26°58′N. Long 118°08′ W.
Sunday—15th—14°56′ N—116°14 W.
Wednesday 18th—9°54′ N—113°17′ W.
Sunday 22nd—5°14′ N—106°45′ W.
—— *29th—1°50* S.—114°55
—— *5th June—19°29′* S.—118°01′ W.
——*12th—26°04* S.—116°31
Friday 17th—30°19′ S.—116°44
Sunday 19th—34°15.—116°38.
—— *26th—47°50.—113°49.*
—— *July 3rd—55°12.—89°5′*
Monday 4th—54°27.—85 21
Sunday 10th—54°10′—79° 07′
—— *17th—55°52′—70°26′*
—— *24th—50°27′—62°13′*
—— *31st—36°41′—38°08*
—— *7th Aug. 25°57′—27°36′*
—— *14th—16°33′* S.—29°21 W.
Sat. 20th—Crossed the Line Long. 35 W.
Sunday 21st—3°29′ N.—35° 15′
—— *28th—12°47′* N.—38°00′
—— *4th Sept. 22°01* N.—51°29′ W
——*11—30°04′* N.—63°23′
—— *18th—41°00—71°30* W.

[*Annotations on verso of title page. They may be notes on dimensions of* Alert.]

Length fore and aft	109 ft.
Lower masts—Main	54 feet
" —fore	52 feet
" —Mizen	48 feet
Topmasts—Main	45 feet
" —fore	43½ ft.
" —Mizen	40 ft.
Main yard—	51 ft.
fore yard—	50 ft.
Cross Jack yard	40 feet
Main Topsail Yard	40 ft.
Fore Topsail Yard	39 ft.

16At the end of the ms., Dana pencilled the notation "Chro-chre-nometer."

Mizen Topsail Yard—	29 ft.	
Beam	27 ft.	

[Presumably a list of Richard Henry Dana Jr.'s seagoing outfit. No date.]

1 Monkey jacket	5.32	5.32
6 checked Shirts (2.90¢) (1.67)	.92½	5.40
2 pair of Thick Trousers	3.00	6.25
4 " " Thin "	.92	3.68
2 Scotch Caps	.37½	.75
2 Tarpaulin Hats	.75	1.50
2 Straw Hats	.12½	.25
1 pair of Boots	3.25	3.25
2 " of thick shoes	1.37½	2.75
5 " " thin "	1.40	7.00
2 " " woolen mittens	.25	.50
1 " " leather "	.50	.50
4 Flannel Shirts		
2 pair of Flannel Drawers		
2 thick waist-coats	2.12	4.25
2 Guernsey Frocks	1.32½	2.75
1 Mattress	5.00	5.00
2 pair of Blankets		
1 piece of Bocking Comforter		
2 Hunter's Cravats		
1 Sea Chest	3.50	3.50
1 Canvass-Bag	.62	.62
2 Blue Jackets	7.00	14.00
2 Oil-Cloth Coats	2.00	4.00
2 Oil-Cloth Trousers	1.00	2.00
2 pair of knit Drawers		
4 pair of Stockings		
Sheath-Knives and Belts		
1 Sou'wester		
Jacknifes		
1 Tin-Pot and Spoon		

[1 page manuscript, Massachusetts Historical Society.]

[Presumably a list of Richard Henry Dana Jr.'s seagoing outfit. It draws together items separately priced in the previous list, which may have been a working draft, and adds prices for some items.]

1 Sea chest	3.50
4 pair duck trousers	3.68

From a painting by M. F. R. de Haas. Courtesy Robert A. Weinstein

"The vessel I am going in is small . . . but a remarkably fast sailer."

1 Blue Jacket	7.00
2 Oil cloth Coats	4.00
2 " " trousers	2.00
1 pair Cowhide boots	3.25
2 pair " shoes	2.75
5 pair Calf skin shoes	7.00
2 pair thick trousers	6.25
2 pair woolen mittens	.50
1 pair leather "	.50
2 Checked Shirts	1.80
1 cotton shirt	.67
2 thick waistcoats	4.25
2 Guernsey Frocks	2.75
2 Scotch caps	.75
1 Monkey Jacket	5.32
[wax?] over for voyage	.25
["] imposition for boots	.53
	$56.75

2 Tarpaulins	1.50
2 Straw Hats	.83
1 Souwester	1.00
4 Jacknifes	.62
1 pair of scissors	.12
1 Sheath Belt	.25
2 Spoons	.8
1 Canvass Bag	.62
1 Tin Pot	.25
	62.02

1 Tin pan	.14
1 checked shirt	.90
2 Sheath knives	.25
	63.31

Purchased of the Effects of Geo. Ballmer,
   deceased;

One Blue Jacket	$3.00
2 White Duck trousers	2.50
	$5.50

Purchased from the Capt's slop chest—

2 Striped cotton shirts	$[blank]

Taken up

1 Sheath Knife	$ .75
1 Red flannel Shirt	2.50
Received from the Steward	4.00
One pound of Wax	1.25
Four yds. of white Flannel	3.00
Received of T. M. Harris	5.00
Received of the Steward	3.00
T. M. Harris	5.00
Steward	2.00

LETTERS OF
RICHARD HENRY DANA, JR.,
1834-1836

Richard Henry Dana, Jr. to Miss Elizabeth E. Dana, Newport, Rhode Island, dated Cambridge, Massachusetts, 11 August 1834. Ms., Craigie House, Cambridge, Massachusetts.

My Dear Aunt Betsey—

Father has just come out from Boston and informs me that we are to sail on Wednesday the 13th, so I have set down to write you immediately. I must thank you in the first place for your letter. I shall take it with me and there will be times when I shall read it with pleasure and profit.

You mention your not having taken leave of me when you set out for Newport. I observed it, and knew the reason. It is not the first time that I have known you to be silent, when others who feel less have said more. I have said but little to you at any time of the great obligations which we are under to you, for they are not of a kind that can be repaid with words. I trust that my conduct is generally a pretty fair representation of what I feel, so that being conscious of what *I feel,* I have a full believe [sic.] that you *know* my feelings from my conduct.

I know very well that you do not think as Aunt Martha once did, that I leave from an impression that I am a burden to my friends. I know my friends too well and I am too vain of myself to believe that. No—my reasons are those which I have often stated before. A natural dislike to being dependent upon others when I am doing nothing for myself; and a believe [sic.] that it will be the best thing for my health and constitution.

You must not think too much of the length and dangers of my voyage. There are hundreds who have been such voyages and are making them now. It is perhaps natural that you should, because there are but few of our family who are often far from home; but those who have friends and relatives constantly upon the sea, think but little of it. At any rate, *I* am travelling upon the beginning of the road of life, and my face is upon the bright side of the picture; I have not yet got far enough to look behind it. You know too, that it is the misfortune of some of the family to think that every thing will go wrong and that "all's for the (worst)." I may perhaps have caught the opposite spirit.

I wish you to give my very best respects to Mr Ellery—explain to him the occasion of my going to sea—and tell him that I hope he will think me a boy who is "up to anything." You may tell him too, that if

I make a good sailor, he may say that it is owing to my Newport blood, and to my fortnights' visit there.

I cannot speak of Cousin Edward and Cousin Harriet, without strong feelings of gratitude and affection. I *felt* that the interest which they have always expressed in my prospects, has not been, as in many, the effect of mere politeness. The particular attention which Cousin Edward paid to my college exercises, and the interest which he has taken in my literary progress, has given me great confidence in myself and great affection for him. Remember me to them very particularly, and tell [them] that they do not know what comfort and confidence it gives to a young man beginning the world, to know that there are some, who feel some sympathy with him in success or failure.

Remember me to Mrs Sedgewick also. I recollect with pleasure the little that I have seen her, and we are all grateful to her for what she has done for Charlotte. You may tell her that C[harlotte] thinks that there is nothing in the world but New York. If we speak of Fresh Pond, she mentions Hoboken; if we speak of Mt. Auburn, she brings up the North River and West Point; and there is nothing equal to what is said and done at Mrs Sedgewick's.

Give my love to Miss Elizabeth and to Ellery whom I have *seen,* and to the rest whom I *know* very well, 'though I have not seen them.

I suppose you have seen by the papers that Father has lost his barn. It took fire on Saturday evening about 10 o'clock, and burned until the next morning at day break. It was seen upwards of thirty miles back in the country. All the western part of Boston was splendidly illuminated, and it is said to have been the most brilliant fire we have had for a long time. There were between twenty and thirty engines present, but it was too far gone to do anything.

I have just returned from another fire. The convent at Charlestown was *set on fire* last night between eleven and twelve, and burned to the ground—the convent itself, barns, chapel, and everything. There has been a story about for a few days of a girl's having escaped and then retaken and closely confined and being in danger of her life. We do not believe it, and from what I can learn from a Protestant family in the immediate neighborhood, the girl was probably insane. However, there was a great excitement—an immense mob collected and set it on fire. The inmates escaped with their lives, but lost every thing else.

Father wishes me to tell you that Mrs Fleming is positively engaged to Geo. B. Emerson.

I am to have a jar of pickles from Mrs Cook, Aunt Martha is making me some ginger cakes, and Charlotte, some hard gingerbread; so that I shall be well provided.

The vessel that I am going in is small, but strong, and a remarkably

From a photograph in the 1880's by E. H. Lincoln. Courtesy Robert A. Weinstein

Full-rigged brig TEASER *tacking ship in Lower New York Bay*

fast sailer; having been built for the smuggling trade. Tell Cousin E[dward] to look out under the shipping list, for the Brig "Pilgrim" Capt. Thompson for California. And now, Aunt Betsey, I must bid you good bye. I have no doubt that I myself shall be able to come back, if I am spared, stronger and more vigorous. As for those whom I leave behind—I can only hope that there will be no change.

Do not let any one forget your dutiful and affectionate nephew—

Richard.

Richard Henry Dana, Jr. to Miss Charlotte Dana and to Edmund Trowbridge Dana, Cambridge, Massachusetts, dated Santa Barbara, California, 1 March 1835 and San Diego, California, 20 March 1835. Ms., Massachusetts Historical Society, Boston, Massachussetts.

Santa Barbara March 1st 1835.

My Dear Charlotte—

Having written a letter to Father, I take this opportunity (s[h]ort and uncertain it is) of saying a few words to you. We have, now that we are in harbour, and discharging our cargo, but very little time to ourselves; so that we have to write and read by snatches. My plan is to write to Ned, aunts three, Cousin Mary, and as many others as I can: but how far I shall be able to carry it, and even whether I shall be able to give you more than a line, is uncertain.

First, my dear Charlotte, I will speak of your music; you cannot tell what sensations I have, when in my night watch, I bring to mind and give my imperfect utterance to, some of your beautiful airs. A few peculiar notes will bring before me the whole scene of some evening passed at home and frequently have I passed many a lonely hour of my night watch, in trying to recollect *even one* of your favorite tunes; and the words are as familiar to me as though I had heard them but yesterday.

St Diego March 20th 1835

You see, Dear C[harlotte], that my letter was interrupted, as I feared. The Captain told us that the "California" would sail in a few days, and that he would give us notice so that we might send, but she sailed without our being informed of it. The Ship "Lagoda" is to sail from the Port, which we shall leave to-morrow, so that I shall have a little time to write you. I hope you are not critical; you must excuse my hand-writing. If you knew where, with what, and on what, I am writing—you would find some excuse. We have had a very pleasant voyage, the principal events of which are, that we have crossed the Equator twice; doubled Cape Horn; been chased one day and a part of the night by a pirate, who could not catch us; and been to Robinson Crusoe's Island. I would send you a few shells and a pressed flower which I picked on that romantic and beautiful island, but there is no opportunity.

When I shall return to our dear home is entirely uncertain; but I hope that two years will not roll over my head, without my seeing you all. This is a beautiful country, a perfect climate, and every natural advantage; but the people are lazy, ignorant, irreligious, priest ridden, lawless, vicious, and not more than half civilized. I prefer being at sea, though we have some pleasant times on shore on "liberty days," which come about once in four weeks to each one. At sea we have the forenoon of every other day to ourselves, and all day Sunday. There is probably no place on earth where the Sabbath is so peculiar a day as at sea. The decks are cleared up, everything put in its place, and no work is done, except to trim the sails to the wind etc., which in the trade winds is seldom necessary. The sailors all dress in their best, and the forecastle and chests put in order, and every one has a book or paper to read, or some other quiet employment. On this day too, we have an extra dinner, i.e. a boiled flour pudding, which is thought a great deal of. There is no disturbance from coaches and chaises, and noisy people, as at home: there is no sound but the noise of [the] great deep. There is an inclination even among the worst sailors, to respect the Sabbath and to read religious books on that day at sea; and in our watch, we went so far as to agree to mend no clothes, or do other *work* for ourselves, after eight o'clock on a Sunday morning.

I forgot to mention in my letter to Father, that there are a great many Sandwich Islanders on this coast, and that I have found several who know Robert Davis's mother; one very smart little fellow sailed from here yesterday in an English Brig bound to Oahu; I told him all that I could about Robert, whom he had heard was in Boston. Mr Jones, the American consul, is expected here in a few months from Oahu.

I have picked up a few Spanish words, and by the help of a Grammar which I have borrowed, I hope to pick up a little Spanish. I have also learned a little of the Sandwich island tongue which is singular enough.

The mate of our brig has just told me that we are to sail for Santa Barbara and Monterey to-morrow; and we must take in ballast this afternoon, so that I must close, and give a few lines to Ned. When you give my love immeasurable to Aunts three, tell Aunt Elizabeth that I took her letter to me from Newport, with me, as she requested and have read it frequently. I am not inclined to a foolish vanity; but I can say that "woman's weapons—water drops" have not filled my eyes, even at the most tender moments of separation, since I left home; except in reading that, and in looking at that small remembrance of one lost to us which you gave me at parting. You cannot say to[o] much for me to Cousins Mary and Sophia, cousin Frank and wife and Prof and Lady Channing. My only wish is that *all* may be spared, and that we may meet again, and once more, even for an hour, form a family circle. I can hardly hope for this, unless it shall have pleased God to give strength to the feeble, and healing to the sick.

I have kept your note and also the one from Cousin Mary, which Father brought me when we were lying in the stream. You say that you will remember me in your prayers; no doubt you all will. It is a great satisfaction to me to think, at different times, that there are many whose thoughts are on me—that I am not away, and forgotten. How many more beautiful Italian airs have [you] learned? Any equal to "O dolce concento" or "Cielo a mi lungli sparinsi." I believe it would melt my heart to hear them.

Good bye my dear Charlotte.

Your affectionate Richard Henry.

My dear Ned—

> "Inter errovis valebavra longi,"
> "Inter ignotus strefictus loquali,"
> "Quod modis, quid aquat requivo,"
> (Carissimus Fratris!)

You must not be critical. You cannot expect good grammar or metre from a sailor. If your vocabulary will supply you with a dactyle, I hope you will make the substitution. Whether it has pleased God to cut me off from all hopes of a literary or professional life, I know not. At all events I feel that I have done my duty in coming to sea; and I can truly say that I am, at heart, lighter and happier, than I was during the last year of idleness which I spent at home. I am now independent, a burthen upon no one, and capable of taking care of myself, in every way. Then I was dependent and useless—a dead weight upon the hands of them to whom I should have been a support—and an object of pity, when I should have been one of hope and pride. My earnest hope now is that the voyage may be short, so that I can return, and God willing, commence a professional life before it shall be too late. At all events, as I said before, I am not like the Huntsman with but one string to his bow, and that broken. I have a means of support and of independence.

Many a time, my dear Ned, have I called to mind the imaginary, or rather, the distortedly real, characters with which we peopled our native town. The Hero of the "little war and of the" Ice . . . the "Bigelow estate"—"the Beck lot"—"I don't know" etc. etc. We had fine sport, to be sure, at [the] expense of our fellow creatures. I hope your character is not like the shuttlecock which needs two blows to keep it again.

View of Timm's Point, San Pedro. The location of the original warehouse was near here

From a photograph taken by William Godfrey, 1871. Courtesy Robert A. Weinstein

385

I expect to find many changes when I return; I dread to find them at home—but I will not speak of that—I mean abroad. How stands the Political world. I suppose old animosities will have been healed, for new to spring up—and old party lines traced in the shifting sands of life, lost; and new ones drawn again for a time to divide, excite, and occupy the mind of "Godlike man." Notwithstanding my moralizing, I believe there were few more zealous politicians than I was; and much would I give for the "Daily Advertiser" sent to me every morning. Apropos How is Uncle Frank, and also Mr Allston? Give my love, respects and duty to them. I can almost see them reading "to-day's," laying aside "yesterday's," and looking forward for "to-morrow's." Remember me too, to Uncle Ned. Would that he might be spared, mind and body; and that we may not, at my return, have to think of him, as of one, whose great intellect is to be known and felt no more! I have many things to ask, about yourself; but it will be too much like carrying on a conversation with Echo. I must make my own answers. How are your eyes? What are you doing? and where are you. I hope that you are well, studying and at home. But may God bless you, wherever you are. I have [not] told you much about the voyage, for I have said everything about it in my letters to Father and Charlotte. Our Captain, we all dislike very much. He is selfish, vain, proud, ridiculous and bad tempered. He has flogged two of the men very badly and for nothing. They will try to make him suffer for it when they return; and I have no doubt they will succeed, for both the mates will testify for them. Our Chief Mate—Mr Amazene—is an excellent man. Calm, quiet, reasonable, good humored. He never would hurt the hair of any man's head. He can not get along with the Captain. The man who came out as 2nd Mate, Forster, has been broken, turned forward. He is rather idle and an indifferent seaman; and I do not know what his character is on shore; but he has had a pretty good education, and is a thoroughly good natured fellow. He thinks of returning in the "Lagoda." I have told him to go and see you all at Cambridge. The new 2nd Mate is a fine fellow. Our Captain has always treated *me* well enough, and will leave the brig in a few months, so that we are well enough off for our officers. Henry Mellus has been unwell and made but an indifferent sailor, so the Capt. has taken him aft to be Supercargo's clerk. Little Sam. Hooper is a real old tar, and is well and hearty. My other messmate Ben Stimpson (son of Dr Stimpson of Dedham) is a clever fellow and will make a good sailor. You recollect that we were in the Steerage when we left Boston; immediately after we left the Cape, the forecastle was enlarged, and we all went forward. You are more independent, more "Ship shape," and have more privileges; than you do aft. We now have a good crew—there is no comparison. I advise every "green hand" to go right into the forecastle. If you see Jim Hodge, remember me to him, and tell him to extend it to his whole family and my friends in Plymouth. Good bye, Dear Ned. I hope you miss me as much as I do you. I am sorry that I can not write a budget.

Richard Henry

Richard Henry Dana, Jr. to Richard Henry Dana, Cambridge, Massachusetts, dated San Pedro, California, 13 March 1835. Ms., Massachusetts Historical Society, Boston, Massachusetts.

Brig Pilgrim off St Pedro,
California,
March 13th—35

Dear Father—

We arrived at the Port of Santa Barbara on the 14th day of January last after a passage of four months and twenty eight days. This is called remarkably short. We had about a week of very bad weather off Cape Horn, but all the rest of the voyage has been very pleasant. When off the Cape, we had rain, hail, snow, head winds and close reefed topsails every night; but it generally moderated before dawn; which was about half past three A.M. By virtue of a plenty of warm clothing, and the necessity of continual motion, I kept myself from freezing; and I found that I—home-bred, gentleman-bred, and college-bred—could stand it as well as the roughest of them. (Don't forget to remember me to Miss Sawyer, and to tell her that I believe that the tippets or whatever they are called, which she knit for me, saved my ears from freezing.) Immediately after doubling the Cape we came into fine weather again, and made a very short passage of eleven days to Juan Fernandes. We spent two days at this romantic and beautiful island. The officers and some of the crew sent letters by a Chilian Brig of War, to the U. S. Consul at Valparaiso, to be forwarded to Boston. As I was one of the watering party, I could not get an opportunity to write even a word, until it was too late: so that I got a good view of the island, its wild goats, wild mountains, and scarce less wild inhabitants; and lost my chance of writing home.

For six weeks after we left the Island we had "Sky sails" set all the time; and made no change of sail, except once or twice shifting "Studding sails," as the wind varied a few points from being directly astern. Any sailor will tell you that these are proofs of fine weather; indeed I cannot conceive of anything finer than that climate and the Pacific. There was not a day when it was too warm, or too cold; but all the time, a beautiful and healthful evenness of temperature.

Strange as it may seem, I have not been disappointed in a sailor's life. Indeed I did not go with the wild, foolish notions which carry many, and which cannot but meet with disappointment. There is no mistake about a sailor's being a hard life—and sometimes with wet—cold—watching—risk and hardship—and cut off from every comfort of "Society, friendship, love, divinely intended for man"; it seems "hard enough"; but there is fine weather again and there is time for reading and writing and other recreations during our watch below; and for thoughts of home and other reflections during the long, star lit, night watch. And then the continuous motion of the vessel; the change of climate, zone, and even hemisphere; the great deep and all its wonders —everything is on a great scale—there is a "something" which is not on land. In addition to this our Brig is a fine little vessel, we have an intelligent and respectable crew, and better men than the Mates (with whom we are principally concerned) I should never wish to sail with. I have increased in strength and bodily vigour, and have not had a sick day, or even a head-ache, since I left you. Putting all these things together, I can say that my voyage has been a pleasant one, and my time has passed swiftly and happily away.

Since the first two or three weeks I have had no trouble with my eyes, and I have great hopes of their complete restoration. To be sure I have not many opportunities of using them, and none at all by candle light, and much may be owing to the exercise, free air, and plain diet; yet I have great hopes that they will be equal to anything that I may be called to put them to.

Soon after we left Boston I began at the very beginning of Bowditch's Navigator, and when we arrived on the coast had nearly finished it. I have worked one or two lunars, can take an observation of the sun, keep a dead reckoning, and work the different kinds of sailing—Plane—Mercator's—Middle Latitude etc. I can say without vanity that when we return, I expect to be a better Navigator than any one on board, for my Mathematical Education enables me to *understand* that which the officers can only work by rule and by the tables.

My Literary Education too I have not entirely neglected. We have a plenty of books and I read them whenever I can get an opportunity. I read the books of Joshua, Samuel and Kings in the Old Testament, Cowper's Correspondence (a present from Dr Channing), also the principal part of his poems, Thompson's Seasons, Cobbett's "letters to young men," etc. also several tales, old and new, and tracts given to some of the crew by Father Taylor. This gentlemen I find is very much liked and respected by the Seamen, and they are all in the habit of going to his church when in Boston. Indeed Father Taylor, Dr Bowditch, and Gen Jackson are the stars of the age in their estimation.

One of our crew is a German, and has lent me an Almanac, Lutheran

Prayer-Book, and a few popular songs which may serve in some measure to keep alive my knowledge of German.

There was one dark day in our voyage which I have not yet spoken of. A few days after we had doubled the Cape, we were aroused one morning by the cry of "all hands on deck" "A man overboard." The vessel was hove aback, the boat lowered, and we sprang into it; and it was not until we were out in the midst of the wide ocean in our little boat; that I had time or thought to ask whom we had lost. It was a fine young English sailor, named Geo. Ballmer, [who] had gone aloft, and fell from the main rigging, one of the ratlines having parted—as we suppose. There was a high sea running, and he was heavily dressed and did not know how to swim, so that there was no hope of saving him. We pulled about for some time, but were obliged to return with heavy hearts to the vessel. No one can have any conception of the feelings of a Ship's company when one of their number, with whom they have been so constantly associated, and separated from the rest of the world, is suddenly taken from them. His watch mates said that on the night before, during his watch on deck, he talked constantly about his parents and home, and of returning to them after this voyage; a subject which he had never before spoken upon.

I have now told you everything that I think can interest you about myself and my voyage; I will now say something about yourself and everyone at home.

To say that I have thought of home and you all, will be saying nothing at all. I think of you always, and with feelings sometimes that I never have had before. The length of our voyage is entirely uncertain, as well as the lives of us all; so that sometimes I feel a terrible misgiving about what may happen before I return: And even now while I am writing, I do not know who may be alive to read. But I can only hope that all is well with you all; and I shall speak of all as if it were so.

I shall not send love to any of the family, for if I cannot write to each one separately and tell what I feel; the common expressions of love and remembrance will be worse than nothing. But there are many not in our household to whom I wish to send love and remembrance. I shall write to Cousin Mary if I have time. Cousin Sophia and Mr Ripley, Cousin Frank and his wife, Aunt and Uncle Dana and Uncle Ned are often in my mind; and many a time have I wished for the "Daily Advertiser," and a pleasant half hour with Prof. Channing and Lady. Often too, of a Sunday evening, have I thought of Mr Allston walking up for Aunt Martha and asking Charlotte for "one more song."

There is hardly one whom I have known, or who has shown an interest in me, whom I do not at some time call to mind. If you should write to Uncle Wm. at Providence, or to Mr Ellery, please to send my respects to them. Dr Channing also, and family, Dr Shattuck and family, and Mr Woods must not be forgotten. My respects to The Rev Mr Adams and Lady, and to "Miss Nancy." You may think me long in my catalogue; but those who have never been "far away at sea," cannot know the strong desire we have of being *sometimes* brought to the remembrance of *all* our friends and even acquaintances.

I commenced a letter to Charlotte and also one to you, from Santa Barbara, in hopes of sending it by the Ship "California" belonging to Mr. Sturgis; but she sailed without our Captain's giving us any notice, so that we lost the opportunity. The letter to you is lost; but Charlotte's I shall continue in hopes of sending it by the "Lagoda."

I said something about the uncertainty and length of our voyage. It is indeed uncertain whether the Brig will ever return to the States; and there is some talk of our being on the coast for nearly two years. This is not what Mr Sturgis assured me, so that I do not believe it. At any rate, we shall return after we have been here long enough to collect the next ship's cargo; for no one will remain on this coast longer than he is obliged to. I prefer being at sea a great deal to being at anchor on some accounts. We have not so many good opportunities for reading, studying and writing as at sea, and are constantly boating and in the water; but hard work and exposure do me no harm, on the contrary I grow strong, and feel remarkably well; and feel that after this, I shall be "up to anything."

I shall attempt to write to Aunts and Ned before the Lagoda sails.

There are many things which I could say if I had time and many more which I shall wish I had said after I have sent this letter; but which I have not now in mind. If I shall ever return to Cambridge and find you all as I left you, in any measure; it will be the happiest day of my life. You cannot give too much love to all.

Your affectionate son
Richard Henry Dana

Richard Henry Dana, Jr. to Richard Henry Dana, Cambridge, Massachusetts, dated Monterey, California, 31 December 1835. Ms., Massachusetts Historical Society, Boston, Massachusetts.

Ship Alert, Monterey,
Coast of California—
Dec 31st—35

Dear Father—

It is now nine o'clock of [the] last day in the year, when I set myself down to write you a few lines. Henry Mellus has just come in and informed me that a Russian Barque, which is lying in this port, is to sail tomorrow morning for Mazatlan and the leeward coast of Mexico, and there is some chance of getting a letter forwarded thence, to the United States. Even on this bare chance, I should have sent a complete budget, had I known of the opportunity before: as it is, I must do as much as I can, and as for the rest, I shall leave it to you to assure all at home that if they are disappointed at not receiving letters—I am still more so at not being able to write.

The Ship Alert arrived on the coast during the month of May last, and by her, I received the packet from home; containing letters from you, Ned, Charlotte, Aunts E[lizabeth] and M[artha], Cousin Mary, Prof Channing and Lady, Dr Channing, Mr Adams, and James Hodge. Those who are at home, or are only absent for a short time, can have no conception of my feelings. I read them all after candle light, and did not percieve any weakness in my eyes. I was at home, in spirit, in [an] instant. They were all that I desired, and more than I expected. Of the letters and remembrances from the family at home, I will say nothing. I *knew* that I held some place in their thoughts and affections; and these proofs of them were, and continue to be, my greatest comfort in my long separation. But there is a peculiar satisfaction, especially to a *young* man, in feeling that he is remembered by others, on whom he has not the same claims. The letters from Cousin Mary, Cousin Harrette and Prof Channing, Dr C[hanning] and Mr Adams, together with messages of love and remembrance from others; gave me great confidence and delight. They made me feel that I had friends to whom I was an object of some interest—that I might not come and go, and no one care for me but my own flesh and blood—that a few years would not make me a stranger in my native place—That those who are often in my thoughts are not entirely indifferent to me.

In your letter to me, you say that Mr Sturgis expects the Ship home in April 1836. *This* must be a mistake, or else *he* is much mistaken in his calculations; for we cannot expect to leave the coast before June next; which will bring us home in the autumn of the year 1836. There is considerable difficulty in procuring hides and tallow so that we cannot expect to be in Boston before the time that I have mentioned. As soon as I received my letters I applied to Capt Thompson, who has taken command of this Ship, to be admitted on board. He said that he had received orders to allow me to return in the Ship, and upon my telling him I should prefer to go on board immediately, he procured one from the ship to exchange with me. My reasons for doing this were, that a large and fine ship like the Alert, is a much more comfortable vessel than a small brig; and that her duty on the coast is pleasanter. Also the custom and style of seamanship are different and superior on board a large vessel, and I wished to become acquainted with

Point Loma from Coronado Beach, San Diego

the ship's company with whom I was to make the voyage home. I have a good crew and excellent officers; and everything goes well. We are employed in trading up and down the coast from St Francisco which lies in 37°49′ N to St Diego in 32° 39′; remaining not longer than three or four weeks at a time in one port. This coast is for the most part very safe, with some good harbors; and a most delightful climate. During the months of Dec. Jan. Feb. March and April we are liable to South Easterly gales of wind and rain; but it is not cold enough for snow and ice. During the rest of the year the light trade winds blow from the N.W. and we are sure of fine weather. From the 10th of May until the middle of October we had not one unpleasant day, nor a drop of rain. Yet we did not suffer from heat or drought. With the help of dews, vegetation flourishes; and I do not recollect one day when we could be said to suffer from heat. At noon, the sun seems to be covered with a thin gauze of ether, which does not interrupt the light, but merely lessens the glaring heat of its rays. I do not believe that there is a finer climate in the world; but the inhabitants are for the most part ignorant, superstitious and lazy—a mixture of the Spaniard and the Indian; nearly all the trade of the country is in the hands of Americans and English. They are obliged to be baptized into the Catholic Church before they can hold property and marry in the country. This costs them but little: and after they have been baptized, repeated their "Padre nuestro," and the Priest has called them "buenos Christianos," they have nothing more to do on the score of religion. They go on, making money by selling diluted rum and brandy to the Spaniards and Indians, at a Real (12½ cents) per glass; cheating the customs,— stealing horses and cattle,—breaking the Sabbath,—marrying and bringing up children to go and do likewise. As is generally the case, the Foreigners excel the natives in following up the vices of the country.

As for myself, I have grown somewhat in stature and I am confident that I have gained a great deal in robustness and strength of constitution. My eyes are certainly much better than they were; and were it not for fear of giving too much ground for hope, I should say that I have very little doubts of their being entirely restored. At all events, if I should be compelled to follow the sea, I shall have gained some hardihood and experience; and if not—apart from the cure of my eyes —the knowledge that I shall have acquired, of all kinds, is not to be despised, and may be of great use to me and others.

All my spare time is occupied in keeping my wardrobe in order and in reading. There are a great many books belonging to the officers and crew, and the Capt. is very willing to lend his. The third Mate is a nephew of Mr Bryant's, and about my age. He is a pleasant and prom-

↩ 393

ising young man and is very obliging to me. A Work of Mad[ame]. de Stael's and Letters of Junius, which I have lately borrowed from him, have given me great pleasure. You can have no idea of the avidity with which one at sea devours books of all sorts, and when we fall in with some standard work, it is a treat indeed. I have continued reading the old Testament, and have just finished the glorious and poetical history of Elijah. Hardly a Sunday passes over my head, without my thoughts turning homeward. I picture to myself the House of worship, and the sound of any, even the most indifferent, music, would be beyond price to me.

Speaking of music, I must speak of Charlotte, and I cannot do that in the third person. No! My dear Sister! wherever you may be, if God has kept you in the land of the living—you do not know what a tie between me and home, those sounds have been, which He has given you the power to utter. Often when alone, have I by their aid, "summoned up remembrance of past time." And often shall I do so again; until, if it be God's will, we shall all meet again round the family circle. I can hardly hope to find that circle unbroken: but I live in that hope.

I cannot thank Ned too much for his letter,—such a fund of news and entertainment—I have read it over and over again. Ned and I know one another too well to have many words pass between us on paper—that is—words of ceremony. Had I time, I would write something to him, with the endeavour to amuse or inform; but I must merely express my hope that he is now able to do something. Of Aunts I need say nothing. The love which I bear them I cannot express; and the debt which I owe them, I never can repay. If I ever in the inconsiderateness of childhood or the vanity of youth, said or done anything to give them sorrow, now is the time that I remember it. But I know that they have long ago forgiven them. From Aunt S. I could not expect *written* love and remembrance, but I received them, and felt them as much through another. Aunt Martha and Aunt Elizabeth's letters I have now by me. If on my return I shall find them yet among the living, the consciousness of being an object to them, of affection and interest will not be the least of my motives of action.

You speak, in your letter of having more of success in the worldly way, and of health's being improved. My heart misgives me, that you might have said such in order to give me comfort. I never had any doubt of your final success in literary popularity; but I [sic.] [if?] your health [is preserv]ed until I return I have nothing more to ask. I must now draw to a close. I desire my love and remembrance to be scattered with no frugal hand. Prof. Channing and Lady, Mr Allston, Dr Channing and family, Uncle and Aunt Dana, Uncle Ned, Cousin Frank and Wife, Mr Adams and Family, Dr Shattuck and family and Mr

Woods, are names which I have set down in my memory. To Cousin Mary, for her beautiful letter, I have nothing to give but thanks; and Messages to Cousin Sophia and Mr Ripley. I must charge Ned with my remembrance to James Hodge, and through him to my friends in Plymouth. There is no one who can inquire after me whom I have not at some time or other, had in my thoughts.

I had almost forgot to mention the Ducks, shoes etc. which I rec'd in very good season. I hope that you received the letters which I sent home by the Ship "Lagoda." I entreat you, My dear Father, not to give yourself one moment's anxiety about me. I am in fine health, and am a[s] happy as one can be, in my situation. The Capt. treats me very well indeed. We have a noble Ship, excellent officers, and a steady and intelligent crew. I have begun to count the months to the time of my return.

May God hasten that time—

Your affectionate son,
Richard Henry Dana

LETTERS OF FRANCIS A. THOMPSON, 1832-1836

Francis A. Thompson to Mrs. Lydia Thompson, Topsham, Maine, dated Santa Barbara, California, 27 October 1832. Ms., Santa Barbara Historical Society, Santa Barbara, California.

Santa Barbara October 27th 1832

Dear Mother

By the first opportunity I hasten to inform you of my safe arrival at this place after a tedious passage of 192 days.[1] I had hard luck the whole passage and especially off Cape Horn. For 5 weeks I was beating and banging off that horrid place. It seemed as though all the Furies of the infernal regions were let loose. Tremendous Gales, Snow and Hail continually, night 18 hours: Sun 9° high and sometimes not seen for a week, a small vessel, all hands wet continually and no chance to dry their clothes. Any person thinking there is pleasure, in going to sea, I would advise them to double Cape Horn the season I did; I think they would change their opinion. I lost my Carpenter off there; poor fellow fell from the Main Topsail yard and broke his head and neck; died in about 10 minutes. He was an Italian: we shipped him in Leghorn in the Candace, was a very steady, trusty man. It required all my energy to keep my crew from giving out; continually making and taking in sail, small vessel, under water most of the time, wet and cold, a bad prospect and no signs of a change, was enough to discourage most anyone. A Brig a short time before from Boston, bound here had her decks swept and had to put back to repair. I stopt at the Island of Juan Fernandez for water and got ashore but fortunately got of[f] again without damage. It seems the D———l has had the whole management ever since I left Boston—it is a hard expression but I cant help it. Alpheus it appears has not gone home yet. I saw a Gentleman that was on board and dined with him 4th of July; he was then collecting Furs on this coast and by all accounts was making a great voyage. He is now at the Sandwich Islands I suppose. By all accounts the Pious missionaries are reigning triumphant there at the present time. A good example of what our country would be, if those cropt eared puritanical

[1]Captain Thompson was in the Brig *Roxana,* owned by Bryant, Sturgis and Co. on this voyage. He sailed from Boston on 24 February 1832 and returned on 16 March 1834.

Rascals had the management of our Government; as they have tryed to get by petitioning to stop the mail etc. About the time we landed the pious Brethren from the Parthian, there were some Roman Catholic Missionaries arrived, who were poor: went to get a living, (and make prosolytes I suppose.) the same as we did, and certainly had as good a right: those poor people after having lived there 2 years; by the intrigues of Bingham and Co. were sent of[f] the Island; landed in a desolate place not within 10 miles of any house and their things hove after them on this Coast! All this is true without a doubt; those people who profess so much love and good will to all men were the means of oppressing, and almost exterminating another society because they had different forms of worshipping the Supreme Being. I am not in favor of the Roman Catholics more than any other sect; I think they are all about alike. Give them power and a plain honest man would be put to the torture because he could not put on a long face and look as hypocritical as themselves. It seems strange that in our enlightened country People are so blind as not to see the deception that is practiced upon them. However every dog will have his day some time, hence they will be down and then they will cry out Persecution. One thing they have done or been the means of doing, which is, stopping the retail of ardent spirits. That is a benefit to everyone and especially to Seamen in General. I had the fortune to have a Mate that would drink 3 quarts per diem and then a person would not perceive it. I soon stopt it, allowed no liquor whatever to be used on board excepting off Cape Horn and then served it out myself. Although I never joined the Cold Water Society I would advise every one that cannot use ardent spirits without abuse to put their name to it as fast as possible. No Man that would keep sober long enough for reason to mount its Throne ever would ruin himself and others by so degrading and beastly [a] practice. When I shall return to America is uncertain. I may in a year and perhaps less time. The Ship California belonging to the same owners will leave here for Boston in about January and I think I shall get away soon after. There are several vessels on the coast and it is sharp work, every one looking out for himself. This place is like all others. Trade is most done by so many entering in to it. I shall write to Alpheus the first opp[ort]unity that offers. He may be on his way home. I hope he is. If I had enough to support myself decently in some Christian country I would leave the salt water to those who think there is so much pleasure to be taken at sea. However I had rather be a Sailor than a Soldier. The night before I left Boston I wrote a letter to you stating I had got 1000$ insurance on my property on board the Roxana. I left the letter in Dixeys room at the Commercial Coffee House not having time to get the policy. Dixey said he would and forward it on to you. If he did not I would you would have it done by some means or other. No doubt Capt Wildes would attend to it. This is a bad coast and I know not how soon I shall beach her. I am now selling my cargo and collecting Hides which will be my return cargo principally. Harding Merrill I have heard is Master of the Brig Convoy. We young men down East can do something yet for a living or at least are not afraid to try. I sometimes wish I could live my life over again. At any rate I shall know what to learn my children. That is, what will be useful to them through life. I did not hear from Hannah before I sailed. I hope she got the money Dixey and myself sent her. I should like to have had young Calvin, think I could make a man of him or do better by him than he will be done by. I want all my Friends to prosper both rich and poor. In a country like ours where there are so many blessings no one ought to suffer for the want of proper necessaries especially if they have relations able to help them.

I hope you enjoy every comfort this world can afford and that I shall see you again in good health and happiness.

I am your affectionate son

F A Thompson

Francis A. Thompson to Alpheus B. Thompson, dated San Diego, California, 5 May 1836. Ms., Santa Barbara Historical Society, Santa Barbara, California.

San Diego May 5th 1836—

Dear Brother

I am now about leaving this Coast but must say I am greatly disappointed in not seeing you before my departure. I have been expecting to hear of your arrival in Monterey every day this long time, but have some suspicion that instead of your coming direct to this Coast as you wrote me,—you have gone to Manila for a better assorted cargo than can be obtained in Woahoo.[2]

The Alert takes 39000 hides and 31000 horns between 7 and 800 lbs. of Beaver and is not deep!! What do you think of that for a California cargo? If I can deliver it in good order in Boston and make a good passage, it is the height of my ambition at present. But that remains to be seen.

I received your letter by Mr Nuttall who goes home with me in the ship, which will make it rather pleasant for me on the passage to have such a pleasant old Codger for a companion.

I am very glad you have got a more comfortable and better vessel to drive around the coast in—for drive you must, if you come here this

[2]This is, of course, Oahu, in the Hawaiian Islands.

season as Messrs. Bryant and Sturgis are determined to carry all before them in this part of the world.

The California is arrived with a good cargo and Assistant Supercargo and another Ship is expected in a few months and should they not have unfavorable accounts from this Coast, it is probable the Alert will be sent back immediately. But it is doubtful if I come in her, *even* if I have the offer, which will depend altogether upon the capricious temper of Mr Robinson at the moment he wrote—I think there will be *fun* between him and his comrade ere long, as it is impossible for a man to put up with some of his *would be* dignified ways at all times. Arthur is just right for him, for if R[obinson] tells him to carry Anneta's Band Box he is just the one who will jump to do it. (Godspeed him say I.)

I rec'd letters from all our Friends who were all well—John was living with his Cousin Isaac who was appointed his Guardian. They all want to see you and your wife very much and think you may return in the Alert. My wife wishes in particular to be remembered by you and has a great desire to see her new Sister. Old Wildes wrote me—wished me to make his compliments to you and your wife and hopes you have written him all the information necessary with regard to the Sch'r Washington and other affairs. He has bought a Ship of 400 tons but does not say what he is going to do with her—some great private expedition I presume.

Wildes and Dixey are freighting Wildes in a new ship of 500 tons and Dixey in the Ship Avis. E. D. Pierce is trading in Brunswick etc. etc.

Charles Hall did not pay up what he owed me (as I always expected) and I took his note payable on demand and (*certainly* before I left St Diego) for ($146) one hundred and forty six dollars in cash and (69) hides and left the note with Abel Stearns for collection, to be forwarded to St Diego by the California, giving him the privilege of taking the hides at the Pueblo cash price and turning over the Cash as soon rec'd. But Hall failed in his agreement and promise to pay. Therefore I shall have to trouble you with an order on Stearns for the am't. when he receives it, which you can either remit to me, or invest in any speculation you may think will be for my benefit. I shall expect to receive letters from you across land and wish you would enclose that list of a California cargo and I will assure you, *no one* will ever profit by it except myself and likewise,—should I get kicked out of employ, whether I could stand any chance to drive a vessel for you or your Partners, if I should make my appearance in these seas again, which God knows I shall not, if I can do better—but it is best to look out in season. I think you might find time to write longer letters than you generally do, and as often as opportunities offer—hoping you may arrive safe here with a good cargo I remain Your Brother

in haste, F. A. Thompson

N. B. I enclose a copy of my letter to Stearns and an order on him for the am't of the note which he has in my favor against C. Hall.

F. A. Thompson

I wish you to pay Mr Burke seven dollars which I owe him for a Box of Cigars. The last time I was in S'ta B[arbara] I forgot to pay him.

F. A. T.

RECORDS ILLUSTRATIVE OF
THE CALIFORNIA TRADE

[Although these documents are of a date about ten years after Dana's voyage to California, there had been little change in the demands of the market on the Pacific Coast during that period, and they illustrate very well the type and variety of goods which were assembled and shipped out to be sold in exchange for hides and tallow. They are excerpts from the Dexter-Appleton Mss. in the Baker Library, Harvard-Graduate School of Business Administration, Boston, Massachusetts. The firm of William Appleton and Co. was an active participant in the California trade.]

Henry Mellus to William Appleton and Co., Monterey, 10 April 1844.

.... Should this arrive in time for the next ship I hope the following list may be of some use in selecting a cargo:

The carpeting should be of a very good quality as the duty on all kinds is 75¢ per v[a]r[a]. even to cost at home $1.50 per Yd. Also some fringe for making the above into rugs of such sizes as may be here required.

Brown Cottons omit entirely.

White Cottons can be omitted in preference to any other piece goods not mentioned. There is a large stock on the coast.

Broad Rimmed Hats omit except made to order by Mr. Robinson. Those by the Brookline and Admittance are not liked and I have many on hand.

Thread 100 lbs. No. 50 and 100 lbs. No. 35. I have none.

300 doz. best spool thread omitting if possible a few of the finest numbers.

Cotton Handkerchiefs. Send only 300 doz. and of the best quality. I have a good stock of common kinds.

Pongees. Omit except large sizes, very fine colors and increase the quantity of silk Bandanas.

Segar paper. Send 500 reams as it is now very scarce.

Broad Cloth. 200 Yds. of the common kind will be sufficient.

Blue Drill. Send 10 cases. None has come in the late ships.

Velveteens. A new kind has lately been brought here about 30 in. wide and is preferable to the old kind.

Sattinets. Fancy colors and very fine quality pay well as the duty is only 15¢ per v[a]r[a]. The duty on Cassimir is $1 per v[a]r[a].

Groceries. It would be well to increase in some things in much demand and always saleable.

Rice 10,000 lbs.

100 Bbls. of sugar would sell readily and if a part of it could be sent in ½ bbls. it would be very convenient.

75 Qtls. Coffee, good quality.

300 Tin boxes Sardines. They sell here at $3 box. The duty is 25¢

100 Doz. Porter.

100 " Ale.

50 " Lemon Syrup.

25 " Sassaparilla.

100 bbls. Flour.

2000 lbs. Almonds

60 Qtls. Tobacco. That that came in the Brookline and Admittance is very much too weak for this market.

50 Qtls. Guayaquil Cocoa.

10 Qtls. Figs to be packed in air tight casks.

50 kegs White lead.

100 Galls. Paint oil

20 " Spirits Turpentine.

2 doz. Soy. 2 doz. Curry.

25 Tin Canasters Salmon.

25 " " Oysters.

2 Iron Safes 3 ft. Square made for holding silver in the bottom and books and papers in the top.

Lead omit, unsaleable and much on hand.

24 Single horse ploughs with 6 extra points each; they are used in vineyards.

Round Bell buttons Plated and gilt with rings to avoid sewing on.

50 Gro. shirt buttons.

20 M. Fluted Percussion caps.

60 doz. Heavy Iron hoes.

10 " Pruning knives.

20 Rms. Wrapping paper.

10 Ps. Burlaps

6 Guaging rods

Loz and Fish lines

2 doz. coffee mills

2 " Mortars

Trunk nails. Iron and Copper Tacks

Iron Try pots. The duty is $2 per Qtl. They are very much wanted.

150 Kegs Nails assorted as for Sizes.
20 Rifles long barrels, to carry a ball 32 to the pound.
1000 Mackerel and Cod Hooks.
2000 lbs. 3/4 in round Iron.
5 Tons Iron hoop assorted sizes with rivets.
20 doz. Morocco not to cost more than $9 doz.
20 doz. Calf skins at $9 doz.
10 M. Corks.
50 lbs. C. Tartar.
10 lbs. Ground Rheubarb.
5 doz. almond oil
20 oz. Se. Quinine.
100 Dishes 15 in. long
100   "   18 "   "
50   "   24 "   "
12 assorted soup Tureens
3 Wardrobes of showy and even gaudy appearance.
20 M. ft. yellow pine flooring, 1½ in. ready planed for use.
10 M. ft. White pine, 2 in and 2.2 in. Plank
10 "   " White pine boards.

List of goods for California in letter of Henry Mellus to William Ap-
pleton and Co., 15 April 1845.

Boots and Shoes as per List.
10 Cases assorted Fine Calico.
2   "   Blue fine figured   "
2   "   "   large   "   "
1 Case fine Patch.
200 Yards Cloth, Blue and Black at $2.50
100   "   "   "   "   at $4.
10 Bales Brown Cotton 33 in. wide or not to exceed 34 inches and
30 yards long.
8 Cases Blue *Jeans.*
200 lbs. Cotton Thread.
1000 Yards Twilled Flannel.
Omit Common Cotton Hose.
Silk and Embroidered Hose as per List.
50 doz. Men's Cotton Hose.
50 pr.[sic] Silk Handkerchiefs.
50 doz. Bandannas. $9. fine quality, large, and very bright colors.
10 doz. Fancy Silk Handkerchiefs largest size. $18. Except 1 yd. sq.
of no sale here.

300 lbs. Wicking.

Ribbon as per List.

50 pairs Velveteens as per Tasso.

4 Cases Blanket Cotton.

Clothing as per List. Clothes per Tasso very badly cut and assorted, blue, black and dark colors are ones wanted. Pants made very full.

Tin Ware. Send more tin pans and omit tin pots otherwise as per list with 12 Bath Tubs.

20 sets black tin measures.

Groceries are always in demand and as large portions can usually be passed as stores, pay an excellent profit. The whole list is not too much, increasing Sugar to 100 bbl. and Rice to 12,000 lbs.

Omit all musical instruments as the Country is full of them.

The Call for Hardware is more than formerly, and a large quantity will sell, particularly articles used in house building. Of the list of hardware, omit pictures, ornamental lamps, Dressers, Cases, work boxes, writing Desks.

Of Furniture send a small-lot, say 1/4 part of the list but to contain more tables than per Tasso.

500 Gunny bags could be sold for $1 each and pay no duties.

3 Tons 5 in. flat Iron for Wheel tires.

10 oz. Sulphate of Quinine.

10 Gross Spanish cards thick and numbered.

250 reams Segar Paper. Very much in demand.

25 doz. Sheep Shears.

100 " Butt Hinges, 2, 3, 4, 5 in.

30 " Axes and Handles.

50 " Wooden Pails.

20 pair Cart Wheels.

100 2 in. Augers.

1000 lbs. Lead.

100 M. finest fluted English Percussion Caps in 1/4 boxes. Much wanted and pay well. The duty is 66¢ per lb.

50 doz. Corn Brooms.

Sewing Silk 80 lbs. Black 40; blue 20; green 10; red 10.

A very large lot of carpenter's tools would sell, if good.

2 Vehicles like the one ordered for Mr. Stearns with Mr. R[obinson].

200 doz. Cotton Handkerchiefs, high colors or not send any.

Some thin dark woolen stuff would sell well for pants in place of Cloth and pay a good profit as the duty is only 12 1/2¢ per vara but the article must be without any mixture of Cotton.

200 Yards Carpeting same as per Tasso with 300 yards black fringe to make rugs with the same on board if wanted.

Crockery as per Tasso and if possible packed in ¼ Crates with an assortment of all kinds in each.

Send 100 doz. heavy pressed Tumblers.

     50 " Plain   "

4 Showy Musical Clocks.

3 Large Organs to wind up, and may cost $100 even in Boston.

100 doz. Horn dress combs to Cost about 150 per doz.

6 Old Tossimed Cap Stills.

200 lbs. Copperas.

25 lbs. Indigo.

300 lbs. Soft Solder or Pewter.

5 bushels Senor Ygnacio's beans (poison). Called here Cabalonga.

LETTERS AND JOURNAL OF RICHARD HENRY DANA, JR., 1859-1860

[*These letters were all written by Richard Henry Dana, Jr. to his wife, Sarah Watson Dana. Dana's journal was destroyed in the burning of the ship* Mastiff *between San Francisco and Honolulu on 15 September 1859. It was reconstructed from memory aboard the ship* Achilles *before Dana's arrival at Honolulu on 27 September. For the period down to the time of the fire, only excerpts from the journal are published to round out the coverage of events in the letters. On his revisit to California in late 1859 and early 1860, Dana made it a practice to include largely family and personal materials in his letters and to mail his journal home in installments. For this period, therefore, the entire text of the journal is presented.*

The manuscripts of both the journal and letters are in the Massachusetts Historical Society, Boston.]

Steamer Star of the West
Off Island of Cuba
July 26, 1859

My dearest wife,

My pilgrimage has begun in earnest, and six of its 200 days are past. I am very well, and trust am using my time profitably for my body and my spirit. I have kept up my religious exercises morning and evening, and it will interest you to know that I go through the same course, in substance, that I do at home—that we did together—and chant (to myself) a canticle, each time, adding the prayer for all at sea. Then some private prayers for my special state. If I can keep this practice up through my whole year, the result will be a blessing to me and mine. Last Sunday there being no clergyman on board, and the captain not thinking himself exemplary enough to perform service, there was none—though there were over 400 passengers. The Episcopalians met together in the Chart-room, some dozen or more, and I read the service, for which they expressed themselves much gratified. It happens that nearly all of our set, at the head of the table, the élite of the boat, are Church people, and 2 or 3 who were not, joined with us. I was glad of this for another reason: for it marked me as a man professing to hold religion in estimation, and it serves to hold me to a corresponding course, and this is aided by my taking no wine or spirit, and my moderate and abstemious living.

The boat has about 100 1st cabin, 150 2d cabin, and 450 steerage passengers, and is dreadfully crowded and hot, but I get along with no head-ache, or fulness of head, or other inconveniences, and sleep better than most of them. We had 3 days of more wretchedness and suffering from sea-sickness than I ever saw. But now all are well, and we have most delicious weather, especially at night. Capt. Davis' letter to the master (Gray) was a good service to me, and gave me many privileges. Our best passengers are Capt. Poor of the Navy, going to take command of the St. Louis, Major Townsend and Lt Myers of the Army, and their families, going to Oregon, to a station there, and some ladies under the charge of these officers—one of whom is from Cincinnati, and knows your school friend Mrs. Dr. Shotwell and speaks highly of her, and of her late husband, who left her a competency. We have Jews in great numbers, and people of all nations, in all classes of the passengers.

I sit alone, at early morning and at night, for some time, to reflect, and this brings you and the dear children, and the home, clearly before me. But I am cheerful and even happy. I have made up my mind (and I wish you to join me in it) to treat this tour of mine as a *pilgrimage,* undertaken for the good of body and spirit, and to earnestly desire God to make it so to me, and I hope that the check to my health and prospects, and the frequent opportunities for solitary reflection, and the solemn effect of absence from all I love, will conduce to that end.

My love to the dear children, each separately. I recall each in order of age, in my prayers. Give my love to Aunts, and Father and Ned and Charlotte, and your own kith and kin. I shall write to Aunts, either via Havana, or via Aspinwall. May God bless you my dearest and most faithful friend and companion.

Yours
Richard

There is a Miss Dana from Michigan on board, niece of A. H. Dana of New York, to whom I was introduced, and desired to look after by her uncle. She is an excellent, honest, matter-of-fact young woman, going to join some brothers, and gives me no trouble. The passengers are a curious study, and in their variety, almost make up for their excess of numbers. We stop 3 or 4 hours at Havana, for mails—which will be interesting to me, and on the Pacific we stop half a day at Acapulco.—

At sea, near Aspinwall,
July 31, 1859. Steamer
"Star of the West."

My dearest wife

I wrote you from Havana, giving you my course and experience up to the day before our arrival there.

Tuesd. night, at 9 o'clock we saw the Morro Light, and lay off and on all night, and entered the harbor at sunrise, Wed. morning. The sight was not so glorious as that described in the early pages of "Cuba and Back," for there was no moon, and the sky was cloudy; but grandeur was added to the scene by the thunder-clouds that lay over the land, emitting lightning every moment from the surcharge of the hot tropical day.[1] The entrance by sunrise was fully equal to that in the Cahawba, and truly magnificent. We were to lie there only four hours, to leave mails and take passengers. I went ashore, and it was like walking in a dream, to find myself back again so soon, among the familiar sights and sounds of Havana. I undertook to guide our party—whom I named to you in my last—the naval and military people and their ladies. We went to La Dominica, stopped in to the old Church of San Domingo and heard the end of the Mass, and drove to Le Grand's to breakfast.

As soon as I came in sight, old Le Grand, who was sitting at his usual post, recognized me, rushed forward and received me as if I were his long lost brother. We ate a Spanish breakfast in his high rooms, and while it was preparing, I stepped into the passages, and there found Antonio and Domingo, just as I left them, both expressing unlimited joy at seeing me. Drove thro' the Paseo de Ysabel, the Puerta de Monserrate, Calle del Obispo, O' Reilly etc. to the Plaza de Armas, thence to the market and bought some pine-apples, aquacerte and cocoa nuts (oranges were out of season) a few sweetmeats, and thence on board. By 11 o'clock we were off at sea again, and never shone a more resplendent spectacle than we had all that afternoon, the city with its castle and fortified hills behind us, the highlands of Cuba under our lee, and the bright, bright blue sea on the other side, more bright and more blue,—it cannot be my fancy only—than elsewhere in the world. At night, lightning over the land. Thursday, Friday and Saturday, in the Caribbean Sea, were as beautiful days as heart would desire, soft trade-wind clouds, bright blue sea, and gentle breezes. Those passengers who drink iced champagne and iced punch, and eat 4 meals a day, complain of the heat, and cannot sleep nights. I do not suffer from it at all. I have had no bad feeling in the head, and believe that I am more free from such troubles than most persons on board. I drink nothing, eat sparingly, and rise at daybreak and take a bath by getting the sailors to turn the hose on me when they wash decks.

We are now to the southward of the sun, and expect to reach Aspinwall Sunday night. Your next letter from me will be from San Francisco.

[1]Dana had visited Cuba in February and March 1859, and his book, *To Cuba and back*, describing the journey, was published later that year. He had travelled from New York to Havana and return in the steamer *Cahawba*.

I have kept my resolution neither to read nor write, and yet I pass my time. The truth is I was made for the sea. It suits me, and I am always content when on it. I can pass time here, when I could no where else. The mere sense of being at sea, the rise and fall of the sea, and the wash of waters against the bows are causes of contentment. We have had two glorious sunsets in the Caribbean, and I fancy that the Tropics are specially favorable to the softest tints of sunset, and to the forming of strange combinations of masses of clouds. Nor has the heat been of the dead, dull, depressing character I was led to fear. When on deck, under awnings, we have breeze enough, and if our staterooms were tolerably arranged, and the number of passengers less, we could be comfortable nights. The poor 2d cabin passengers, whose staterooms have no ventilation, sleep all over the decks. It is hard to pick one's way among them.

The steerage passengers sing, at night, and we have at last got up a singing party aft, which is pretty good. The songs in the steerage are mostly of a sentimental cast, about home, love, parting, meetings, death, etc., with interspersing of negro melodies.

I have kept my religious exercises faithfully, find them a great comfort, protection, and resource, and they are the strongest reminders to me of home. When I call up the faces, the little baby always comes up with her crying face and rolling tears, just as she looked when I took my leave of her, and she would not notice me.

When you receive this you will know that I have reached Aspinwall in health and safety, on the 31st July. It will be as late as the 12th or 14th August before I land in San Francisco. The Caribbean Sea, instead of a dead heat, has been very agreeable.

As we are getting ready for entering port this evening, I doubt if there will be any service to-day. But I shall have the pleasure of going over the service with you all. I do hope that if you let the house, you will go to a place where there is an Episcopal Church. If you do not, you and the children will be adrift from all the regular services, and from the anniversaries and course of the Christian Year, which I shall be following.

Give my love to each child, wherever it may be. Tell them how I recall each separately in my mind, twice a day, in the Collect for Grace. So, love to all the Chestnut Street family, and Aunt Martha, and Wethersfield, and Canandaigua, and to Mrs. Channing.[2] Name me to the Wheatons also.

Yours everywhere and everywhere,
Richard

[2]Mrs. Dana had family living in Wethersfield, Connecticut and Canandaigua, New York.

Steamer "Golden Gate"
Off Acapulco
Sat. Aug. 6, 1859.

My dear child—

I wrote you first from Havana, July 27th, then from Aspinwall, July 31st.

We arrived at Aspinwall after midnight Sunday night, 31st July, and at 9 A.M. of Monday, August 1st, took the cars and crossed to Panama, and before 2 P.M., we were on board the noble steamer Golden Gate, at anchor in the outer bay of Panama. So, on my birthday, I crossed a Continent! In the morning, I was sailing on the Atlantic, and in the evening I was sailing on the Pacific, and at noon, I crossed the Continent.

Aspinwall is the most dismal place I ever saw. I doubt if the Almighty intended it for a dwelling of man. It is a tropical swamp, a torrid stagnant marsh. In the morning, exhalations are drawn up from it by the sun (it is only 7° N. of the Equator.), looking like smoke from burning meadows. A waste of mangrove swamp, with large stagnant pools of yellow water, is all you can see for miles,—with a rich morbid tropical vegetation, dying and reviving, decaying and renewing simultaneously. The inhabitants are chiefly negroes, who seem to do well enough in this climate, but the white look wretchedly. They are coffee-colored, bloodless, sunken-eyed, with all blood drained out, and all stamina shaken out by intermittent fever. This was chosen for the depot because it is the best landing place at the narrowest part of the Isthmus. The houses are placed on made-land, filled in by the R. R. Co. We remained on board the vessel until the cars were ready, and spent only about half an hour at the American Consul's, which is the best place in the wretched hole. Besides intermittent fever, they had some yellow fever there; but no one seemed to fear it. The U. S. Frigate Roanoke, a noble steam screw, lay there, and the sloop-of-war St. Louis, and their officers and men came ashore, and Capt. Poor left us there to take the St. Louis.

Glad we were to leave the "Star of the West"; for, now I am clear of her, I am willing to say that she was a filthy, ill-managed, overcrowded concern. I had privileges and attentions, and got on well enough; but I never saw so much suffering among passengers from disgust, sea-sickness, and inconveniences of all kinds.

The first half of the way over the Isthmus was flat and low, swampy, miry,—with the richest vegetation, rich and profuse to morbidness, gorgeous flowers, gorgeous butterflies, dense jungles, luscious fruits, palm-trees, mangoes, bananas, plantains, oranges, limes, pine-apples,— with little negro hamlets of thatched hovels, standing in the mire, and negro women with four flounces to their white gowns, without shoes or stockings, stepping about in the mud.

The last half of the way, the country becomes hilly, dry, and picturesque, with distant mountains,—beginning of the Andes I suppose, for we are in South America, Panama and Aspinwall being in New Granada,—and then comes the first view of the Pacific. Panama is an interesting old town, on high land, surrounded by high hills, with the open sea before it, and mountains behind it. It is the antipodes of Aspinwall. The houses are of stone and old, in Spanish style, and there are several churches. The Bay of Panama is noble. I have seldom seen a grander view than the sunset view from the deck of our steamer, as we got under way from the Bay of Panama. The Bay is sprinkled with islands, all of which are high and steep, and some even mountainous.

(The U. S. Sloop-of-war Vandalia lay at Panama.) The Golden Gate is a noble steamer, as large as the Persia, and with more commodious arrangements, for the freedom of the Pacific from violent gales, permits the building upwards and outwards, which would not be safe in the Atlantic. We have a bathing room and I take a bath of sea water every morning. The saloons are large, the order and discipline excellent. The state-rooms are scrubbed and washed out every day, and fresh saucers of chloride of lime placed under the wash stands, and in all parts of the boat where smells are likely to generate. The captain and surgeon inspect all parts of the boat daily. She is also a fast sailer. The passengers feel as if they had been transported to Elysium,—especially the poor steerage passengers, who here are decently and comfortably situated farther [?] of which they were before.

Tuesday the mountainous land of New Granada was in sight all day and the sea was broken by mountainous islands. There is no picturesque coast on the Atlantic below Massachusetts Bay, until you come to the Spanish Main of Brazil. Not so, the Pacific. It is a beautiful Ocean too, and we have had very fair and not over-hot weather since we left Panama, and we have been saved from all sickness, so far.

As for myself, I am perfectly well. I live very simply and by rule, sleep a good deal, keep cool and clean, read none at all, drink nothing but tea or water.

I have kept up the lessons and my semi-daily exercises, with great pleasure, and I hope with profit. I want you to join with me (I believe I said this in a previous letter) in dedicating this voyage as a pilgrimage for the good of my soul, mind and body. I hope that I shall not fall back from these feelings and this way of life.

Sat. Aug. 6. Shall be in Acapulco in a few hours. Lie there three or four hours, and then sail for San Francisco, where we expect to arrive the 14th.

The Pacific Mail Steamship Co's steamer GOLDEN GATE

From a lithograph in the Eldredge Collection. Courtesy Mariner's Museum, Newport News, Va.

My home in Cambridge is often in my thoughts, and pictured to my mind, and I go over all the dear forms and faces gathered there. If it shall please God to re-unite that family group, I hope that we shall live together with ever more happiness, at least more wisely and prudently with more regard to health and all the laws that govern human existence.

Don't forget to order your Transcript wherever you go. After this, I shall direct my letters to Boston, not knowing if you are at Cambridge.

Now, may God bless you for a dear, faithful wife, and keep you for a reunion between us on earth. But still, we *must* learn to say "Thy will be done." Take care of your own health! Exercise, Ride horse-back, Don't economise on health. You must look fresh and young and healthful when I return.

Love to each dear child, Sally, Charlotte, Lilly, Rosamond, Richard and baby crying [in] the passage way.

Yours
Richard

I send you back one of the leaves of verbena that you gave me. They have been a delight to me, and breathe the breath of *home,* on the high seas. Your hair-chain I wear, that is if it is not too hot.

San Francisco, Cal.
Aug. 15, 1859

My dearest wife,

I wrote you from Havana July 26th, from Aspinwall July 31st, and from Acapulco Aug. 6.

Now, here I am in San Francisco, on the "Coast of California"! It is incredible to me.

I came here in the Alert and it was a solitude, woods, deer and Indians. Now, here is a city of 72,000 inhabitants, with immense commerce and all the arts of civilized life. John Felton gave me a dinner yesterday as good as could be had, at the Café Riche, and they are building of stone for private purposes, while the Government has forts, arsenals and lighthouses, all of the highest character.

I had a pleasant passage, and a very rapid one, in the Golden Gate. We arrived off the mouth of this Bay Sat. night (Aug. 13) about 10 o'clock and went through the Golden Gate by bright moonlight, and came into the crowded wharves before midnight. I am at a large hotel, the Oriental, which is well kept.

Sat. 20th, I shall take a little steamer to San Diego, Santa Barbara etc. I intend, also, to visit the big trees, mines, falls and springs. As I have only had one day here, I have seen but few persons; but—with them, my visit seems to be a matter of a good deal of interest.

View across the Golden Gate from Fort Point, San Francisco

From a photograph by Edward Muybridge, 1867. Courtesy San Francisco College for Women

As the mail leaves early this morning, I shall not write much, and my observations are not of much value yet. This is a strange place, and a jumble of all nations and characters. Some streets are inhabited by Chinese. French and Germans are numerous. Every enterprise, good or bad, is carried on with freedom and zeal. On Sunday, nearly all shops open all day, theatres, race-courses etc, yet Churches and Sunday Schools full and flourishing. Part of the city of plank-roads, and part paved, and so on.

I met a party of gentlemen yesterday who spoke in the highest terms of Capt. Stone. They said he ought to have been born in the times of knighthood. (I mean Mrs. Parker's brother).

I am in very good health—and have been "guarded from the dangers of the sea, from sickness and every evil to which we may be exposed." I keep my resolutions and practices. Help me in them, by your prayers, for no man is sufficient—still less I.

My dearest love to the dear, very dear children, and to the home in Berkeley St., whether it is now a home or not. Love to Manchester, and Wethersfield and Canandaigua.[3]

God bless and keep you and us all

Yours ever

Richard

[JOURNAL]

Sunday Aug. 14th [1859.] . . . Visit U. S. Marine Hospital—Political jobbing, neglect of furniture for sick, failure of apparatus for heating, etc. Enormous money jobs, waste, nothing done.

Visit city hospital—not much better, but not so large expenses.

Deliver letter to Archbishop Alemany—Large Roman Catholic Church of St. Mary. Working Catholic clergy and sisterhoods. General respect and popularity of Bishop Alemany. Visit School and Orphan Home of Sisters of Charity—School of Presentation Nurses and Hospital of Sisters of Mercy. All creditable institutions.

Went to Roman Catholic Church on Feast of Assumption. Sermon was not article of Faith, but *general and pious belief* that the Blessed Virgin Mary resumed her body, at death, and it was taken with her.

Windmills in general use here to raise water for irrigation and household purposes. More than 200 in the city.

Charles R. Bond, assessor of taxes, attentive—takes me to ride. Go to the Mission. This looks like 1836, and is the only thing that does.

Felton takes me to San Mateo. Visit the fort, at entrance of harbor. Great work—not completed.

Ditto, the fortifications on Alcatraz Island.

[3]Dana had built a house at 4 Berkeley Street in Cambridge, Massachusetts. Members of the family spent summers at Manchester, Massachusetts.

From a photograph by Edward Muybridge, 1867. Courtesy San Francisco College for Women

View looking across San Francisco Bay
towards Yerba Buena Island, from the Presidio

Part of San Francisco is built over the water on piles, streets, shops, and all, the sea flowing under them. Part is on made land. Rest is on sand hills. No grass, no trees. Some flower gardens, with artificial irrigation in summer. Dreary sandhills form the background. Bay is capacious and grand.

Strong wind from sea, every day at about 11 o'clock, and blows until night—very strong—dust. Climate cold, all summer. People wear woolen clothes and thick flannel underclothes. Overcoats worn a good deal in afternoon. Thin clothes—never. Very healthy except for consumptives or rheumatics. Children strong and healthful.

From the testimony of the best citizens, I think the Vigilance Committee was a necessity. It certainly was effectual. As a general rule, every good citizen is in its favor, and every bad citizen against it.[4]

Jews and Chinese very numerous here. Jews, a business and political power. Chinese disfranchised, but very numerous—chiefly in the lighter labors and in trades. Signs in streets, of Chinese names. Generally, are under 5 year contracts with China companies and merchants, who pay them and employ and let them out. These contracts are legal and respected—I think.

Lawyers practice champerty and maintenance. Not illegal. Injurious to the profession. Land-title lawyers been a curse to the city. Professional morals low—very low.

San Francisco
Aug. 19, 1859

My dear wife,

I wrote you from this place by the overland mail of the 15th, the day after my arrival; and as the Camanches may have got it, I will repeat that I arrived here Sunday morning after a very pleasant trip from Panama via Acapulco.

I have been treated with every attention and kindness, public and private, been invited to deliver the address on the anniversary of the settlement of California, to lecture before the Mercantile Library Association, Seamen's Fr[iend] Society etc, etc, and made member of the chief club, and met everybody worth seeing here, I believe, and have been taken to see the chief public institutions and buildings, and one per[son] offered to answer my order for wines and liquors, to entertain my friends, so long as I should be here.

I leave tomorrow morning for Santa Barbara, San Pedro and San Diego and shall be back here about the 26th Aug. and then go to visit the mines and big trees.

I am in excellent health and like the climate. It is October weather

[4]The San Francisco Committee of Vigilance of 1856.

The Mission San Francisco de Assis

From a photograph by George Fardon, 1856. Courtesy Kodak Research Laboratories

here, without rain, all summer, warm—not hot—from dawn to noon, and cool or cold the rest of the 24 hours. The chief vegetables and fruits and flowers are to be had summer and winter alike—I speak of the *coast* climate. In the interior, the summers are hot, and the winters cold. This absolute certainty of no rain, is singular. I can hardly yet make it real to myself.

Did I tell you that the Jews and Chinese are very numerous here, and Chinese costumes, signs and businesses abound[?] The Jews are a power here; and so are the French. Tell Charlotte I have called on the Roman Catholic bishop, (who is universally esteemed here) and visited the institutions of the Sisters of Charity and Mercy and of the Presentation Nurses, which are all the Roman Catholic institutions here—the college being in the interior. The Sisters of Charity were much pleased to have the line from Sister Ann Alexis. They have a very good Asylum here, and ditto the Presentation.

I have dined with Bishop Kip and with William Duer (late of New York) and several others and seen a good deal of Felton, Pringle, Dr. Holman (and Mrs.), C. R. Bond (who stands well here)—as does William Bliss (Mrs. Bancroft's son), Dr. Adams' brother Sam a druggist and about every hour some one makes my acquaintance, especially the acquaintances, who inquire into 1834-6.

As this letter may be for general use, I will add a P. S. on a separate sheet.

Yours etc—etc—etc—
Richard

[JOURNAL]

Sat. Aug. 20. Steamer Senator, for the leeward ports—to visit San Diego, Santa Barbara etc. Among passengers is Capt. John Wilson, who commanded the brig Ayacucho in 1835, 6 (Two Years before Mast)—long talks over old times. He is now one of the richest and most respected rancheros in California. I was at his wedding, in Santa Barbara—to Doña Ramona. He has large family—rancho in San Luis Obispo.

Point Conception! What recollections associated with it! Now has lighthouse.

Aug. 21. Santa Barbara. The first place I saw in California in 1835. Land in the surf, on the beach. Amphitheatre of mountains—Mission in the rear—islands on the sea side, and a roaring surf! Call on Mr. Alfred Robinson. Lives at house of Noriega—Now (the children) called De la Guerra. Don Pablo de la Guerra, (Two years etc.) receives me. Robinson's daughter, a belle.

Call on Doña Angustias, (Two years etc. danced at Robinson's wed-

From a photograph taken in 1875. Clark Collection, Courtesy Peabody Museum, Salem, Mass.

The steamer SENATOR *at Monterey*

ding) still a fine looking woman. My book gives her great celebrity, on the coast.

Judge Fernald, a young lawyer of Santa Barbara, attentive. Grapes, olives, wine making, and sheep raising.

Aug. 22. San Pedro. The point—the beach—the hill! This was our hated spot—place of toil and exposure. There, too, is the Dead Man's Island.

Good deal of trade here—now steamer to carry freight to an upper landing at head of creek. Phineas Banning, owner of the steamer and line of coaches to Los Angeles—very attentive to me. Coaches; six horses each, half wild—run all the way. Level pampa for 30 miles to Los Angeles. Few trees, no grass, alive with squirrels. (Told that snake, squirrel and bird occupy the same hole)

Los Angeles, prosperous, growing. All engaged in grape growing. Vineyards everywhere. Hot, but dry, and not unpleasant. Meet here Henry Mellus, my shipmate in Pilgrim, and his brother Frank, both settled here. Married sisters, Mexican women.

Dine with Mellus. Takes me to ride, to visit the vineyards—Grapes, olives, figs, peaches, pears and melons. Can raise fruits and flowers in every month in the year. Excellent climate for such, but too dry for wheat.

Of the people of Los Angeles of 1835, 6, see John Temple, Stearns and Warner. The former become immensely rich. At Stearns', met Don Juan Bandini (Two years etc.) and his wife, Doña Refugio, still beautiful, daughter of Don Santiago Argüello, (then, 1836[)] commandante of S[an] Diego.

Meet here a brother of George B. Emerson, who has been much abroad.

Return in P. M., on a run of 30 miles,—tearing rate—to San Pedro....

San Diego (Cal.)
Aug 23 1859

Mrs. R. H. Dana Jr.
Boston Mass.
My dear Sally—

As I can send to you by the Los Angeles Mail, of tomorrow, I write you a word from here,—for it interests me deeply, and I hope will you, to know that I am again here.

I have been to Santa Barbara, landed in the surf on the beach, been to the town, and seen all that remained of my old acquaintances—ran in to San Pedro, landed, went up to the Pueblo de Los Angeles, dined with Mellus, met Don Juan Bandini (see Two years etc.) and the once beautiful,—and still fine looking Doña Angustias (see Ditto, Robin-

↩ 421

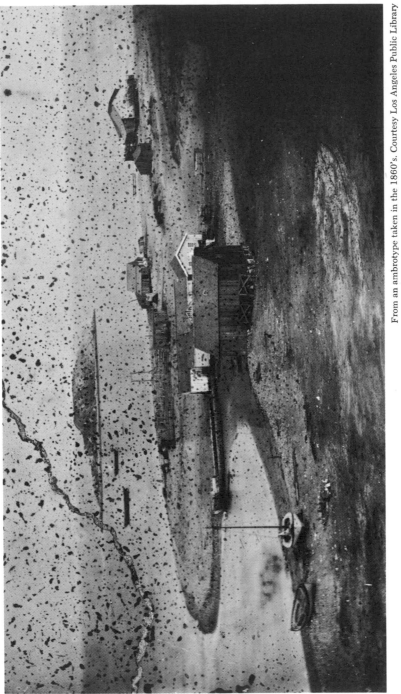

From an ambrotype taken in the 1860's. Courtesy Los Angeles Public Library

A view seaward from Timm's Point, San Pedro showing Dead Man's Island

son's wedding), and last and chief—have spent a day at San Diego. I sat on the beach, walked over the hills where we cut and dragged our wood and chased cuyotas, and killed rattle snakes, and have hunted up the few bricks that indicate the place of the Kanaka's Oven—all the hide-houses are gone—walked to town, cantered to the Mission as I did on my first visit in 1835,—and how I did ruminate, and how inexpressibly strange it was to me,—as I walked over the ground where we cleaned hides, and where the vats stood, and where we worked and walked—all are gone, whites, Kanakas—all.

This trip has been the great motive of my visit to California, and it has been all I hoped, and more—I cannot express it. You can have no idea of the interest that is taken in my visit,—the number of persons who remember me (or think they do) and the number who have read my book—everybody has read it—and I am met with kindness and earnest inquiries and congratulations at all points.

When I stood alone, on top of San Diego hill, and saw all that scene before me,—I had been a heathen had I not thanked God for my prosperity and happiness since, and for having been allowed to see this day.

I shall write fully and more soberly from San Francisco.

In haste,—good bye,
Richard

[JOURNAL]

Wed. 24 Aug. San Pedro again. Master set me ashore at the old landing, I to walk to the new. Searched out the old spots. The landing and hill nearly gone by land-slides. Old house still standing. Stood on old spot where spent so many dreary hours—imagined little Pilgrim at anchor in offing, and old work, and shipmates—

Up to Los Angeles again. Breakfast with Banning—*present,* 2 Melluses, Capt. Hancock (U.S.A.) and wife, Lt. Merchant (?) U.S.A. just returned from expedition to the desert. (News of Major Armistad battle just come in.) Mr. Emerson, and others.

Lunch at Mellus'. Nearly same people—Wilson also. Down to San Pedro in 3 hours—full run all the way. Ran one mile without lynch-pin.

Last looks at San Pedro, at sundown.

Stopped at Santa Barbara, for an hour. Judge Fernald sent me off box of Santa Barbara wine.

Point Conception—Stopped at San Luis Obispo and landed Wilson —Cordial invitation to visit him at his ranch—obliged to decline it— Passengers from San Diego to San Francisco, a Dr. Hoffman, intelligent man and a German gentleman by name of [blank in manuscript], a man of extraordinary acquirements and knowledge of belles lettres

From a photograph taken about 1880. Courtesy Craigie House, Cambridge, Mass.

The De la Guerra adobe, Santa Barbara

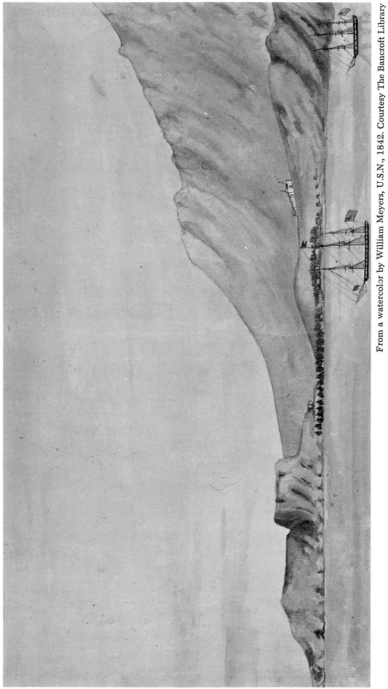

From a watercolor by William Meyers, U.S.N., 1842. Courtesy The Bancroft Library

Santa Barbara, California

View of Los Angeles, 1857

From a lithograph by Britton and Rey. Courtesy History Division. Los Angeles County Museum

425

and science, in all languages. His English is scientifically good—Valuable information from him as to history and condition of California.

Friday evening 26 Aug. enter Golden Gate again—Fort, lighthouse, Alcatraz Island, Angel Island, Sausalito Bay, clipper ships at anchor, town, opposite coast of Contra Costa. Oriental Hotel again. . . . .

San Francisco (Cal.)
Sep. 9, 1859

My dearest wife,

I have the letters from you and Sally (with postscript from Grandpapa) of Aug 1st, and the letters from Charlotte and Lilly of Aug. 12th.

My last letter to you was from San Diego of Aug.23d. I *did* remember and observe the wedding day on the 25th.

Since I have left home I have been 34 days in steamers, 6 in the saddle, 4 in stage coaches and on 6 or 7 at rest.

From San Diego, I returned to San Pedro, Los Angeles and Santa Barbara, and reached San Francisco Aug. 26th, and started the next day for the mines, falls and big trees. I went to Stockton, the valley of the San Joaquin, across the Stanislaus and Tuolomne, to the Mariposa country. There I spent two days with Col. Fremont, visiting his mines and mills with him, and thence took horse and guide for the Sierra Nevada. I was six days on this trail, visiting the Big Trees, the famous Yosemite Valley and Falls, the mines, placer diggings etc., camping out at night, and seeing none but hunters, Indians and miners. I killed a rattlesnake with seven rattles, which I will try to send to you. I have seen trees 95, 97 and 103 feet in circumference at 1 foot from their base, with their lowest branches 160 feet from the ground; perpendicular rocks 3800 feet high, water-falls 2500 feet, etc etc. It is very grand.

I returned just in season to find a noble clipper ship, the Mastiff, sailing for the Sandwich Islands and I sail in her tomorrow—the 10th.

Think of my sailing for the Sandwich Islands! When I am in cheerful modes [sic.], I ask what I have done that I should be so favored,— with what I so love—the sight of the new strange places, and this precious revisit to California.

Let one of the children write to Mrs. Smith (or Mrs. Olmstead) that I wrote Canning [Smith] and got no reply, and now have written to the Post Master of the place, to learn whether he got my letter and where he is. His place was too distant for me to visit it.

Tell the girls I made Fremont's acquaintance on horseback, on a trail, in the mountains. He is a hero, every inch of him, so quiet and yet so full of will and courage and conduct! Mrs. Fremont is true blue, full of courage and talent, and they have two noble boys, 8 and 4, brought up in wild life, riding and going bareheaded.

426 ⇥

The Golden Gate looking eastward. Angel Island in the center

I have had very good health—yet I occasionally am reminded that I am not *perfectly* well—Yet these reminders are slight—such as a few years ago I should not have thought of.

I keep up my lessons and exercises, and one of their chief comforts is their connecting influence with you and the children. I am trying to be a good man—and you will help me—

The letters from home were very nice, and I am glad of the success in letting the house. Your next letter will tell me where you are to pass the year, but then I shall be in China.

Ask Uncle Ned to see or write to Geo. Sumner, (or to Charles direct) to have a good letter or two of introduction in Calcutta sent to me there, to my address.

My dearest love to you. Next to each dear child in order. How often I go over the precious list and call up each face and form and voice!

May the Lord, who has kept me so far, preserve me to meet you in health and prosperity.

Yours
Richard

[JOURNAL]

Sat. Sep. 10. 10 A.M. Set sail, in the noble clipper ship "Mastiff" for Sandwich Islands. This ship is bound to Hong Kong, stops at the islands to land mail and few passengers, and has 175 Chinese steerage passengers on board. William O. Johnson, Master. His wife on board. Cabin passengers—George Clifford of San Francisco, merchant—(brother of Governor Clifford of Massachusetts). Charles C. Harris, Esq. of Honolulu, a lawyer, young Mr. James H. C. Richmond of New Bedford, going to Honolulu to enter into business, and a Jew (?) named Shanburger. Ship of about 1200 tons, and said to be one of the best American ships afloat, and captain a high reputation.

Beats out of harbor exceedingly well—quick in stays. Last view of San Francisco hills, islands, forts, lighthouses, Golden Gate—and its fogs and strong N. E. winds—

First three days of passage; the coast fogs and cold hold on. Then clear, fair Pacific Ocean weather, and light winds—

Enjoy highly life in a sailing vessel—so much better than a steamer. No noise, no smell of oil, no tremor, as still as country after city—and the interest in the sails, winds, duties of seamen etc. Become intimate with Captain Johnson—German by birth, well educated—a library on board which cost some 12 or $1500 and all other things to match—plate, cutlery, furniture, provisions, etc. The ship his home and his idol and chief subject of conversation—He owns 1/4 of her, and took her from the stocks, built in Donald McKay's best manner—

Chief mate is [blank in ms.] Bailey of New Bedford, Second mate

The San Francisco waterfront, 1867, looking southeast from Rincon Hill

429

Johnson of Salem, 3d mate a Frenchman, and crew of about 20 men—
All newest fashions of rigging.

Captain Johnson and wife very fond of animals—has on board a
large English mastiff, of 125 lb. weight, "Watch," two English spaniels,
two spaniel pups, a King Charles spaniel—two tame kangaroos, two
walloughbees, a Java cat, pigeons, hens etc. a cow and calf, large number pigs etc. "Boy Jap" to take care of stock. "You Jap" "You Jap"—
"Kangaroos had no hay" "That dog no water" Constant attention to
these animals. The mastiff follows Johnson everywhere, a perfect
guard. . . . .

At sea
Off Honolulu
Sep. 26, 1859

My dear wife

Join with me in thanks to Almighty God for preservation from a
great peril. You will have read, in the paper sent to you, the accounts
of the burning of the ship Mastiff at sea, on the 15th inst., and in my
rough draft of a journal, which I send with this, you will get all the
material facts—so I will not repeat them here. I am entirely sure that
we had a wonderful preservation. If no ship had been in sight and near
enough to reach us without long interval, all would have perished.

Fire at sea, 500 miles from the nearest land, with a herd of ignorant,
terrified half civilized passengers on board, is a terrible thing, you
may well suppose. Had it not been for the Chinamen—had we had only
the crew and cabin passengers, we could have done something without
a ship in sight; but with them, little or nothing.

I had been to my stateroom and read the lessons and psalms, and
gone on deck again, it being nearly five o'clock, when the alarm was
given. At first I thought it would be easily put out, but when the fatal
fact was made known that all below was on fire, and the ship could not
be saved—which was in five or ten minutes after the alarm,—and the
smoke became suffocating, the Chinese ran aft frantic or paralyzed by
fear, and we had to draw revolvers and take to belaying pins to beat
them back, and in all the confusion, the powder was to be got out, the
boats launched and filled, and the sails and yards managed so as to stop
the ship and enable the other ship to come up with us—you can form
some idea of what was before us.

I can truly say, on reviewing the events, that I did not lose my presence of mind for an instant. I mention this, as a satisfaction for future
cases. I suggested several things to be done, and kept my post, pistol
in hand, until Capt. Johnson asked me to see his wife (the only female passenger) out of the ship. I did so and went in the first boat with
her to the Achilles—the ship that came to us,—and made no attempt to

Looking out to sea through the Golden Gate

save anything of my own, for I did not dare to leave the deck, as all were needed to aid in keeping back the Chinese and lowering the boats. After I got safely on board the Achilles, which was about 2 miles off, and Mrs. Johnson was taken care of, finding one of the Mastiff's boats had no officer in it, I took command of her, managing a steering oar aft, and made several trips between the two ships, taking the poor Chinese from the burning wreck and placing them on board the Achilles, I am glad to say without accident or mishap, my dearly bought experience in boating and seamanship standing me in good stead. While I was so employed, the faithful steward had taken from my room and sent on board the Achilles my trunk, valise, carpet and hat box, so that I lost nothing except a few things that were lying about my room, not of much value. I lost my journal, which is my only serious loss, and have been obliged to write out a new one—which I send you herewith to keep for me. I doubt if you can read it. It is mere heads and dates. I lost my favorite little Prayer Book, which you all will remember,— the limber bound one, with the cross on it, that I always took to church —but saved the little Bible you gave me the day I left home. I lost Dr. Palfrey's 4 parts with my notes, and 2 old coats—which I believe is all my loss. The saving of all my clothing, letters of introduction, letters of credit and books, has been a great convenience as well as avoiding of expense; and here I am, save [sic.] and well, at my port of destination, as if nothing had happened (I write so for on the day we enter the harbor of Honolulu to send by a vessel, if one is ready to start. If not, I shall add post scripts up to the day of sending the letter.[)] After 2 or 3 weeks here, I go to China. Please inform the office that I expect to leave China for Calcutta by Jan 1st so that letters and papers must be sent to Calcutta which would not reach Hong Kong by Jan. 1.

As we are coming to anchor, and I am to go ashore to help Capt. J. with his Chinese and his pilfering sailors, I must bid you and the children a hasty good bye and God bless you. If Capt. Johnson calls to see you, you will find him a well informed and well principled man, and a warm friend to me.

Yours
Richard

P.S. Honolulu Oct. 2, 1859—Here I am, spending Sunday in Oahu, among Kanakas, Missionaries and Whites—the dream of my youth! And how I do like Oahu. It is far the most delightful and interesting place I have seen since I left home. And I like the natives, the climate, the scenery, and all. It has as much charm of tropical life as Cuba, and is not so hot and is healthy—the constant trade winds keep it cool except for the direct sun at mid-day, and the occasional showers keep all green. I went to the great native church this morning, and saw a congregation of 1000 Kanakas preached to in native tongue by Dr. Armstrong, and then to the Bethel, where Mr. Damon preached on the loss of the Mastiff. I am to have a private interview with the king tomorrow, and have spent an evening with a female chief, Pauwahe (Mrs. Bishop) who is a dignified interesting young woman, English bred, and seen most of the chief people here, as my journal shows you. Tuesd. Oct 4 I shall leave for Hawaii, to visit the volcano of Mauna Loa to return here by the 15th, and then to sail for China. My bodily health is excellent and spirits good. Occasionally I am reminded that my head is not so strong and insensible as my foot, but in the main, I am well there, and no doubt much better. I am sure I have taken the right course in making a tour round the world, for the succession of objects present, and to come, keeps me interested and makes the time pass. I may send a few things from here, via New Bedford, which you may get in 4 or 5 months—but am not sure—to Mr. Arnold's care. You may lend my journal to the families, if it is legible, and anyone cares to read a mere list of events, without description or reflections—an out-line—As I cannot know where you all are, I imagine you all as in the Cambridge home—which is the most pleasant and natural thing.

This delightful and improving voyage is not my own—It is the gift of others, and I am continuing to try to regard it as a pilgrimage for the good of soul and body,—not for my own pleasure or will.

Love to each dear child. Tell them, and also tell Chestnut St. and Wethersfield etc that I do not write to them all because I wish to keep myself clear of books and pens,—but desire much to write them.

Yours as ever
Richard

[JOURNAL]

[*15 September 1859.*] . . . Now attempt to save the animals. The cat and one pup are smothered. Cow and one hog too large. The 2 walla-bees are smothered. Save the two kangaroos, all the large dogs, and numbers of poultry, pigs and pigeons. Captain Johnson asks me to come on board and have a *calm conference* to see if anything more can be done. I do so. Very much fatigued by exertions in my boat, espe-cially the steering oar, and head and lungs full of smoke. Captain John-son says all between decks a mass of fire, and will soon burst out through deck. . . .

Flames burst out through deck at main mast. Now, nearly dark, and flames glow over the ocean. Mrs. Johnson anxious lest her husband stay too long. Two figures on the quarter deck—now disappear, and the last two boats come off. Captain Johnson comes aboard and the poor, noble Mastiff is abandoned.

↩ 433

Flames mount the rigging, catch the sails and all a mass of fire. Main and mizzen mast fall. Foremast stands long, then drops, and only a burning hull.

Captain Hart of the Achilles, a generous, frank British sailor, takes Captain Johnson by hand. Now the excitement over and his duty done —the magnitude of the loss comes over him, and he says over and over— "My ship Mastiff! My ship Mastiff! Is it possible she is gone!" Like the mourning of David over Absolom—. . . .

[JOURNAL]

Sunday Dec. 11 [1859] Arrive at San Francisco.[5] Pass "heads" at sunrise, beat in ag[ainst] strong head winds. Noble bay, and striking points —yet no wish to see it again. Land at noon. Tehama House kept on European plan—More convenient and economical for me. Comfort of dressing and washing and room enough. In Architect, had no stateroom, but slept in cabin, and no private place at all.

A good dinner, neat furniture, fresh meats and vegetables, and excellent cooking, at French Restaurant. No one can conceive the comfort of it, who has not been through a bad voyage at sea. Landed too late for A.M. Service. No afternoon Service. At 7 p.m. went to Vespers in the Roman Catholic Cathedral. Full, but not like the music. An Irish sermon. Said Scripture assures us that ¾ of the seed is lost. The parable says that three of the 4 *parts* are lost—but not which was the larger, or that were equal.

Monday, Dec. 12. Ride horse-back to Mission, before breakfast. Horses good and cheap. No vessel up for China. Fear long delay. Glorious weather here—like our warm October weather, and grapes, pears and apples in market, and flowers growing in open air—Dine tête-à-tête with Felton. Introduced to Judge Norton, thought to be the best judge in California.

Tuesday Dec. [*13*]. Ride to cemetery, horse-back. Fine view from cemetery of Pacific Ocean, Bay, City and Golden Gate. Site good, but no trees over 15 feet high—all scrub. Must be so here, I fear.

Dr. Morison, brother of Rev. of Milton, etc takes me to ride to the beach. By far the grandest surf ever saw. Breakers break 8 or 9 deep, and the outer ones are fearfully high.

Dine with Felton, Abel Guy, the very rich banker, Koopmanschap, a German merchant, who is aiding me to go to China, and a Mr. Liès, a lawyer of Santa Barbara, French origin educated in Paris, speaks Eng-

---

[5]Dana remained in the Hawaiian Islands until November 1859. Finally, despairing of getting a ship from Honolulu to Hong Kong, he decided to return to San Francisco to make another start from there. He took passage from Honolulu in the bark *Architect* on 16 November 1859.

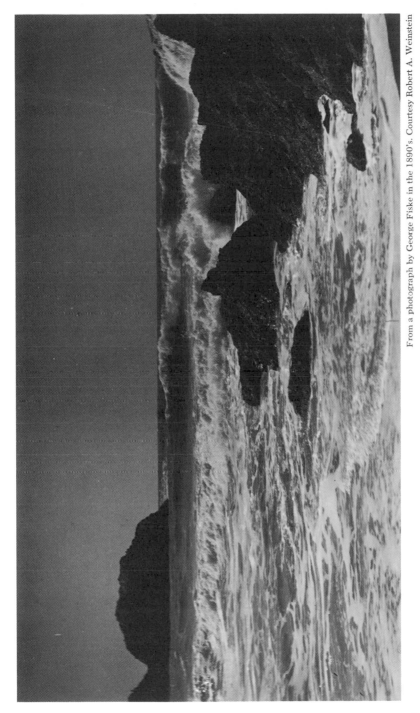

From a photograph by George Fiske in the 1890's. Courtesy Robert A. Weinstein

By far the grandest surf ever saw . . .

435

lish perfectly, and is very clever, brilliant, drank rather too much and is a mere pleasure seeker. These are Felton's friends,—all too fast and too loose for my taste. Edward Hoar, brother of Rockwood, left here the reputation of brilliant talents and reckless life,—the Sargent Prentiss of Young California.

Felton's first introduction to a judge of the Supreme Court, Wells, a few days after his arrival here, in 1853. Wells was leaning against a wall, with a revolver in his hand, and inquiring for "that G— d— s— —— b——" that had told a story about him—gave his other hand to Felton.

Usual interest here, on good security is 2 percent a month, and that allowed to compound. Principal doubles in between 2 and 3 years. Reasons given are (1) want of any system of credit, by which paper doubles and triples the actual specie (2) the risk there is as regards the value of all Security, merchandise, from fluctuations in market, and real-estate from that cause and the doubts over all titles. Fluctuations is more owing to being no market near here, and all goods sent here must be sold *here* or kept.

Wed. Dec. [14]. Yesterday I returned my horse to wrong stable. They took it, thinking I meant to lodge him there. Called at the right stable to-day, and found they had been in alarm. Did not know me, even by name, and the owner had been censuring the hostler for letting a horse to a stranger without getting his name, and the hostler had just said "Well, if I could not trust that man, I could not trust my own father. If a man ever had an honest face, he had. He looked like one of our *first bankers.*" I entered, just at the height of it, as they were about sending off for a search, and said—"I'll take that horse again, if he is in."

"He has not been here. He is not returned—"
I insisted that I returned him, but on looking further, I saw that I had gone to a stable just like it, at the next block, where the horse was quietly breakfasting. They were a good deal relieved.

Rode to a high hill, which gave grand view of Bay and entrance and town.

Bark Early Bird is up for Hong Kong—for Jan. 1st. This is probably the earliest vessel. Great loss of time. Yet, consolation is that I am in a healthful, invigorating climate, with nothing to trouble me, and sufficient employment to keep me from being dull. Shall employ interval in going to Sacramento, Almaden mines, Navy Yard, etc. . . .

Spent evening at Bishop Kip's. Met a Mr. Olney, a Rhode Island man, who held high military command under the Vigilance Committee. Vigilance Committee had determined to destroy the U. S. Ship John Adams, if she fired on the town. Olney says most of the naval and military officers sympathized with the Vigilance Committee.

Met in street, Mr. Stien, of Brattleboro' Vt. He has come here to

From a photograph by Edward Muybridge, 1867. Courtesy San Francisco College for Women

North Beach and the Golden Gate from the top of Telegraph Hill

437

reside. Invited me to call upon his wife, and says her health is much better in California.

Thurs. Dec. 15. Rode to Presidio. Troops target shooting. Clipper coming in under her fore and aft sails—pretty sight, hear song of sailors. Fine situation of Presidio.

Breakfast with Governor-elect Latham, Judge Parsons, Felton, Liès, Hemstead and Casserly—very pleasant—extravagant breakfast,—given by Parsons. Conversation clever, but on personal topics, anecdotes etc. only. Stories of fights in courts. Man drew pistol on Parsons. John Conness fought before Hager J. in Court, and he let it go through. In another case, before Hager Judge, this conversation took place

Wilson (counsellor), "I desire a delay on account of absence of my client. ["]

Blake (counsellor) "Of course she is absent. She is on a tour of f——n through the States."

Wilson. "You are a liar."

Blake. "I claim the protection of the Court."

Hager J. "I don't see that any injury has been done on either side yet." . . .

Walk through the narrow alleys between Jackson and Pacific St. at night, where the Chinese live, in little rooms. There are Coolies, under contracts, and kept at this business by their owners and importers.

Friday Dec. 16. Visit camp of "Digger Indians" in outskirts of the city. Several hundreds, captured and transported to a "Reserve" as thievish and predatory. Very ugly and rather squalid.

Called on Mrs. Major Leonard [?] and Mrs. Lawler (Miss Price), and dine with latter. Nice little house, with view of harbor, bay and town, being on top of Telegraph Hill. Frankly says she has been perfectly happy in her marriage, and seems to be so, and Lawler says he shall always keep her so. Pleasant to see life begin in that way. She gave up a great deal for him.

Streets of San Francisco covered with plank boards, and frequent "man-traps" and "horse traps" in carriage ways and side-walks. All San Francisco is built on sand, that is not built on water and hence the planking.

3ᵈ Artillery, Col. Merchant, at the Presidio. Calls from Drs Holman and Hastings, Mr. Fred Billings (lawyer), Bond, Capt. Thomas of E. Adams, [?] etc. etc.

Sat. Dec. 17. Attended Court to hear Judge Norton give his weekly batch of opinions. He is said by all classes, parties and callings, to be the best and ablest Judge that ever sat in California. The confidence in his integrity and ability is unlimited. His great feat of memory consists in giving opinions in a long list of cases, having before him only the names of parties, referring to names, dates, places, amounts, points taken, cases relied upon, and his own reasons,—all *on terms*. It is almost beyond belief. To-day, he gave about 10 or 15 opinions, all in that way. His language is concise and clear, and reasoning good. He decides about 1500 cases a year. In most cases, the parties have a choice of tribunals, among the District Courts, and Norton is such a favorite that the other Court is a sinecure. . . .

(Did I mention that, in coming upon the coast, we had a mirage of the Light House on Farallon? The Light House is a cone. By the mirage, it looked like an hour-glass,—two cones, one the actual building and the other the inverted image, touching it?)

To-day, in my morning's ride, saw men ploughing and others hoeing between rows of vegetables just coming up (Dec. 17th). There has been no rain for more than two weeks, the finest of our Oct. weather—yet this is the rainy season.

Sunday Dec. 18. Ride to Mission Dolores before breakfast. All building fitted into chapel, and mass saying there.

Trinity Church at 11 A.M. Rev. Mr. Thrall preacher. Fair congregation, rather *genteel*, no audible responses, excellent singing and playing, but choice of tunes and chants as bad as can be. No Church like the Advent!

3 P.M. to Vespers at Notre Dame des Victoires, the French Church. The contrast between that and the Cathedral is that between a Paddy Church and a French Church. At Notre Dame des Victoires everything is as neat, clean, and orderly as it is possible to imagine. The vestments of priest and altar boys beautiful and in better taste than I ever saw in a Roman Catholic Church, and the music excellent. Chanting, all Gregorian, slow and grave, and several beautiful hymns sung, in one of which I found myself shedding tears, mais pourquoi—je ne sais pas. What with the good taste, the neatness, the devout attention of the congregation, the exquisite music, the odour of the incense, and the slow and reverent steps and genuflections of the priests,—the effect was better than ever saw in a Roman Catholic Church. Short, familiar sermon, in French, by the Abbé Blaine.

7.30 P.M. to the Confirmation at Grace Church, with my friend Capt. Blanding, late U.S. District Attorney, and captain in the Palmetto Regt, in the Mexican War,—an excellent fellow. Odd, that the two most religious, moral, and gentlemanlike men I have met at the Bar here, should be from South Carolina, Blanding and Pringle,—both are vestrymen of Grace Church. Church crowded, singing worse than at Trinity, i.e., voices and playing very good, selections of tunes abominable. They know absolutely nothing of the resources of music in the Church, by way of chant and hymn,—sounded like second rate opera.

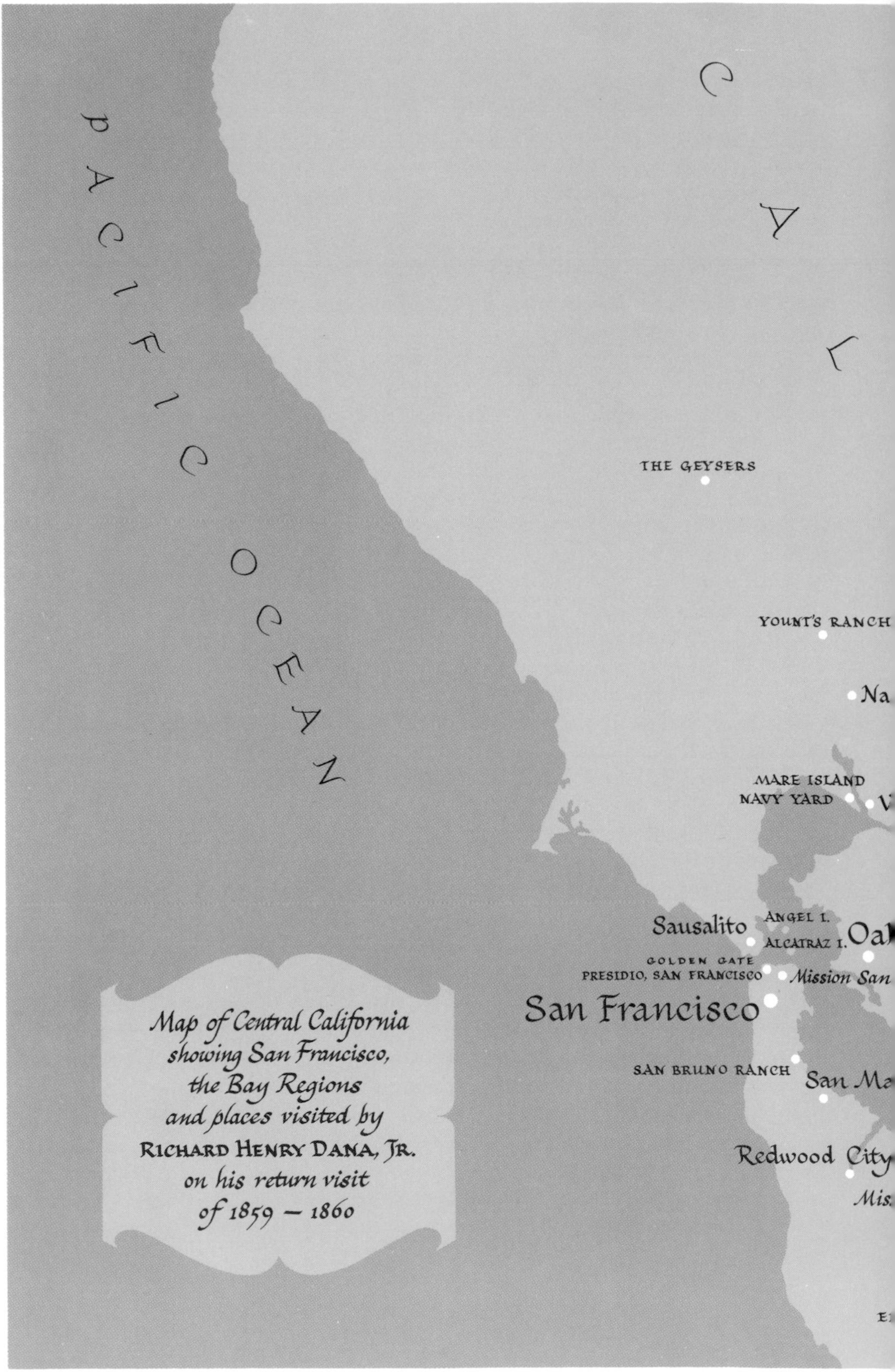

C
A
L

P
A
C
I
F
I
C

O
C
E
A
N

THE GEYSERS

YOUNT'S RANCH

Na

MARE ISLAND
NAVY YARD

V

Sausalito   ÁNGEL I.   Oa
              ALCATRAZ I.
GOLDEN GATE
PRESIDIO, SAN FRANCISCO   Mission San
San Francisco

SAN BRUNO RANCH   San Ma

Redwood City

Mis

E

Map of Central California
showing San Francisco,
the Bay Regions
and places visited by
RICHARD HENRY DANA, JR.
on his return visit
of 1859 — 1860

Feather

River

Yuba

River

River

River

Marysville

River

Sacramento

Sacramento

River

O

Stockton

R

co de Assis

Leandro

Lorenzo

N

San Joaquin

Stanislaus

River

Mission San Jose

River

a Clara San Jose

Tuolumne

nta Clara

GUADALOUPE

River

A

A MINE   NEW ALMADEN

Twenty six confirmed, and among them an *ex* Member of Congress and leading lawyer, and another lawyer, a reclaimed inebriate. Rest were young. The sermon and address by Bishop Kip were nothing—absolutely nothing! Even B. Garth's stereotype would have been a relief. No allusion to anything practical,—duties, reading, self-examination, discipline, habits of prayer, sacraments and preparation for them, public worship etc.—but vague, superficial talk! How *can* a man do so, with such an occasion, and such a company of hearers. Bishop Kip is a gentleman, but a superficial man, in thought and in feeling, humble and kindly but no grasp and no zeal.

Took tea with Blanding, at Martin's. He told me about the battles his regiment was in, from Vera Cruz to Mexico. He joined with 1100 and brought home 250. At Cherabusco, more than half the Regiment on the ground was killed or wounded, including Col, Lt. Col and Major. Quitman was the best volunteer general, after Persifor Smith. Shields, rash and careless of lives, and not trustworthy as to truth, if his own reputation concerned.

Mond. Dec. 19. Ride to Presidio. Warm, June morning and cloudless sky. So far, San Francisco winter is delightful.

Sent journal and letter by steamer of Dec. 20th.

Tu. Dec. 20. Sent journal and letters to wife and Mr. Parker, by steamer.

10 A.M. took steamer for Mare Island, (Navy Yard). On board found Mr. Edward L. Stanly, late Member of Congress from North Carolina, now of California, on his way to his ranch, in Napa Valley, General Vallejo (Don Guadalupe Mariano) and his son-in-law Frisbie, and, above all, old Mr. Yount, the famous pioneer and woodsman, the first white settler in Napa Valley. All invited and insisted on my going to Napa. Glad to do it—as Napa Valley is the pride of California and the Geysers one of its greatest curiosities, and old Yount is alone worth a journey there. Agreed to meet Stanly at Napa City tomorrow.

Landed at Navy Yard, Mare Island. Spent night at Com. Cunningham's, where met Miss West, fellow-passenger from New York. The Russian officers, from the 2 men-of-war steamers, were spending day there, Com. Popoff, 2 lieuts, and 8 or 10 middies, all young,—all spoke more or less English and French, inquiring and polite.[6] Com. Popoff and one lieutenant were at Sebastapol.

Examined, with them, the docks. Russians lunched, waltzed and took leave early, to go back to San Francisco. Old Com. Cunningham,

[6]The steam corvettes *Novick* and *Rynda* (10 guns each) under the command of Commodore A. A. Popoff, Imperial Russian Navy, arrived at San Francisco on 11 December 1859, 35 days from Japan.

alone at end of table, oblivious of all guests, barely knowing anything, sticking to his bottle after all left.

Com. Cunningham takes the Naval Constructor, Hanscomb, and goes all over the new steamer, the Saginaw, with me. Neat boat, side wheel, light draft, first naval vessel built by us in Pacific. Go to Model Loft etc. Yard very large, and on a plan of magnificent proportions, if ever completed. Make acquaintance of Colonel Turner, a Virginian, his wife daughter of Key, the poet. He is Engineer, and a very kindly, hospitable and honorable man. Wife clever, and good children. Also, Captain McDougal and Bissell, very civil and attentive, all.

Vessels here are Independence, 50, Receiving Ship, Decatur sloop of war, in ordinary, Saginaw, and 2 small steamers.

The officers like the position of the yard—healthy, safe from attack, remote from city and deep water. Use the native laurel for ship timbers, is very hard, cuts like lead and fine polish.

Wed. Dec. 21. [Mare Island] Up early. Capt. McDougal waits on me, and sends me over to Vallejo in a Yawl. At Vallejo, breakfast at Frisbic's and meet General Vallejo, and his younger daughter, La Señorita Jovita, at school in San Francisco, and wives of Frisbie and his brother, both daughters of Vallejo. Frijoles for breakfast.

General Vallejo remembers me as a boy in the Alert's boat, in 1836. He repeats some of my conversation with him then. He was Commandant of Presidio.

The Vallejos, Guadalupe and Salvador, owned nearly all Napa and Sonoma, having princely estates, but have little now, Guadalupe by bad management, and Salvador by that and gambling.

General Vallejo got the capital placed here, on condition of his puting up Public Buildings at his own expense. Did so, expended $100,-000, but after 2 sessions was moved to San José and the town fell to pieces, the houses (wood) *moved off* etc.[7] Within 5 years, has increased to 4 or 500 inhabitants and is promising. Doubt if Vallejo gains by it; but Frisbie does, who owns most of the land here. All Vallejo's daughters are rather handsome, in the Mexican style, and are full blood whites.

Took coach for Napa City, which reached at noon. Ride up Napa Valley is beautiful. Never saw so much land under the plough in the same space, except in England. Great fields, level, rich, no undergrowth, fair sprinkling of large trees, and distances so great that the men are ploughing by flagstaffs, as a pilot would steer his ship. Peculi-

[7]The capital of California was moved from San José to Vallejo in 1852. After a week's sojourn there, the legislature moved to Sacramento. In 1853 the legislature returned again briefly, moved to Benicia, and thence to Sacramento once more which was designated the official capital in 1854.

arity of valley is that [it] is enclosed by high hills, river wandering through it, lands nearly level, and small hills, green to top, dotted over the valley, which can easily ride round or over—rising like artificial mounds. Napa City, small town of say 1000 inhabitants, Court House, 2 or 3 churches, etc.

Stanly there with buggy and pair of mules. He has a ranch just below, said to be very valuable ($100,000 or so.) Land here varied from $50 to $100 per acre. Rich in grains and fruits.

Napa Valley. Reached Yount's towards night. He has a principality here, of some 12000 acres, from mountain to mountain, and running lengthwise of the valley, the Napa Creek running through its centre. He owns a large mill, and has some 100 or so Indians encamped near his house, whom he employs. He lets his land at about $5 per acre a year—very much troubled with squatters. Lately married an intelligent middle aged woman, well educated etc, from New York, who takes care of his affairs, keeps his accounts, sees he is not cheated, and pays off his debts, for the old hunter had no business habits or knowledge. He had a former wife, and has children and grandchildren, but all have left him except a granddaughter, Lilly Yount, about 12 years old, at school at San Francisco and now at home for Christmas—strong, hardy and fine looking girl. She owns 1000 acres of this land, which is a large fortune.

Old log house, modernized, one story, huge chimney and large logs at knee timbers burning on the fire. Hearty welcome.

In evening, old man tells me his Indian stories and his life. Born in North Carolina Burke County in 1794, left home at 15, for Kentucky (or Tennessee), in war of 1812-14, joined Mounted rifles and fought the Indians for 2 years, advanced to be lieutenant and great reputation for courage and skill in woods and with rifle. After peace, takes to hunting and trapping, and engaged in it until 1843, incessantly, hunting over Arkansas, Texas, New Mexico, etc., and trapping the Colorado, Gila etc. Frequent fights with Indians and bears, panthers etc. Several times besieged in camp by Indians and fights for days. Says, with great simplicity, that never killed an Indian for the sport of it, *for game,* but only in fight, when necessary. He was the first white man that came into Napa valley. It was then full of Indians and grizzly bears. Built log hut, and fought the Indians for several months. Once besieged in his hut for several days. Indians had only bows and arrows, and he had rifle and pistol. Usually he had 3 or 4 men with him, whites or friendly Indians. Where house now stands, scene of sev[eral] fights.

Grizzly Bears ("Grizzlies") he has killed hundreds of. In one day, he and Spaniard killed eight. Spaniards lasso them and get a tree between them, and so the lasso holds the bear at distance,—always mounted.

444 ⇦

(Story of the Mexican who got lasso round bear's nose, and it came off)

Yount's famous dream, as told by him to me.

He was living then in the valley, in 1843. He had never been over the mountains, by the N. route, but only by the Southern, and knew nothing of it. Dreamed that walking in strange place, large mountain, a white chalk rock, river and trees, all as plain as if seen them, and came on large travelling party, men, women and children, "Snowed up," starving to death, eaten their animals and begun to eat their own dead. Awoke, fell asleep and dreamed the same again. Troubled and after lying awake some time, fell asleep and dreamed it all a third time. So much impressed that believed it a Divine Revelation, went off to some hunters who knew the route, told them the dream and described the scene. They said they knew the place from his description. This confirmed him and them, and Yount gave $70, and others contributed. General Vallejo etc, and party went out. At the very spot, as seen by him in his dream, (and they went by that) they found a party, just in that condition, and relieved and brought them in. This is known as the "Donner Party," and their story made a great impression on the public at the time. A large portion of them perished.[8]

All I can say is that Yount believes what he tells, of this dream, thinks it was divinely sent, and the people in the Valley corroborate him so far as came to their knowledge, i.e., his telling the dream, with the minute description of the spot, the party going out on the faith of it and finding them there. Gen. Vallejo told me that it was true, so far as he knew of it. Yount is a man of unimpeachable integrity, and moderate and reasonable in his views, and does not exaggerate.

Yount's Ranch is called Caymas, an Indian name.

Th. Dec. 22. In this Latitude, prob. °38 N, breakfasted open door [sic] few remaining strawberries on vines, and some strawberries in bloom, grapes still on vines, and fresh flowers in bloom. The creeping vines over the verandah are in luxuriant bloom. Best of weather, wood fires and open doors. This is California winter.

Left for the Geysers. Detained until noon by a pompous old half lawyer, Col. Fisher, who is drawing Yount's will, and wished Stanly to look at it. Glad he did.

Old man give us bottle of wine of his own make. I like it. It has no spirit, but pure juice, pressed by hand. Better so. The skin and seeds of the grape should not go in.

Reached McDonald's at night, after delightful ride up valley. Above Yount's, on his land, is a white sulphur warm spring at temperature of °90. As get higher, land is rougher, stones appear, few stone walls, etc. Evergreen oak, and the common deciduous oak droops, almost like

[8]The Donner Party crossed the Sierra Nevada in the winter of 1846-1847.

willow, with mistletoe and has long pendents of thin hanging grey moss, all among the leaves. Very pretty. Trees are large and come right out of the sod, as in English parks. No clearing to be done, but plough right in. The Napa Valley is Lake George, dried up, turned to rich soil, level, with little hills sprinkled over the level, and large trees alone and in clumps.

At McDonald's large wood fire in stone chimney, sticks 4 feet long and 1/2 dozen on at a time. McDonald is away, and his wife and 3 children, a hired man, a Norwegian, called Brady. Mrs. McDonald is neat, pretty and obliging, about 30 years old. Asked her how she came to California, said, "Over the Mountains." "Had hard time, then." She made no reply and did not wish to pursue the topic. Stanly and I both stuck with it, and asked Brady about it. Brady told us she was of the Donner Party, that Yount's party rescued. In that dreadful time, she lost father, mother (names were Graves) 2 sisters and brother-in-law, there, and a brother and sister died after got in. She was then a young girl of about 15. The Graves family did not eat their dead; but some of the party did so. The family were 11 in all, of whom 5 survived, all now living in California and 2 married near her.

A Methodist Circuit rider spends night here. His first words, in dark, simple reply to Stanly's question how far came from to-day, "Well, Sir, from Clear Lake, only"—were uttered in so solemn a tone, as if were last he expected to utter in this life,—a rebuke, a warning, a final testament and benediction—all in one—revealed the Methodist preacher.

Frid. Dec. 23. Started on horseback, (Stanly and I) with Brady for guide, for the Geysers. Fine mountain scenery, large Trees. Little, twinkling leaf of evergreen oak. Reach Geysers in 4 hours 45 minutes.

Spend 2 1/2 hours wandering in the cañon and over the little hills. A space of 1/2 mile square, all devoted to hot springs, sulphur steam, coming from ground and rocks and steam bursting out from hill sides, through little fissures, as big as steam boiler pipe, and with all the noise of escape steam in steam boat. Obliged to speak loud, when 200 feet off. Two cauldrons of stuff as black as ink, bubbling at boiling heat. Rest as color of water, more or less colored by green and yellow of sulphur. One pretty little cool spring of pure water, impregnated with sulphur and soda, pleasant to drink.

One Cañon (ravine) is burnt over, and devoted like a Gehenna, to these fires, steam escapes and boiling discolored emissions. Through it all runs a quiet stream of pure water, over the rocks.

House stands prettily, and hot sulphur water conducted to baths in pipes. Scenery in neighborhood is pretty, mountainous scenery.

Heavy fog sets in. Rain threatens. Start off at 2.30 P.M., with fear of being caught out in dark and rain. Push on at quick speed. At 5 o'clock, is pitch dark, heavy rain, and can see nothing. Single file, but can see neither Stanly nor his horse, nor can see the guide or the guide's horse. Call out, at intervals, not to lose each other. Several streams to ford, and occasionally a fallen tree. Guide loses the trail,— for we are on an Indian trail. He says he can follow the stream, and knows the hills,—which we can see against sky, though we can see nothing against the ground. Only know we are in water by the splashing of horses feet. Chance of spending night out in rain, in woods, rather gloomy. Cross stream again. Knows where he is. See light! It is McDonald's. Get lost in the yard, as cannot see fence, or barn or shed.

Glad to get to fire and lights and change of clothes and warm supper. Mrs. McDonald nearly given us up.

Rain hard, all night, pattering on roof. Not cold, not at freezing point, probably.

Sat. Dec. 24. Still heavy rain. Brady reports streams so swollen that cannot get buggy over. May have to stay here several days. Dreary prospect. Stanly lately married, sent wife to Sacramento, to spend Christmas with her brother Judge Baldwin. He to meet her there to-day. She not know he has gone to Geysers. Must go on. Walk to house of one Keyes, $\frac{1}{2}$ mile off. He knows a ford, not much over the buggy floor. We go over on horses. The driver over [in] buggy. All right, on other side. But not off before noon. Cannot get to Napa in this state of roads, to-day.

Go on as best we can. Heavy rain, muddy roads and deep streams to ford. At dark, get to little shop, about 2 miles from Yount's. Must give up Yount's, as too dark, and large stream to cross, neither of us knowing where. Wagon at door, which turns out to be from Yount's, and returning there. God-send. Follow it and get into Yount's at 7 P.M. Cordial welcome. Mrs. Yount we find to be an intelligent, well educated woman, from New York, and very useful to Yount. Miss Lilly there, too, the old man's favorite. There is a simple, natural courtesy in Yount's manners, which is delightful. His receptions and leave-takings are models. He is a gentleman, roughened by 40 years hardy adventure, and not a boor half polished.

(His story of Glass, the hunter. Wounded by a grizzly, shoulder torn, neck open, wind pipe open, one flank gone. Major ————, commander of the party, obliged to leave him, paid man and boy $400 to stay with him and bury him when he died. Came in, after 2 days, reported dead and decently buried. Glass ate berries in reach, drank water, killed rattle snake, cut off head and tail, pounded up and ate rest. So, for 2 mos. crawl a little. Walk with cane. At last, got into fort. "How far to fort?" "Well, 200 miles, or so," Man and boy given up to him to punish. "If God forgive them, I will."

Next time, Glass wounded by arrow, companion cuts out the stone by razor. Get well. Next time, betrayed into Indian village, guns taken, Glass and six others, run for it—pursued, 5 killed. "Bill" says last saw old Glass run round rocks, and Indians soon after walking over 'em. Bill got in and in few days in comes Glass—Next time, last seen making for thicket pursued by Indians. Gets in, nearly starved. Last of Glass, is that leaves a fort, to camp in open air, and is found on rock, killed by Indians.)

All over California, the Americans hail from some state. All are emigrants. Men and females are described as from Virginia, Carolina, Missouri, Illinois, or from the New England states. State feeling very strong, yet the usual repugnancies of New England and the North against the South, and *vice versa,* are softened by intercourse, interchange, and tie of common interest in the new State.

State pride of Californians very strong. Remote, severed by ocean and Rocky Mountains from rest of world, and have a peculiar climate, and peculiar habits and history.

Pleasant night at Yount's. Still rains. Mrs. Yount just got home from below, tired, and no attempt at Christmas Eve.

Old man says "Gentlemen, I sort of believe in punishment," and goes on to say that some of the Donner Party had left a sick man to his fate—may have been their punishment. Inclined to believe in spiritual manifestations—"cannot limit power of spirit."

Sund. Dec. 25. Sunday and Christmas. But Stanly must go on to Napa, and telegraph to his wife at Sacramento, or they will be in distress. Been so kind to me, and all on my account that came off here— so I accede to suggestion, and our whole Christmas, is spent on a rainy, muddy road. Afternoon, too late for Church, arrive at Napa City. Spend afternoon and evening in tavern bar-room, as no fire-place in any other room, where billiards are playing. But Stanly and I have some reas[onable] and agreeable conversation. All our journey, have had agreeable conversation. Stanly has anecdotes of Congressional life, politics etc. He is Republican, now, and opposed to extension of slavery, a churchman, communicant. Delegate to the late General Convention at Richmond (1859). He tells me he has seen the letters between Mr. Randolph and his cousin Judith, after she had married Governeur Morris and had a son,—John writing an infamous letter to Morris, reviewing her unf[ortunate] story. Morris knew it all. Showed her the letter, and she replied. He says if Jack did not bleed and blush, it was because he could not. He must have been crazy.

Mond. 26 Dec. Steam Boat at Napa City, 10 A.M. for San Francisco via Mare Island, and Vallejo. At Mare Island, shake hands with Com. Cunningham, Capt. McDougal etc. on wharf, and Miss West goes to

San Francisco, under charge of Com. Cunningham's son. (Don't like her manners. Attends to nothing but what relates to herself or her friends—so let her alone.)

This is surely a grand basin, this Bay, or series of bays. There is little Benicia, and now Mare Island and Vallejo are hidden. Here is Alcatras, and there the narrow Golden Gate! and there the town—Yet a dreary fog lies over all—

Reach my rooms at Tehama House before dark. This trip makes me less regret my revisit to California.

Tuesd. Call on Mrs. Dr. Hastings and lunch there. Dined with Bishop Kip, to meet the new Bishop of British Columbia, a delightful man, serious, well bred and well toned; with a peculiarly pleasing voice.[9] He preached at Church of Advent in evening, an excellent sermon, in agreeable, solemn, conv. manner, earnest, simple and cultivated taste etc.—in fact he is worth the Bishop and all the clergy of California put together. Church of Advent is Low Church, and a McAllister family affair, with great pulpit in middle, no altar to be seen—but beautifully dressed with flowers and evergreens—

(Wrote by mail of Dec. 30th and sent journal to Dec. 29th.)

Th. Dec. 29/59. Rose early. 8 A.M. take stage coach for San José, to visit quicksilver mines etc. Seat with driver. Pass old Mission of Dolores and the San Bruno ranch, and go over the new road cut into the bank by the side of the Bay. Rough country and no trees until come to San Mateo. Here few large, and rich soil. Capt. Macondray's country house and farm, in pretty place. Public House of San Mateo the best looking edifice out of San Francisco I have yet seen.

Now, all the way, rich, flat country—a large "land lake" as Dr. Bushnell says. After rains, is very muddy. Never saw mud before, even in Cambridge—our soil is not deep enough. Coast Range in sight, with snow on its highest tops, across the Bay.

Redwood City, the Shire town of San Mateo County, a mere mud hole, on a slough, running up from the Bay, 6 sloops there. Trade in redwood timber.

Now comes Santa Clara valley. The live oak abounds here, and the sycamore—the same as our sycamore or plane tree. As far as eye reach, this land lake of rich alluvial, with no undergrowth, and large trees sprinkled over it. Ranchos and farms abundant. Some, have pretty houses, and some rather approaching the stately. All ranchos and large farms have names. These often painted on the gate-way. The Spanish are the prettiest names—but the land here is chiefly held by Americans and British. One is "Menlo Park."

[9]The Rt. Rev. George Hills was consecrated Bishop of Vancouver Island and British Columbia in 1859. He arrived at Esquimalt, Vancouver Island on 5 January 1860.

Three men in field, mounted. One rides towards us. "How well that man rides—beautifully!" *Driver* "Don't he? I'll bet! He is one of the best riders in California." I "Who is it?" *Driver* "Don Secundino Robles. He used to own most of this country here; but has sold or lost most of it, and lives in that little house."

This is the way with most of the old Spaniards—

Now come to pretty little town of Santa Clara, one of the oldest of Missions, established about 1770.[10] Here is the Mission, its old adobe walls, its gardens and orchards, but in good order and preservation, for it is the seat of the Roman Catholic College. Additions have been made to it, and the effect of the whole is pleasing, the venerable—the active and useful. Wish had time and letters of introduction, and could stop and see the college. Driver says it is the best college or school in California, about 120 pupils. Town grows little, but San José eclipses it, in trade and population, and is the county town of Santa Clara County.

In outskirts of Santa Clara are the Agricultural Fair Grounds, with Race Course, etc., etc., well got up.

This is near head of the Bay. The vessels, steamers etc. stop at Alviso, some 6 miles from Santa Clara and San José.

The valley goes on to San José. This is a large thriving town. It was the Second Pueblo established by the Spaniards, Los Angeles being the first. It was known in the North as "the pueblo," as Los Angeles was in the South, and they were distinguished as the Upper Pueblo, and Lower Pueblo. The Mission of San José is some 12 or 14 miles off, on the North side of the Bay.

The two large buildings in San José are the Church and the School. The Church was the old adobe church, which looked rather old and crumbly, but was solid, and the Spaniards were not willing to have it pulled down. So brick walls were built outside the adobe walls, a kind of veneering, making them some 7 feet thick, and two wings and a chancel added, making a very large and fine looking building.

The school is kept by the Sisters of Notre Dame, for girls, and has nearly 200 scholars, and stands very high in public estimation. It is a large brick building, with large grounds enclosed by a wall.

Spent night at a French inn, where cooking was excellent, service as good as in Paris, and prices high. Large wood fire, in bar room, and all the frequenters are French. Great deal of talk round the fire, politics, Napoleon, Austeriche, Les Anglais, [illegible], Espagne, Italy etc.

Young gentleman from Mr. Laurencel, comes over to spend the night: to drive me to the mines tomorrow.

---

[10]The Mission Santa Clara was founded in 1777.

Advertisement of Hamlet, to be played in the little theatre, Mr. and Mrs. W. C. Forbes.[11] Go in and see 2d and 3d acts, and can stand no more. Yet interesting to see how this great play interests and affects an audience of farmers and traders and miners and their families, acted as badly as possible. In closet scene, when ghost comes in, Hamlet falls flat on floor, and is picked up by his mother. In the play scene, after hitching himself up to the king, in watching his countenance, fairly staring him out of countenance, when king springs up, and goes off, Hamlet seizes him by the shoulders, shakes him, as he would a pickpocket he had detected,—amid great applause. In scene with Horatio, he hugs him in his arms, at "as I do thee"—and when he disjoins, he says "Something too much of this"—and so on, and so on. Yet it is an attractive play, in their hands, in San Francisco, and Hamlet called twice before the curtain in one night.

Great French bed, 4 or 5 beds deep, curtains etc. and clean.

Frid. Dec. 30. Up early, and off to the quicksilver mines. Leave the valley, and come to broken, hilly country.

One long vein runs across these hills, several miles in length, but held by different owners. The oldest and most southerly mine is called the New Almaden. That is not in operation, being under an injunction, in trust by U. S. for possession, and they do not ever permit any one to enter it. Ergo, do not go there, but to Mr. Laurencel's mine, the Enriquéta, named for his daughter. This is the name of the mine, village, etc. Mr. Laurencel's family being in San Francisco, he boards at the Enriquéta Hotel, a little place, but kept by Frenchmen, and, of course, well kept. Breakfast there, at 9 o'clock. Two intelligent gentlemen, besides Laurencel, speaking French, Spanish and English, and latter very fairly. In this little, remote place, we discuss English and French drama, Rachel, etc. They, though French, agree with us about the old French drama.

A Frenchman can make good bread anywhere, even in Boston. A Yankee can make good bread nowhere.

To the mine. High up the hill. Tunnels cut in, and shafts sunk. This mine only been in operation 6 or 8 months. One shaft is 60 feet deep. Went down it, by candle lights, ladder—a single timber, notches cut in it. The quicksilver ore is found only in the vermillion rock. These vermillion streaks run through the other formations. When pieces are broken and brought out to light, picked over by hand, and those that have the red streaks are accepted. These accepted pieces have from six to forty per cent of quicksilver, in weight, the average being about 15 per cent.

11James Stark built the first theatre in San José in 1859. He and his wife played there with great success.

These pieces are first crushed under stamps, moved by steam, then washed in troughs, shaken by steam, when the ore goes to the bottom, and the earth is taken off;—then another washing and shaking, until the ore-bearing earth is pretty well separated. It is then dried, in large pans, and then put into furnaces, and kept in them four hours. In this heating process, the quicksilver evaporates and ascends into retorts, is collected, passed through water, in syphons, and then spits out, drop by drop, into iron receivers. Then is bottled off in iron flask, with iron stoppers screwed in.

Most of the workmen work on contract, by the job, or, as they say, tribute work—All the mines do so, working in companies, and are paid by the weight of accepted stone, accounts being kept with each shaft.

Each shaft and tunnel has a name,—usually of a patron saint, and at entrance of one is a framed print of the Infant Jesus.

One year ago, not a house here. Now Enriquéta is a village of 40 or 50 houses, with Post Office, etc.

Two or three miles below is another mine, just opened, and worked by a Balt[imore] Company, called Guadaloupe, and a village begining. If these 3 mines, Almaden, Enriquéta and Guadaloupe, succeed as they promise now, there will be 10,000 people in these hills in a few years.

The quicksilver is carried by mules and wagons to Alviso, the head of the Bay, and shipped for San Francisco. San José is the market town of all these miners.

The discovery of the quicksilver mines was from inquiries made of the Indians as to where got red paint for their faces, etc and they showed these rocks, with streaks of vermillion—

Lunch, and left very good friends, for San José, which reached at dark. Dine at my French house—Could not stand another night of the drama, and knowing no one, spent night in the bar-room, at the open fire. I like these French people. They are laborers or journeymen, yet are so polite, and more *civilized* than any other people in the same class of life. Drink very little, and smoke and talk.

Amusing violent, theatr[ical] dispute between 2 of them, and appeals to "amour propre," "parole d'honneur" etc. If it had been on stage, would have been [too] vehement for English or American tastes.

Sat. Dec. 31. Stage coach early, for San Francisco, down the other side, the East side of the Bay.

East side of the Bay, San José Mission, San Lorenzo, San Leandro, and the great grants of the Soto and Castro families, who own some three leagues of land apiece,—forms a glorious agricultural country— Great land lake, between the Coast Range of mountains and the Bay— some 4 to 10 miles wide, a perfect level, except at the foot of the hills, no undergrowth, and trees enough to make shade here and there. Houses well placed under the trees, Fine views of mountains and the great Bay. If the Napa Valley is Lake George, turned to land, this valley,—the Alameda Valley, is Lake Champlain ditto. Napa is more beautiful and picturesque with better near views. This is on a larger scale, with grander distant views—Napa has the great advantage of water, all summer. This is dry in summer, but not so dry as Santa Clara Valley. The latter, in very dry seasons, loses its crops by drought.

Visit old Mission of San José. Church is standing, and in good order, and is now in use. The orchard also. But the ruined adobe walls are all that show the rows of Indian huts, which the Christianized Indians held under these great mission principalities.

(Old Mr. Yount, by the way, spoke very favorably of the condition of these missions and of their treatment of the Indians, when he came here first.)

Oakland, in Contra Costa County, is a large town, a popular suburb of San Francisco, and though only 6 or 8 miles off, across the Bay, has a different climate from San Francisco. (See Dr. Bushnell's reasonings on these facts.) It is not as cold or windy in summer, and trees grow well there. It is, indeed, a grove of live oak, almost hiding the houses. Large steamers go from here to San Francisco every few hours.

Reached my hotel, in San Francisco, at dark. Had neither dined, lunched nor breakfasted,—only cup of coffee, with bread dipped in, before [I] left San José. Dined. Spent evening at my room, and to bed early—although all the city is alive with New Year's Eve, balls, music, street processions, singing, etc. Do not feel in humor for it. Feel too serious, away from home, end of a year, etc.

Auction rooms (night auctions) have drinks and music and buffoons, to draw people in.

Signs here "Ici on parle Francais," "A qui se habla Espagnol" etc.

California phrases—*Spondulics*—Cash, ready money.

> *Dry up.* Stop, hold one's tongue.
>
> *Gone in.* Dead, given up.
>
> *You bet.* Certainly, doubtless.
>
> *First Rate,* used familiarly—for very well.

Ask a girl of 12 or 14 how she is, or how her mother is—she says "First rate, Sir."

No paper money and no copper here. Smallest coin is ½ dime. Small pieces go by *bits* i.e. for ½ shilling, or 12-½ cents, but a dime is always taken for a bit.

At restaurants, dinner of canvass back duck is 50 cents, and of chicken is 75 cents, and eggs are 12½ cents apiece.

The Mission San Jose

From a copy of a daguerreotype made in 1856 by Carleton E. Watkins. Courtesy Robert A. Weinstein

Monday, Jan. 2. Observed as holiday, for New Year's, Counting rooms and many other places closed. Calls on friends, as in New York. All "receive," unless sickness or calamity, and then place basket or plate at door to receive cards. Called on *Mesdames* Kip, Lawler, Blanding, Ewer, Morrison, Thompson, Hastings, Macondray and Holman. [Part of page cut away here.]

(Last notes sent by Steamer Mail, to Jan. 2d)

Jan. 3. Tuesday. Took steamer "Queen City," 4 P.M., for Sacramento. Sacramento is the capital, and the Legislature and Supreme Court are in session there. Steamer is a Mississippi style, high pressure, one cabin running the whole length of the boat, uninterrupted by machinery, and makes great show. Prices are "high pressure," also. No accommodations for sleeping except state rooms, and these are $3 apiece, for one night, and not provided with anything but a bed; and for toilet, you must go to barber's shop and wash *coram omnibus,* and wipe on a roller. I made some complaint to clerk of boat, for which I suppose he set me down as a "bloated aristocrat."

After leaving the Bay, and getting into Sacramento River, country is low and level and stream full, as a passenger said, like the Mississippi. The Sacramento is growing shallow from the immense quantity of dirt thrown into its waters above by the gigantic hydraulic mining operations, which settles on bars below the city. The steamers often ground on these, now, where 5 years ago there was water to spare. Marysville, on Feather River, is in danger of losing all its navigation by that cause.[12]

Wed. Jan. 4/60. At Sacramento. St. George Hotel, kept by General Hutchinson, who has been mayor of Sacramento, and is General of militia and vestryman of Grace Church, etc. Large and first style hotel, excellently kept. Top full of politicians. A *sub.* in the Custom House, a Mr. Joseph E. Lawrence, came up in boat to promote the interests of the Collector, Mr. Washington, as candidate for U. S. Senate. The election of Senator in Broderick's place, is the great thing now, and absorbs all attention.[13] Every prominent man in the state is a candidate, and all are on the spot, making personal canvass, with their retinues. The San Francisco Bulletin says that the Custom House, Mint, Navy Agency, Post Office etc. are all removed to Sacramento, *pro temp.*

No sooner got to hotel than a Boston client salutes me, one Hill, who has come here to dodge an order of Supreme Court for custody of child. Then, a man comes "Is this Mr. Dana of Boston?" "Yes, Sir."

[12]Marysville is at the confluence of the Yuba and Sacramento Rivers rather than being on the Feather River.

[13]Senator David C. Broderick was killed in a duel with Chief Justice David S. Terry on 13 September 1859.

Sacramento in 1855

Sacramento Illustrated, San Francisco, 1855

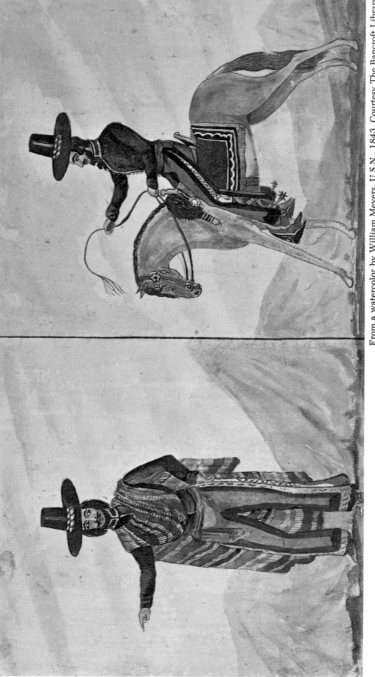

From a watercolor by William Meyers, U.S.N., 1843. Courtesy The Bancroft Library

Costumes in California

"You don't remember me. My name is Ryan." Still, I don't recall him. "I repaired your father's house, at Manchester, in 1846." "Oh yes, you were the carpenter, etc." and I began to inquire patronizingly after his success here, when he told me he was here as Senator from Humboldt County! I had to come down several pegs. He was neatly dressed, carried himself erect and straight, and had quite an air, full of tongue, and, I suspect, a thorough going party hack, with none but California scruples. I met him afterwards in the Governor's private rooms, full of importance.

To Supreme Court room. In lobby, found Chief Justice Field. He is from Berkshire, brother of David Dudley Field, etc., etc., also Baldwin and Cope J. J., and was introduced to numberless lawyers, who were all either *ex* judges or colonels, or generals—Crittenden, Campbell, McDougall, Williams, Hoag, etc. *Baldwin J.* is quick and fertile, but hasty, *Cope J.* is new and slow, but sensible. *Field C. Jus.* is the chief power. The Bench now is honest, learned and independent; and, for the first time, has public confidence. *Terry C. Jus.*, was the last of the ruffian and *buyable* order. Heard two questions argued, one touching the case of Terry, late Chief Justice, indicted for killing Broderick.

Only difference between manners of these judges and ours is in their familiar and free intercourse with the bar, off the bench. At adjournment, they come down into the Bar and talk with the members; and sit and smoke in the lobby, with the members. This is wrong, and will die out, as all tendencies in California are in a conservative direction. I have been told by Field, Governor Latham, the Governor elect, and several leading democratic politicians, that the sentiment of the state is almost unanimous in favor of removing the judiciary from political influence, of having the judges appointed by the Governor, instead of by popular election, and giving them a life tenure; and that the Democratic party would take the responsibility of recommending this if a Convention should be called. Several gentlemen have told me the people would even sustain a system of retiring pensions for judges who have served for long periods.

Field tells me that the Reporter of their decisions makes dreadful work, being a political appointee, and the new Governor is to recommend to Legislature to authorize the Court to appoint its own reporter. He thinks the last few volumes must be re-edited, and says they would give Horace Gray $20,000 to come out here and do it;—for he thinks Gray the model reporter.

A statute, drawn by Field, when he was in the Legislature, provides that the usages and rules of the miners, in their several localities, shall be received in evidence, and, when not in conflict with the Constitution and laws, shall govern. This is in lieu of a code of mining laws, and is far better; for the character of mining in different localities varies so much, and the needs and interests of the miners, that a general code would be impracticable. This system delights the miners, and the judges say that the rules and customs which have come before them are almost always sensible and just, though always verging on the severe and the summary. When magistrates were scarce, and before this statute, the miners in each region had their organizations, their written law, their summary tribunals, and banished, flogged and hanged delinquents, without hesitation or scruple. Without this, they could not have lived. They still keep up their organizations and rules, and make preliminary inquiries, like grand juries, but almost always take the delinquent in to the nearest magistrate, and don't interfere afterwards, unless they have reason to think the magistrate releases him improperly,—in which case, they still sometimes take him and try and punish him by their own tribunals,—but a decision of a *Court or jury* they always obey. The Supreme Court is very popular with the miners, as its decisions have sustained their rules, their water rights, and their investments, however rudely cared for by them.

Field tells me he was Alcalde of Marysville in 1850, before regular organization of counties and courts, had no definition or limit to his authority or jurisdiction, took unlimited jurisdiction over all cases brought before him (short of capital punishment), held the law in his own breast and declared it for each case, *pro re natâ*, made novel writs, *in rem* or *in personam*, as he pleased, and the most curious judgments, but such as justice and the state of society required. Having no jails, and no houses but of canvass, and no jailers or Sheriffs, no criminal could be confined longer than they could hold him in hand; so he used to order flogging, lashes on bare back, by installments, and where restitution was possible, or some important disclosures desirable, the lashes were to cease, at end of any installment when the required act was done. Under this system, order reigned in Marysville. Subsequently, he got his acts and records recognized by the Legislature, which protected him, and on them all the land titles of the town rest. He also told me that from 1849 to 1856, he never went into Court or Legislature without a pair of Derringers in his pocket and a Bowie knife under his coat, and that he was advised to do so by the judges, who did the same—all men did. If a man was not ready to fight, either on the spot or by duel, he could hardly live, certainly not tolerably, in California. Now, no man is armed, (except some rowdies who would be so anywhere) and a man may refuse a challenge on grounds of principle, if his life sustains him in the position.

Called on Miss Dana, my fellow-traveller here from New York, at the home of her brother-in-law, one Culver. Talked over the "Star of the West" etc. Nice, little helpless, innocent thing. Evening at Field's rooms—anecdotes of California life 1850-3—almost incredible. *Inter alia,* he arrived at Marysville with 18¢, and in 6 months made $60,000 by professional practice and some lots bought on speculation—lost it in suits and political contests in a year more, and made another fortune at the bar.

Thursd. Jan. 5. Rain and mud— all day and night.

Called on Rev. Mr. Hill, the Episcopalian clergyman. He complains of the want of religious interest, and habits of Church going—indifferent, lax etc; but attentive and kind of him personally, and many good traits in the people.

Called on Rev. Mr. Beckwith, late Principal of Punahou School, whose wife is daughter of Dr. Armstrong, the missionary at Honolulu. He is in temporary charge of a Presbyterian Society here. He left Punahou on account of Mrs. B's health.

Mrs. B. showed me daguerrotypes of all the Punahou scholars, which were given to them, on their departure. Pleasant to see the faces of the Gulicks, Armstrongs, Parkers, Lymans, etc. etc.,—those excellent, intelligent, kind young men and young women.

To the Legislature. State House a long, brick, building—one story in height. Assembly and Senate Rooms well enough. No business of consequence. Long conversation with Don Pablo de la Guerra, who is senator from Santa Barbara District. He saw San Francisco twice destroyed by fire, a large city, of shanties and canvas houses chiefly, but large and full of goods and business, in the morning, and nothing standing at night, and rebuilding the next day. This, twice—Once, while fire raging, saw an old woman clearing off the coals and hot ashes and putting up a cloth tent with a board and a few bottles. His companion said "We ought to encourage such industry as that—Let's take a drink." His anecdotes of early times—and impositions on the old Mexican holders of land—(which the judges tell me is true), they paying taxes and all their lands held by squatters whom no law would eject. Later decisions are returning to them their rights. Don Pablo is an intelligent, cultivated man, and is a noble of Spain, by right of birth.

(An ignorant judge in San Francisco, on a petition for Hab[eas] Corpus, entered judgment against the petitioner for the amount he owed the man who was illegally restraining him).

Dined at Governor Latham's. Latham a young man, clever, not more than ordinary in other respects, and a regular politician. Mrs. L. the best mind of any woman I have met since I left home, and few better have I ever met, if any—ill health, pale, sallow—Is daughter of Dr. Birdsall, now or late of the army. She is rich and so is Latham. *Ex* Lt. Gov. Purdy was present. After gents left to look after the caucus, had long and interesting conversation with Mrs. L. on theological subjects, on which she perfectly understands herself.

Introduced to Livingston, of the Alta, Gen. English ex Treasurer of California, etc.

Friday Jan. 6. Epiphany, and, as I am a man of leisure, feel it my duty to go to Church. Found the only Episcopal Church in the city locked—evidently the day forgotton or omitted. (Mr. Hill complained of want of interest, in his people.) The only other church to keep the day, is, of course, the Roman Catholic, and I go there, where, in the rain and cold, dull day, in a shell of a church with bare brick walls on inside, mortar standing out, and holes not yet closed in the roof, was a congregation of not less than two hundred; and yet there had been an early service before this. I never saw a more still, attentive and (to all external appearance) devout congregation. One priest only,—the only one here. He has a day school for boys under the Church; and seven Sisters of Mercy, recently arrived, have a girls' school of about 200 scholars, also under the church in a damp, dreary place, with bare walls. They have bought a lot for a school and convent, and will soon build. At the end of the side aisle was a representation of Our Lord (being Christmas season) lying in the manger,—a figure of the virgin, of the size of life, standing before the child which is lying on the floor of the small place, and over it is a thatched roof, and grass lying about it,—all actual.

Congregation chiefly Irish, but some others.

To the Legislature. Met Mr. Billings of San Francisco, who introduced me to several members and notables. Don Pablo de la Guerra and Don Andrés Pico are the only men of Spanish descent in a Senate of 40 members, in a country which was Mexican 13 years ago! In the Assembly, of 80, there is but one Mexican. Both branches very young men, mostly between 23 and 35, few over 35. Ryan sits reading his newspaper and voting grandly on yeas and nays. My friend De la Guerra is thought able and intelligent, and has the most of a patrician look of any man here.

Called on Mrs. McDougall. Her husband is candidate for the U. S. Senate, so he is out. Mrs. McD. is in poor health, reminds me of Miss Wheaton, and is an intelligent, well educated woman. Met there the handsomest woman I have seen in California, wife of Mr. Stewart, a lawyer and member of Assembly, and daughter of *ex.* Senator Foote of Mississippi.

Sacramento is on a dead level and low, has been flooded several times and twice burned up. Now, a levee of 10 feet high is built round the city, and all the ground in occupation raised to that level, as they are now raising Chicago. It is laid out in regular rectangular blocks, like

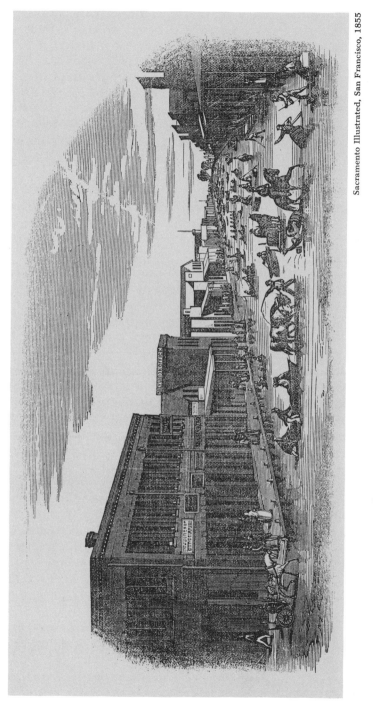

Sacramento Illustrated, San Francisco, 1855

Sacramento . . . has been flooded several times . . .

461

Philadelphia, the streets being wider. The streets parallel with the river are named by numbers, and the cross streets by letters. In some streets, trees are set out. More brick houses, in proportion, than in San Francisco, and all wooden houses are now prohibited. Awnings of wood, i. e. piazzas, are built out to the whole width of the sidewalks, giving protection against sun and rain. These are generally made strong enough for promenading on their tops from the windows of the second stories, which are used as parlors. The Episcopal and one Presbyterian Church are handsome, of brick, with climbing roses, etc. The Roman Catholic Church is a large shell, and there is a huge deformity of a Methodist Church.

The statement that the rivers Sacramento, Feather and Yuba are badly filling up by the quantity of earth sent down by the immense hydraulic mining operations is confirmed to me.

The City and County of Sacramento built a hall for State Agricultural Fairs, in less than 60 days from first sod cut—a hall of brick, 140 x 100, the largest hall in U. S. unsupported by pillars. Inauguration of Governor Latham and Inauguration Ball to be there—(Obliged to buy a view of Sacramento from a young artist—sent it home by mail.)

Sat. Jan. 7. Rode out with two *ex* governors of California, Johnson and Purdy, to visit Sutter's Fort. Little of it remains—only the adobe angles and one adobe house.

Rode to house of Col. Zabriskie, father in law of Gov. Johnson, where saw 3 fine looking women. Mrs. Z., and the 2 daughters, Mrs. Johnson, and Miss Annie. They have fine figures and classic features. The Col. a New Jersey public man, of some note,—now in reduced circumstances. His house is on the only rising ground in the neighborhood of Sacramento.

Called on Mrs. Latham and Mrs. McDougall, and Mrs. Stewart. Latter is handsome and bright, but poverty of acquisitions and topics. Mrs. L. admits that the politics of California are and have always been very corrupt, and that most of the votes in the Legislature are purchasable by office if not money and that arrangements to give offices for votes are not concealed or thought dishonest by the greater number. She says political life is closed to any man who does not do such things.

Met two Democratic judges who doubt if the people would favor a judiciary for life by Executive appointment, at present; for politics are too corrupt to trust so long terms to the appointment of any governor, or any convention—yet they think that is the true tenure, and should be aimed at. At present, all is too much tentative and fleeting—people, offices and laws.

All praise Don Pablo's speech, in 1855, on the extension of the statute of limitations as to land titles. It was made in the Senate, in

Spanish, and was a noble plea for the Old Californians and their rights, and carried the Senate and Legislature, and probably saved the State from the disgrace of a great robbery.

Met Major Gillespie, who was in active work here in the war of 1846, 7, commanding at Los Angeles. He was besieged there and capitulated, but with honors of war. He was present at the action of San Pasqual, where Don Andrés Pico, with 70 men, defeated General Kearny with sev[eral] hundreds, and at several other actions where Pico distinguished himself. He says Pico was as brave as a lion, and the soul of honor. Pico is now in the Senate, sitting by the side of Don Pablo, the only representatives of the old regime.

Sunday Jan. 8, 1860. To church. Day reasonably pleasant, yet not above 40 persons in church, of whom only 8 or 10 were women—very muddy, to be sure, but not raining—. Yet good sized church, well furnished empty pews, etc. But I fear brother Hill is enough to provoke a good deal of staying at home—, "The bottomless - ev - pu - at" (Bottomless pit) etc. *degoutant.*

Met Marshal Tukey in street, who saluted me. Met a lawyer, partner and friend of Gov. Latham, who thinks Latham honest and capable etc., yet he boasted how in the Convention wh[ich] nominated Latham (the contest being between him and Weller), he "traded Weller out of his boots,"—got Cope, a lawyer from the mountains, to run for Supreme Court Judge, to be voted for by Latham's friends, and Cope's friends to go for Latham, and so on as to Members of Congress, State offices of all sorts—"Yes, Sir, Weller was 10 ahead on the first ballot, and before next morning Latham was 10 ahead. He worked it round by getting these offices and tickets against each other, and traded the Weller people out of their boots before they knew it." This lawyer is a reputable man, and does not think these things dishonest, so no money is paid down as a bribe.

(Telegraph, yesterday, that the "Early Bird" will not sail before Wednesday—so shall stay over the inauguration.)

The universal habit of "drinks" here, tells especially on the politicians. The candidate for Speaker had to be dropped because he got on a spree which lasted over the election day, and there was a drunken row at the Legislative caucus Friday night. One member drew a knife on another, who drew a pistol and instantly as many as 20 pistols were cocked. This stopped the fight. It was too serious. (The question is gravely discussed whether A. *did right* in drawing his knife, etc.) The best man among the Senatorial candidates is McDougall,—but his habits have been very bad, and his state is now critical,—wh[ich], they say accounts for his wife's ill health. (Intemperance is the worst vice in a husband a woman can suffer from, for it is constant, public, and mortifying.) So, the best two orators on the Republican side, Judge Tracy and Col. Baker are the same way; and ex Gov. Johnson, my entertainer of yesterday, was "as tight as a peep" in the hotel the night before, and not quite straight yesterday, and he told me he was taking care of a young lawyer from the mining region, who could not get away unless a friend forced him off before the morning drinks began. While I was calling at Mrs. McDougall's, her husband came in rather boozy.

Lawrence, whom I supposed to be a New York fast man and a mere Court House democratic politician, turns up a "Spiritualist," in the technical sense. He tells me he was a disbeliever in immortality, and, of course, in Christianity, and in all spiritual powers,—saw the rappings, mediums etc. (among good private circle at home), was led to think and read, and came to a belief in the immortality of the soul, its active state after death, spiritual agency of angels and saints, miracles etc.,—thinks there should be prayers for the dead, invocation of Saints, etc., making the World of Spirits practical parts of our religion. How little we know of what is going on in men's minds! I had seen him here canvassing for his friend for the Senate, and thought him a man that would laugh at the mere mention of a religious subject. So, I find that Mrs. Latham and Mrs. McDougall, in the whirl of bed politics, have given anxious attention and are now giving it, to the highest of subjects, and know their grounds. And *per contra,* how often men of good reputation and high professions have *no* religious or spiritual life or thoughts *whatever.* We are deceived both ways. Spent the evening in Field's room. His wife has come—a very pleasant and pretty young woman from Virginia, with cordial manners, and knows how to blush, —a lost art in California. They were in Brookline in September and gave me late news from my friends there.

Major Gillespie married a daughter of Duane of Philadelphia, has been unfortunate here, tried to be elected clerk of the Senate, but the caucus set up another man, who, of course, would be elected, but Gillespie's old opponent of the war of 1847, Don Andrés Pico, made a speech in his favor, detailing, as a generous foe, his good conduct in the war, and expressing his astonishment that *Americans* should refuse to sustain a man who had shed his blood for his country's cause, and spoke so feelingly and well, that Gillespie received *every vote.*

There are three great interests in California, mining, agricultural and commercial. At present, I think that, in political and economical questions, the mining is the most powerful of these,—not in wealth or numbers probably, but in unity of interest. In questions touching their affairs, they are one man. (In this interest is included, of course, those who depend on them,—the mechanics and traders in mining regions.) Next is the agricultural, the richest and most numerous, but divided into various interests, grain growing, wine growing, cattle raising, etc., and large rancheros and small yeomen. The members of the Legislature are spoken of as from mining districts, or agricultural districts. The commercial interest is almost solely San Francisco.

The practice of hailing from the state of previous residence is so general, that the state is put in the city directory—thus: "Brown, John, druggist, 105 K. St. (Penna.) etc," and men, permanent residents, are introduced as Mr. A. B. from Georgia, or Massachusetts, etc.

Found out the member from Mendocino County and inquired about Canning Smith. He says Canning is clerk of the County, which is a good office. I inquired how he was succeeding, his character etc., as a relative,—he replied, being a Southern chivalry man—"Well, Sir, him and me has had a difficulty, and I prefer to say nothing about him,—except that in his office he is thought an efficient man and good clerk." (Sent by mail from Sacramento Jan. 9, 1860—to that date)

Inauguration, in large Agricultural Hall (120 x 100, instead of *140* x 100 as I said before). Three companies of militia. Gov. Weller introduced Latham, and Latham, (previously sworn in, at the Legislative Hall) delivered his inaugural address. No allusion to national pol-[itics.] Loud and pretty good voice. Large audience. Not order enough. Boys making noise. Judges of Supreme Court, *ex.* governor, etc. on platform.

Don Pablo introduced me to Don Andrés Pico, who has old Spanish manners.

A humbug named Warren, (editor of a paper here) has just been married, and told Mrs. Field he had married a woman who was "sound on all the progressive principles of the age."

The Chinese Chapel—a small brick building, arranged inside exactly like a Methodist Chapel, open pews, middle aisle, small square pulpit at head of the aisle. A few small tables about the pulpit were filled with pamphlets or unbound sheets, like tracts—in Chinese.

Inauguration Ball at the Agricultural Hall—complimentary ticket for me—including carriage. Arrangements of dressing rooms, supper room, etc. excellent. A hall of 120 x 100, no pillars, and very high roof, the best dancing hall I ever saw. Large assembly, nearly all dance. Many fine looking women, and many very costly dresses. Mixed with them, the common rustics, with ungloved hands. *Ex.* Gov. Weller and wife, Gov. Latham and wife, Lt. Gov. Downey and wife (a Mexican, cousin of Mrs. Henry Mellus), Chief Justice Field and wife, McDougall and wife, and innumerable ex. governors, ex. judges, etc. with wives and daughters. Weller is a coarse, tobacco spitting man, with inattentive manners, and I had but few words with him.

Sacramento Illustrated, San Francisco, 1855

Chinese Chapel, Sixth Street, Sacramento

Tuesd. Jan. 10. Parting calls, and took boat at 2 P.M. for San Francisco. Beautiful sail down the river. (Better site for city below, and reasons why failed.) Felton on board. Tells me the secret that Latham is to be nominated Senator to-night—all arranged—the word is "combination," which means jobs, trades, etc. Latham is as honest as any of them, and more free from trammels. Capt. of Steamer tells good stories of early California life, the infamous, murderous *wag*, Ned McGowan etc. (Ned McGowan's funny account of his man killing the Dutchman —"the only place he was mortal" etc.—his *infernal machine* etc.) (Also, of Ned Marshall and Senator Foote—"That or *rain*"—fellow with window sash over his neck "running yet"—) The "same old drink."

At *San Francisco*, 9 P.M., and my hotel and long night's rest.

Wed. Jan. 11. The Bark "Early Bird" sails to-night. Called on Mr. and Mrs. Stanly. Letter from Fremont etc. Fine large French ship to sail for Hong Kong in 10 or 12 days. Should like to go in her, for advantage of speaking French—and would wait that time were I not already out of season in the East. Two weeks may make the difference of my visiting or not visiting a country, escaping a quarantine or not etc.

To-night, I hope to see my last of California—

"A few short hours, and he will rise to give the morrow birth,
"And I shall hail the main and skies,—but not my mother Earth."

(The captain of the steamer came from Panama with Edm. D. Otis, and says he was a capital fellow, cheerful and full of fun and courage and the favorite of everybody—So, in San Francisco, but he fell away, and got to driving a job wagon, and was taken home by compassion, and died on the passage.) (Felton speaks very well of Bruce Upton, and says he was respected and liked here and his failure was owing to over-confidence.)

(Sent journal and letters from San Francisco by mail of Jan 13th, to date of Jan. 11th.)

Sunday Jan. 15, 1860. At sea, onboard bark "Early Bird" four days out from San Francisco.

We sailed from San Francisco Wednesday night, Jan. 11th, about midnight. As this was my 8th time of passing the Golden Gate, I did not care to see it, and went on board, put state room in order and "turned in," and waked up next day (Thursday), about 7 o'clock, with gentle rolling of the ship, to find myself at sea, the Golden Gate in sight and the hills of the Coast Range. Calm or light winds all day. Next morning, Friday, out of sight of land, and glad am I to see the last of California, and to be on the broad Pacific, every hour bringing me nearer to China.

View looking north from San Francisco showing Angel Island, Alcatraz and the Marin Coast

From a photograph by George Johnson, 1857. Courtesy Robert A. Weinstein

THIRTY-THREE YEARS AFTER

[The following pages are those which Dana wrote in 1869 as the concluding section of his new edition of Two Years before the Mast. *They were included in the chapter entitled "Twenty-Fours Years After," but obviously contain information and materials which came to him up to the actual time of writing.]*

It is time my fellow-travellers and I should part company. But I have been requested by a great many persons to give some account of the subsequent history of the vessels and their crews with which I had made them acquainted. I attempt the following sketches in deference to these suggestions, and not, I trust, with any undue estimate of the general interest my narrative may have created.

Something less than a year after my return in the *Alert,* and when, my eyes having recovered, I was again in college life, I found one morning in the newspapers, among the arrivals of the day before, "The brig *Pilgrim,* Faucon, from San Diego, California." In a few hours I was down in Ann Street, and on my way to Hackstadt's boarding-house, where I knew Tom Harris and others would lodge. Entering the front room, I heard my name called from amid a group of blue-jackets, and several sunburnt, tar-colored men came forward to speak to me. They were, at first, a little embarrassed by the dress and style in which they had never seen me, and one of them was calling me *Mr.* Dana; but I soon stopped that, and we were shipmates once more. First, there was Tom Harris, in a characteristic occupation. I had made him promise to come and see me when we parted in San Diego; he had got a directory of Boston, found the street and number of my father's house, and, by a study of the plan of the city, had laid out his course, and was committing it to memory. He said he could go straight to the house without asking a question. And so he could, for I took the book from him, and he gave his course, naming each street and turn to right or left, directly to the door.

Tom had been second mate of the *Pilgrim,* and had laid up no mean sum of money. True to his resolution, he was going to England to find his mother, and he entered into the comparative advantages of taking his money home in gold or in bills—a matter of some moment, as this was in the disastrous financial year of 1837. He seemed to have his ideas well arranged, but I took him to a leading banker, whose advice he followed; and, declining my invitation to go up and show himself to my friends, he was off for New York that afternoon, to sail the next day for Liverpool. The last I ever saw of Tom Harris was as he passed down Tremont Street on the sidewalk, a man dragging a hand-cart in the street by his side, on which were his voyage-worn chest, his mattress, and a box of nautical instruments.

Sam seemed to have got funny again, and he and John the Swede learned that Captain Thompson had several months before sailed in command of a ship for the coast of Sumatra, and that their chance of proceeding against him at law was hopeless. Sam was afterwards lost in a brig off the coast of Brazil, when all hands went down. Of John and the rest of the men I have never heard. The Marblehead boy, Sam, turned out badly; and, although he had influential friends, never allowed them to improve his condition. The old carpenter, the Fin, of whom the cook stood in such awe, had fallen sick and died in Santa Barbara, and was buried ashore. Jim Hall, from the Kennebec, who sailed with us before the mast, and was made second mate in Foster's place, came home chief mate of the *Pilgrim*. I have often seen him since. His lot has been prosperous, as he well deserved it should be. He has commanded the largest ships, and when I last saw him, was going to the Pacific coast of South America, to take charge of a line of mail steamers.[1] Poor, luckless Foster I have twice seen. He came into my rooms in Boston, after I became a barrister and my narrative had been published; and told me that he was chief mate of a big ship; that he had heard I had said some things unfavorable of him in my book; that he had just bought it, and was going to read it that night, and if I had said anything unfair of him, he would punish me if he found me in State Street. I looked at him from head to foot, and said to him, "Foster, you were not a formidable man when I last knew you, and I don't believe you are now." Either he was of my opinion, or thought I had spoken of him well enough, for the next (and last) time I met him he was civil and pleasant.

I believe I omitted to state that Mr. Andrew B. Amerzene, the chief mate of the *Pilgrim,* an estimable, kind, and trustworthy man, had a difficulty with Captain Faucon, who thought him slack, was turned off duty, and sent home with us in the *Alert.* Captain Thompson, instead of giving him the place of a mate off duty, put him into the narrow between-decks, where a space, not over four feet high, had been left out among the hides, and there compelled him to live the whole wearisome voyage, through trades and tropics, and round Cape Horn, with

[1]Pacific Steam Navigation Co.

nothing to do—not allowed to converse or walk with the officers, and obliged to get his grub himself from the galley, in the tin pot and kid of a common sailor. I used to talk with him as much as I had opportunity to, but his lot was wretched, and in every way wounding to his feelings. After our arrival, Captain Thompson was obliged to make him compensation for this treatment. It happens that I have never heard of him since.

Henry Mellus, who had been in a counting-house in Boston, and left the forecastle, on the coast, to be agent's clerk, and whom I met, a married man, at Los Angeles in 1859, died at that place a few years ago, not having been successful in commercial life. Ben Stimson left the sea for fresh water and prairies, settled in Detroit as a merchant, and when I visited that city, in 1863, I was rejoiced to find him a prosperous and respected man, and the same generous-hearted shipmate as ever.

This ends the catalogue of the *Pilgrim's* original crew, except her first master, Captain Thompson. He was not employed by the same firm again, and got up a voyage to the coast of Sumatra for pepper. A cousin and classmate of mine, Mr. Channing, went as supercargo, not having consulted me as to the captain. First, Captain Thompson got into difficulties with another American vessel on the coast, which charged him with having taken some advantage of her in getting pepper; and then with the natives, who accused him of having obtained too much pepper for his weights. The natives seized him, one afternoon, as he landed in his boat, and demanded of him to sign an order on the supercargo for the Spanish dollars that they said were due them, on pain of being imprisoned on shore. He never failed in pluck, and now ordered his boat aboard, leaving him ashore, the officer to tell the supercargo to obey no directions except under his hand. For several successive days and nights, his ship, the *Alciope,* lay in the burning sun, with rain-squalls and thunder-clouds coming over the high mountains, waiting for a word from him. Toward evening of the fourth or fifth day he was seen on the beach, hailing for the boat. The natives, finding they could not force more money from him, were afraid to hold him longer, and had let him go. He sprang into the boat, urged her off with the utmost eagerness, leaped on board the ship like a tiger, his eyes flashing and his face full of blood, ordered the anchor aweigh, and the topsails set, the four guns, two on a side, loaded with all sorts of devilish stuff, and wore her round, and, keeping as close into the bamboo village as he could, gave them both broadsides, slam-bang into the midst of the houses and people, and stood out to sea! As his excitement passed off, headache, languor, fever, set in—the deadly coast-fever, contracted from the water and the night-dews on shore and his maddened temper. He ordered the ship to Penang, and never saw the deck again. He died on the passage, and was buried at sea. Mr. Channing, who took care of him in his sickness and delirium, caught the fever from him, but, as we gratefully remember, did not die until the ship made port, and he was under the kindly roof of a hospitable family in Penang. The chief mate, also, took the fever, and the second mate and crew deserted; and although the chief mate recovered, and took the ship to Europe and home, the voyage was a melancholy disaster. In a tour I made round the world in 1859-1860, of which my revisit to California was the beginning, I went to Penang. In that fairy-like scene of sea and sky and shore, as beautiful as material earth can be, with its fruits and flowers of a perpetual summer—somewhere in which still lurks the deadly fever—I found the tomb of my kinsman, classmate, and friend. Standing beside his grave, I tried not to think that his life had been sacrificed to the faults and violence of another; I tried not to think too hardly of that other, who at least had suffered in death.

The dear old *Pilgrim* herself! She was sold, at the end of this voyage, to a merchant in New Hampshire, who employed her on short voyages, and after a few years, I read of her total loss at sea, by fire, off the coast of North Carolina.

Captain Faucon, who took out the *Alert,* and brought home the *Pilgrim,* spent many years in command of vessels in the Indian and Chinese seas, and was in our volunteer navy during the late war, commanding several large vessels in succession, on the blockade of the Carolinas, with the rank of lieutenant. He has now given up sea, but still keeps it under his eye, from the piazza of his house on the most beautiful hill in the environs of Boston. I have the pleasure of meeting him often. Once, in speaking of the *Alert's* crew, in a company of gentlemen, I heard him say that that crew was exceptional; that he had passed all his life at sea, but whether before the mast or abaft, whether officer or master, he had never met such a crew, and never should expect to; and that the two officers of the *Alert,* long ago shipmasters, agreed with him, that, for intelligence, knowledge of duty, and willingness to perform it, pride in the ship, her appearance and sailing, and in absolute reliableness, they never had seen their equal. Especially he spoke of his favorite seaman, French John. John, after a few more years at sea, became a boatman, and kept his neat boat at the end of Granite Wharf, and was ready to take all, but delighted to take any of us of the old *Alert's* crew, to sail down the harbor. One day Captain Faucon went to the end of the wharf to board a vessel in the stream, and hailed for John. There was no response, and his boat was not there. He inquired, of a boatman near, where John was. The time had come that comes to all! There was no loyal voice to respond to the familiar call, the hatches had closed over him, his boat was sold to another, and he had left not a trace behind. We could not find out even where he was buried.

Mr. Richard Brown, of Marblehead, our chief mate in the *Alert,* commanded many of our noblest ships in the European trade, a general favourite. A few years ago, while stepping on board his ship from the wharf, he fell from the plank into the hold and was killed. If he did not actually die at sea, at least he died as a sailor—he died on board ship.

Our second mate, Evans, no one liked or cared for, and I know nothing of him, except that I once saw him in court, on trial for some alleged petty tyranny towards his men—still a subaltern officer.

The third mate, Mr. Hatch, a nephew of one of the owners, though only a lad on board the ship, went out chief mate the next voyage, and rose soon to command some of the finest clippers in the California and India trade, under the new order of things—a man of character, good judgment, and no little cultivation.

Of the other men before the mast in the *Alert,* I know nothing of peculiar interest. When visiting, with a party of ladies and gentlemen, one of our largest line-of-battle ships, we were escorted about the decks by a midshipman, who was explaining various matters on board, when one of the party came to me and told me that there was an old sailor there with a whistle round his neck, who looked at me, and said of the officer, *"He* can't show *him* anything aboard a ship." I found him out, and looking into his sunburnt face, covered with hair, and his little eyes drawn up into the smallest passages for light—like a man who had peered into hundreds of northeasters—there was old "Sails" of the *Alert,* clothed in all the honors of boatswain's-mate. We stood aside, out of the *cun* of the officers, and had a good talk over old times. I remember the contempt with which he turned on his heel to conceal his face, when the midshipman (who was a grown youth) could not tell the ladies the length of a fathom, and said it depended on circumstances. Notwithstanding his advice and consolation to "Chips," in the steerage of the *Alert,* and his story of his runaway wife and the flag-bottomed chairs, he confessed to me that he had tried it again, and had a little tenement just outside the gate of the yard.

Harry Bennett, the man who had the palsy, and was unfeelingly left on shore when the *Alert* sailed, came home in the *Pilgrim,* and I had the pleasure of helping to get him into the Massachusetts General Hospital. When he had been there about a week, I went to see him in his ward, and asked him how he got along. "Oh! first-rate usage, sir; not a hand's turn to do, and all your grub brought to you, sir." This is a sailor's paradise—not a hand's turn to do, and all your grub brought to you. But an earthly paradise may pall. Bennett got tired of in-doors and stillness, and was soon out again, and set up a stall, covered with canvas, at the end of one of the bridges, where he could see all the passers-by, and turn a penny by cakes and ale. The stall in time disappeared, and I could learn nothing of his last end, if it has come.

Of the lads who, beside myself, composed the gig's crew, I know something of all but one. Our bright-eyed, quick-witted little coxswain, from the Boston public schools, Harry May, or Harry Bluff, as he was called, with all his songs and gibes, went the road to ruin as fast as the usual means could carry him. Nat, the "bucket-maker," grave and sober, left the seas, and, I believe, is a hack-driver in his native town, although I have not had the luck to see him since the *Alert* hauled into her berth at the North End.

One cold winter evening, a pull at the bell, and a woman in distress wished to see me. Her poor son George—George Somerby—"You remember him, sir; he was a boy in the *Alert;* he always talks of you—he is dying in my poor house." I went with her, and in a small room, with the most scanty furniture, upon a mattress on the floor—emaciated, ashy pale, with hollow voice and sunken eyes—lay the boy George, whom we took out a small, bright boy of fourteen from a Boston public school, who fought himself into a position on board ship, and whom we brought home a tall, athletic youth, that might have been the pride and support of his widowed mother. There he lay, not over nineteen years of age, ruined by every vice a sailor's life absorbs. He took my hand in his wasted feeble fingers, and talked a little with his hollow, death-smitten voice. I was to leave town the next day for a fortnight's absence, and whom had they to see to them? The mother named her landlord—she knew no one else able to do much for them. It was the name of a physician of wealth and high social position, well known in the city as the owner of many small tenements, and of whom hard things had been said as to his strictness in collecting what he thought his dues. Be that as it may, my memory associates him only with ready and active beneficence. His name has since been known the civilized world over, from his having been the victim of one of the most painful tragedies in the records of the criminal law.[2] I tried the experiment of calling upon him; and, having drawn him away from the cheerful fire, sofa, and curtains of a luxurious parlor, I told him this simple tale of woe, of one of his tenants, unknown to him even by name. He did not hesitate; and I well remember how, in that biting, eager air, and at a late hour, he drew his cloak about his thin and bent form, and

[2] Dr. George Parkman was murdered by Professor John White Webster in Boston in 1849.

walked off with me across the Common, and to the South End, nearly two miles of an exposed walk, to the scene of misery. He gave his full share, and more, of kindness and material aid; and, as George's mother told me, on my return, had with medical aid and stores, and a clergyman, made the boy's end as comfortable and hopeful as possible.

The *Alert* made two more voyages to the coast of California, successfully, and without a mishap, as usual, and was sold by Messrs. Bryant and Sturgis, in 1843, to Mr. Thomas W. Williams, a merchant of New London, Connecticut, who employed her in the whale-trade in the Pacific. She was as lucky and prosperous there as in the merchant service. When I was at the Sandwich Islands in 1860, a man was introduced to me as having commanded the *Alert* on two cruises, and his friends told me that he was as proud of it as if he had commanded a frigate.

I am permitted to publish the following letter from the owner of the *Alert*, giving her later record and her historic end—captured and burned by the rebel *Alabama*:—

"New London, March 17, 1868.

"Richard H. Dana, Esq.,

"Dear Sir,—I am happy to acknowledge the receipt of your favor of the 14th inst., and to answer your inquiries about the good ship *Alert*. I bought her of Messrs. Bryant and Sturgis, in the year 1843, for my firm of Williams and Haven, for a whaler, in which business she was successful until captured by the rebel steamer *Alabama,* September, 1862, making a period of more than nineteen years, during which she took and delivered at New London upwards of twenty-five thousand barrels of whale and sperm oil. She sailed last from this port, August 30, 1862, for Hurd's Island (the newly discovered land south of Kerguelen's), commanded by Edwin Church, and was captured and burned on the 9th of September following, only ten days out, near or close to the Azores, with thirty barrels of sperm oil on board, and while her boats were off in pursuit of whales.

"The *Alert* was a favorite ship with all owners, officers, and men who had anything to do with her; and I may add almost all who heard her name asked if that was the ship the man went in who wrote the book called *Two Years before the Mast;* and thus we feel, with you, no doubt, a sort of sympathy at her loss, and that, too, in such a manner, and by wicked acts of our own countrymen.

"My partner, Mr. Haven, sends me a note from the office this P.M., saying that he had just found the last log-book, and would send up this evening a copy of the last entry on it; and if there should be anything of importance I will enclose it to you, and if you have any further inquiries to put, I will, with great pleasure, endeavor to answer them. Remaining very respectfully and truly yours,

Thomas W. Williams."

"P.S.—Since writing the above I have received the extract from the log-book, and enclose the same."

The last Entry in the Log-Book of the Alert

"September 9, 1862.

"Shortly after the ship came to the wind, with the main yard aback, we went alongside and were hoisted up, when we found we were prisoners of war, and our ship a prize to the Confederate steamer *Alabama.* We were then ordered to give up all nautical instruments and letters appertaining to any of us. Afterwards we were offered the privilege, as they called it, of joining the steamer or signing a parole of honor not to serve in the army or navy of the United States. Thank God no one accepted the former of these offers. We were all then ordered to get our things ready in haste, to go on shore—the ship running off shore all the time. We were allowed four boats to go on shore in, and when we had got what things we could take in them, were ordered to get into the boats and pull for the shore—the nearest land being about fourteen miles off—which we reached in safety, and, shortly after, saw the ship in flames.

"So end all our bright prospects, blasted by a gang of miscreants, who certainly can have no regard for humanity so long as they continue to foster their so-called peculiar institution, which is now destroying our country."

I love to think that our noble ship, with her long record of good service and uniform success, attractive and beloved in her life, should have passed, at her death, into the lofty regions of international jurisprudence and debate, forming a part of the body of the "Alabama Claims";—that, like a true ship, committed to her element once for all at her launching, she perished at sea, and, without an extreme use of language, we may say, a victim in the cause of her country.

R. H. D., Jr.

Boston, May 16, 1869.

APPENDIX A
VESSELS

Achilles. Ship. British. Built at Sunderland, England, 1854. 578 tons.

Admittance. Ship. American. 501 tons. On the California Coast, 1843-1845.

Alert. Ship. American. Built at Boston, 1828, under direction of Noah Brooks, master carpenter. 2 decks. 3 masts. 398 18/95 tons. 113 ft. 4 in. x 28 ft. x 14 ft. Square stern, no galleries, billet head. Owners, 1828: Alfred Richardson, Boston, and Theodore Lyman, Waltham, Massachusetts. Owners, 1830-1843: William Sturgis, John Bryant, and various associates, Boston. Owners, 1843-1860: Henry P. Havens, Thomas W. Williams, and various associates, New London. Vessel was engaged in whaling. Apparently bark rigged in 1856. Owner, 1862: C. H. Chapell, New London. Captured and burned by C.S.S. *Alabama* 9 September 1862.

Ann McKim. Ship. American. Built at Baltimore, 1833. 494 tons. Dismantled at Valparaiso, Chile, 1852.

Architect. Bark. American. Built at Rockland, Maine, 1855. 399 tons. 127 ft. x 28 ft. x 12 ft.

Avon. Hermaphrodite brig. American. 88 tons. 16 men. John C. Jones, owner. Made two or three trips from Honolulu to California in 1834-1835.

Ayacucho. Brig. English. Tonnage given in various customs house documents as 300, 232, 204, 160. Traded between California and Hawaii and California and Callao, Peru, 1830-1835.

Blonde. Frigate. English. Built 1819. 46, 42 guns. Renamed *Calypso* in 1870.

Bolivar. Brig. American. Tonnage given in various customs house documents as 224, 212, 202, 193, 180. Owned by Americans at Honolulu. Traded between Hawaii and California and on the California Coast, 1832-1844.

Brandywine. Frigate. American. Built 1821-1825, at the Washington Navy Yard. 1726 tons. 44 guns. Burned at Norfolk Navy Yard, 1861; raised and sold 1867.

Cabot. Ship. American. Built at Duxbury, Massachusetts, 1832. 339 tons.

Cahawba. Side-wheel steamer. American. Built at New York, 1854.

1643 tons. Chartered by U.S. War Department 1861; purchased by U.S. War Department 1864; sold by U.S. War Department 1865. Abandoned 1867.

California. Ship. American. Built at Medford, Massachusetts, 1831, under direction of George Fuller, master carpenter. 2 decks. 3 masts. 369 2/95 tons. 117 ft. 6 in. x 26 ft. 3 in. x 13 ft. 1½ in. Square stern, no galleries, figure head. Owners, 1831-1845: John Bryant, William Sturgis, and various associates. On the California Coast repeatedly 1831-1845.

Catalina. Brig. Mexican. Tonnage given in various customs house documents as 161, 160, 138. 13 men. On the California Coast repeatedly 1831-1844.

Clementine. Brig. English. Tonnage given in various customs house documents as 160, 93, 76. Traded between Hawaii and California 1835-1839.

Constellation. Frigate. American. Built at Baltimore, 1797. 1278 tons. 36 guns. Rebuilt 1805-1812. Broken up at Norfolk, 1854.

Convoy. Brig. American. 137 tons. 13 men. Traded on the California Coast and to Hawaii, 1830-1836.

Cortes. Ship. American. 382 tons. On the voyage on which *Pilgrim* met her at Juan Fernandez, she departed New Bedford 20 July 1834 for the Pacific whaling grounds. She returned to New Bedford 5 November 1837 with 2320 bbl. sperm oil.

Decatur. Sloop-of-war. American. Built at New York Navy Yard, 1839. 16 guns. Sold at San Francisco 1865.

Diana. Brig. American. Tonnage given in various customs house documents as 199, 170. Traded on the California Coast, to Hawaii, the Columbia River, and Alaska, 1835-1838. Renamed *Kamamalu,* 1837, Went aground near Santa Barbara, April 1838.

Dublin. Frigate. English. Built 1812. Sold 1885.

Early Bird. Bark. American. Built, Newcastle, Delaware, 1856. 525 tons.

Facio (also referred to as *Fazio*). Brig. Mexican. 11 men. Owned by Johnson and Aguirre. Traded on the California Coast, 1833-1835. Went aground at San Pedro in 1835. *Pilgrim* aided in getting her afloat.

Golden Gate. Side-wheel steamer. Built, New York, 1851. 2067 tons. Owned by the Pacific Mail Steamship Co. Burned off the Mexican Coast in 1862.

Independence. Receiving ship. American. Built at the Boston Navy Yard in 1814 as a 74-gun line-of-battle ship. Altered to 54 guns in 1836. For many years after the Mexican War was a receiving ship at Mare Island. Sold and burned 1914.

John Adams. Sloop-of-war. American. Built at Norfolk Navy Yard, 1830. 18 guns. Sold at Boston, 1867.

Lagoda. Ship. American. Built at Wanton, Massachusetts, 1826. 292 tons. Owned by Bryant, Sturgis and Co. when she was trading on the California Coast in 1833-1835. Engaged in whaling 1841-1877. Became a coal hulk at Yokohama 1890 and was broken up at Kanagawa in 1899.

Loriot (Dana spelled her name *Loriotte*). Hermaphrodite brig. American. Built at Plymouth, Massachusetts in 1828. Tonnage given in various customs house documents as 90, 76, 70. Traded on the California Coast 1833-1837.

Mastiff. Ship. American. Built by Donald McKay at East Boston, 1856. 1030.70 tons. 168 ft. 10 in. x 36 ft. 6 in. x 22 ft. Burned at sea, 1859.

New England. Ship. American. Built 1834. 375 tons. When spoken by *Pilgrim* she was on a whaling cruise in the South Atlantic grounds. She had departed Poughkeepsie, New York, 7 June 1834, and returned 3 August 1836 with 800 bbl. sperm oil, 2000 bbl. whale oil.

Persia. Side-wheel steamer. Built 1856 by Napier, Glasgow. 3300 tons. 376 ft. x 45 ft. Owned by British and North American Royal Mail Steam Packet Co. (Cunard Line). Sold in 1868; engines removed and scrapped 1872.

Pilgrim. Brig. American. Built at Medford, Massachusetts, 1825, under the direction of Sprague J. James, master carpenter. 2 decks. 2 masts. 180 56/95 tons. 86 ft. 6 in. x 21 ft. 7½ in. x 10 ft. 9¾ in. Square stern, no galleries, figure head. 1825: Joshua Blake, Francis Stanton, George Hallett of Boston, owners. 1831: Charles Hill, Boston, owner. 1832: William F. Weld, Boston, owner. 1833: Arthur Lithgow, Jr., Boston, owner. 1834: Samuel Hooper, John Bryant, William Sturgis, John Bryant, Jr., owners. 1837: Nathan Godfrey, Portsmouth, owner. 1837: William Sheafe, Edmund Q. Sheafe, Nathan Godfrey, Portsmouth, owners. 1839: Mark W. Sheafe, Portsmouth, owner. 1841: Robert Haley, Boston, owner. Lost 1856.

Queen City. Side-wheel steamer. American. Built, San Francisco, 1854. 379 tons. Abandoned, 1861.

Rialto. Ship. American. Built at Kingston, Massachusetts, 1834 by Joseph Holmes. 459 tons.

Roanoke. Steam frigate. American. Built at Norfolk Navy Yard, 1855. Sold, Chester, Pennsylvania, 1883.

Rosa. Ship. Sardinian or Genoese. 425 tons. 24 men. Trading on the California Coast, 1834-1835.

Roxanna. Brig. American. Built, Bath, Maine, 1822. 241 tons. Owned by Bryant, Sturgis and Co. Traded on the Coast of California, 1832-1833.

Royal George. Line-of-battle ship. English. 100 guns. Sank at Portsmouth with heavy loss of life, 1782.

Sachem. Ship. American. Owned by Bryant, Sturgis and Co. Traded on the California Coast, 1825-1827.

Saginaw. Side-wheel steamer. American (U.S. Navy). Built at Mare Island Navy Yard, 1859. 453 tons. Wrecked on Ocean Island Reef, 1870.

St. Louis. Sloop-of-war. American. Built, Washington Navy Yard, 1827-1828. 18 guns. Sold after the Civil War.

Senator. Side-wheel steamer. American. Built at New York, 1848. 754 tons. Operated on the Sacramento River and then on the California Coast until her engines were removed and she was sold to Australian owners in 1884.

Sitka. Bark. Russian. 202 tons. On the California Coast, 1835-1838.

Star of the West. Side-wheel steamer. American. Built at New York, 1852 for Cornelius Vanderbilt. 1173 tons. Was running from New York to Aspinwall for the United States Mail Steamship Co. in 1859. Chartered by the U. S. Navy Department to attempt the relief of Fort Sumter in 1861. Seized by the Confederates at New Orleans, and burned to prevent her falling into Union hands in 1862.

Tasso. Bark. American. 314 tons. Engaged in trade on the California Coast, 1841-1848.

Vandalia. Sloop-of-war. American. Built at Philadelphia, 1825-1828. 700 tons.

Wilmington and Liverpool Packet. Ship. American. 384 tons. First whaling cruise, 1820-1823. Made whaling cruise to the Pacific Ocean grounds, departing New Bedford 14 November 1833 and returning 16 August 1836. Took 2700 bbl. sperm oil. Condemned in the Sandwich Islands, 1845.

APPENDIX B
PERSONS

Adams, The Rev. Mr. Nehamiah, Jr. (1806-1878). In 1834, he left the "Shepherd Congregational Society" to become pastor of the Essex Street Church, Boston.

Alemany, The Rt. Rev. Joseph S., Archbishop of San Francisco, in 1859.

Allston, Washington (1779-1843). Uncle by marriage of Richard Henry Dana, Jr.

Amerzeen, Andrew B. (also spelled Amazeen, Amerzene) (1806-1838). Born Epsom, New Hampshire. First Mate of *Pilgrim* on voyage to California in 1834-1835. Returned to Boston in *Alert*. The crew list of *Pilgrim* of 1834 describes him as residing in Portsmouth, New Hampshire, 5 ft. 8½ in. tall, of light complexion and with brown hair.

Anson, George (1697-1762). Visited Juan Fernandez Island in H.M.S. *Centurion* in 1741.

Argüello, Santiago (1791-1862). Diputado and comisionado for San Diego Mission, 1831-1835. Alcalde of San Diego in 1836.

Armstrong, Richard (1805-1860). Arrived in Honolulu as a missionary in 1832.

Arthur, James P. German. Mate of ship *Brookline* on the California Coast 1829-1830; master of Bryant, Sturgis and Co's ship *California* on four or five voyages to California, 1834-1846. Bancroft describes him as a skilful mariner, but close-fisted and not popular on the coast.

Baker, E. D. An active Whig in California politics in 1853. A Republican politician in 1860.

Baldwin, Joseph G. Associate Justice of the California Supreme Court in 1859.

Ballmer, George (listed as Bellamer on the crew list). Dana calls him an English sailor. The crew list calls him a United States citizen, born and resident in Boston, 21 years of age, 5 ft. 4 in. in height, light complexion and brown hair.

Bandini, Juan (1800-1859). Resident of San Diego and officially inspector of customs for California in 1835-1836. He died at Los Angeles.

Bandini, Refugio Argüello. Second wife of Juan Bandini.

Banning, Phineas T. Laid out the town of Wilmington, California in

1858. Operated the stage-coach line between San Pedro and Los Angeles.

Beckwith, Edward G. Principal of Punahou School, Honolulu, 1854-1859.

Billings, Frederick. Partner in the firm of Halleck, Peachy and Billings, attorneys-at-law, San Francisco in 1859.

Bingham, Hiram (1789-1869). Missionary in Hawaii.

Birdsall, L. A., Dr. Boarded at the Brannan House, San Francisco in 1859.

Bishop, Bernice Pauahi. Hawaiian chiefess. Died 1884.

Bissell, Simon B. Commander, U.S. Navy and in charge of receiving ship *Independence* at Mare Island in 1859.

Blake, Maurice C. Judge, County Court of Probate and Court of Sessions, San Francisco in 1859.

Blanding, Lewis and William were attorneys-at-law with offices together in San Francisco in 1859.

Bond, Charles R. City and County Assessor, San Francisco in 1859.

Bowditch, Nathaniel (1773-1838). Author of the *American Practical Navigator*.

Bradshaw, John. Master of a number of trading ships from Boston on the California Coast: *Franklin* 1827-1828, *Pocahontas* 1830-1832, *Lagoda* 1834-1835. Died in 1880, aged 94.

Brown, Richard. First mate of *Alert,* 1834-1836. On the crew list of the ship shown as born and residing in Marblehead, Massachusetts; age 25 in 1834, 5 ft. 4 in. in height, dark complexion and brown hair.

Burke, James W. Born in Ireland. Came to California as a trader in 1824 and settled in Santa Barbara in 1828 where he lived until his death about 1878.

Bustamente, Anastasio (1780-1853). A Mexican general and politician.

Casserly, Eugene. Attorney-at-law in San Francisco in 1859.

Channing, Edward Tyrrell (1790-1856). Boylston Professor of Rhetoric and Oratory at Harvard College, 1819-1851.

Channing, William Ellery (1780-1842). Unitarian clergyman. A cousin of Richard Henry Dana, Jr.

Conness, John. A California politician. Nominated for lieutenant governor in 1859. Elected to the U. S. Senate in 1863 to succeed Milton S. Latham.

Cope, W. W. Associate Justice of the California Supreme Court in 1859.

Cunningham, Robert B. Captain, U.S. Navy and Commandant of the Mare Island Navy Yard in 1859.

Damon, Samuel Chenery (1815-1855). Sent to Honolulu in 1842 to be chaplain for the American Seamen's Friend Society.

Davis, Charles H. Commander, U.S. Navy in 1859.

Davis, Robert. Born in Honolulu. Brother of William Heath Davis. Educated in Boston. Came to California Coast in 1839 as clerk of *Monsoon*. Died in 1872.

Downey, John G. Elected Lieutenant Governor of California in 1859 and succeeded Milton S. Latham as Governor in 1860 when the latter resigned to enter the U. S. Senate.

Duer, William. County Clerk, San Francisco in 1859.

Emerson, George Barrell. Resident in Cambridge in 1834.

English, James Lawrence. Partner in the firm of Edwards and English, attorneys-at-law, Sacramento. Treasurer of the State of California, 1856-1857.

Ewer, The Rev. Ferdinand C. Rector of Grace Church, San Francisco in 1859.

Faucon, Edward H. (1806-1894). Master of *Alert* and *Pilgrim* on the California Coast 1835-1837. He was born in Boston. According to *Alert's* crew list he was 5 ft. 6 in. in height, had dark complexion and brown hair.

Felton, John B. Partner in the firm of Whitcomb, Pringle and Felton, attorneys-at-law, San Francisco in 1859.

Fernald, Charles. Born at North Berwick, Maine in 1830. Came to California in 1849 and to Santa Barbara in 1852. In 1859 he was a county judge.

Field, Stephen Johnson (1816-1899). Chief Justice of the California Supreme Court in 1859. In 1863 he was appointed to the U. S. Supreme Court.

Foote, Henry Stuart (1804-1880). Elected to the U. S. Senate in 1847 and Governor of Mississippi in 1851. He resigned in 1854 and moved to California returning to Mississippi in 1858.

Foster, George. (Dana spells his name Forster in his ms.) Second Mate in *Pilgrim*, 1834. According to the crew list he was born and resided in Scituate, Massachusetts. He was 23 years of age in 1834, had a light complexion and brown hair.

Frémont, Jessie Benton (1824-1902). Daughter of Senator Thomas Hart Benton and wife of John Charles Frémont.

Frémont, John Charles (1813-1890). Frémont, a controversial character, had run for President of the U. S. on the Republican Ticket in 1856. In 1859 he was devoting himself to the operation of mines on his Rancho de las Mariposas in California. Its title had been confirmed to him in 1855.

Frisbie, John B. Born in 1823 and came to California in 1847. He was prominent in business in Vallejo, California in 1859.

Gillespie, Archibald H. Came to California with dispatches for Larkin and Frémont in 1846; returned there overland in 1848; and spent much of the rest of his life there, dying in San Francisco in 1873.

Guerra, Ana María de la (1820-1855). Daughter of José de la Guerra y Noriega. Married Alfred Robinson.

Guerra, María de las Angustias de la. Daughter of José de la Guerra y Noriega. Married Manuel Jimeno Casarín and later Dr. J. C. Ord.

Guerra, Pablo de la (1819-1874). Son of José de la Guerra y Noriega. State senator from Santa Barbara County for several terms.

Guy, Abel. Banker and commission merchant in San Francisco in 1859.

Hager, John S. Judge of the 4th District Court, San Francisco in 1859.

Hancock, Winfield Scott. Captain, U. S. Army, 1859.

Hanscomb, Isaiah. Naval Constructor, Mare Island Navy Yard in 1859.

Harris, Thomas. Seaman in *Alert*, 1834-1836. Dana calls him an Englishman but the crew list gives his birthplace as Charlestown, Massachusetts and his residence as Boston. In 1834 his age was 40, he was 5 ft. 8½ in. tall, had a dark complexion and dark hair.

Hastings, John. Physician, San Francisco in 1859.

Hatch, James Byers. Third Mate in *Alert*, 1834-1836. The crew list gives his birthplace and place of residence as Springfield, Massachusetts, his age in 1834 as 19, his height as 5 ft. 7 in., his complexion and hair as dark. Died about 1894.

Hempstead. (The San Francisco *Directory* for 1859 lists no "Hemstead.") Charles H., Superintendent, U. S. Branch Mint, San Francisco. David B., notary public.

Hill, Charles. Came to California from Boston in 1832. Was a trader in Los Angeles, 1833-1836.

Hill, James (1813-1904). Seaman and later Second Mate in *Pilgrim*, 1834-1837. According to the crew list, he was born in Pittston, Maine and resided in Boston in 1834. He was then 21 years old, 5 ft. 10 in. tall, and had a light complexion and brown hair.

Hill, The Rev. W. H. Rector, Grace Church, Sacramento in 1859. From New York, married.

Hinckley, William Sturgis. Nephew of William Sturgis. Came to California in 1830. Was master of *Volunteer, Avon* (1834-1835), *Diana* or *Kamamalu*. Died in California in 1846 at the age of 39.

Hoar, Edward S. Practiced as a lawyer in Santa Barbara for a few years after 1853; then returned to Boston.

Hodge, James Thatcher (Harvard 1836). He died in 1871.

Holman, Francis A. Visiting physician and surgeon, City and County Hospital, San Francisco in 1859.

Hooper, Samuel. Employed by Bryant, Sturgis and Co., Boston in 1836.

Hutchinson, C. I. Keeper of the St. George Hotel at 4th and J Streets in Sacramento in 1859. He was listed in the directory as married and coming from Wisconsin.

John. The crew list of *Pilgrim* gives John Linden, born and resident in Sweden, and a Swedish citizen, as the only seaman named "John." He was listed as 27 years of age, and was the oldest seaman aboard. Height 5 ft. 7 in., light hair and complexion. The carpenter, John Holtz, was 37 years of age, born and resident in Germany and a German citizen, whatever that may have meant in 1834. He was 5 ft. 11 in. tall with a light complexion and dark hair.

Johnson, J. Neely. Came to California in 1849. Was elected Governor on the Know-Nothing ticket in 1855. He died in 1872.

Jones, John Coffin, Jr. Born in Boston. He was long a merchant and U. S. Consul in Honolulu with close business relations with California. He came to California in 1838, settled in Santa Barbara in 1841, and returned to Boston in 1846.

Kearny, Stephen Watts. Brigadier General in command of the overland expedition to New Mexico and California in 1846. He was Military Governor of California in 1847.

Kip, The Rt. Rev. William Ingraham (1811-1893). Elected missionary Bishop of California in 1853 and arrived at San Francisco in 1854.

Koopmanshap, Charles. Merchant, San Francisco in 1859.

Latham, Milton S. Born in 1829 in Ohio. Came to California in 1850. He was elected to the U. S. Congress in 1851 and remained until 1856 when he was appointed Collector of the Port of San Francisco. In 1859 he was elected Governor of California and the next year he resigned to take a seat in the U. S. Senate.

Laurencel, Henri. Resident of San Francisco in 1859.

Lawrence, Joseph E. Entry-Clerk, U. S. Custom House, San Francisco in 1859.

Leonard, Hiram. Paymaster with rank of Major, U.S. Army, 1860.

Liès, Eugene. Resident of Santa Barbara where he was variously treasurer, assessor, county clerk, district attorney, and member of the state legislature.

Livingston, Henry B. Reporter, *Daily Alta California,* San Francisco in 1859.

Macondray, Frederick W. Commission merchant, San Francisco in 1859. He was the owner of a ranch at San Mateo, California.

Marsh, George P. True name said to have been George Walker Marsh, an Englishman shipped on *Alert* at San Pedro in the autumn of 1835.

McAllister. The Rev. F. M. McAllister was rector of the Church of the Advent, San Francisco in 1859. The vestrymen included Cutler Mc-

Allister and Hall McAllister. The church was established in 1858 with the Rev. Mr. McAllister as its first rector.

McDonald, William. Came to California in 1846. Married Eleanor Graves of the Donner Party in 1849. Lived in Sonoma County and acted as a guide to the geysers for many years.

McDougal, David. Commander, U.S. Navy and Assistant to the Commandant, Mare Island Navy Yard in 1859.

McDougall, James A. (1819-1867). Came to California from Illinois in 1849, settled in San Francisco and began a law practice. He was elected Attorney General of California in 1850, a member of the U. S. Congress in 1853, and to the U. S. Senate in 1860.

McGowan, Edward ("Ned"). Notorious California politician.

Mellus, Francis ("Frank"). Came to California in 1839 at the age of 15. He became a clerk for Alpheus B. Thompson of Santa Barbara. In later years he was clerk, travelling agent, and junior partner for the firm of Mellus, Howard and Co. He settled in Los Angeles and died there in 1863.

Mellus, Henry. Born in Dorchester, Massachusetts, and came to California as an ordinary seaman in *Pilgrim* in 1835. He became agent's clerk. In 1834 he was 18 years of age, 5 ft. 7¾ in. tall, dark complexion and dark hair. He remained in California, and later returned as agent or supercargo of vessels of Appleton and Co. including *Admittance* and *Tasso*. He formed a partnership with W. D. M. Howard in 1845. Settled in Los Angeles in 1859 and died there in 1860.

Merchant, Charles Spencer. Lieutenant Colonel, U. S. Army and Commandant of the Presidio at San Francisco in 1859.

Myers, William. First Lieutenant, U.S. Army in 1859.

Norton, Edward. Judge of the 12th District Court, San Francisco in 1859.

Nuttall, Thomas (1786-1859). Resigned as Curator of the Botanical Garden, Harvard College to accompany the Wyeth Expedition to the Pacific Coast. Visited California in 1836 and returned to Boston in *Alert*.

Nye, Gorham H. Master of various vessels trading on the California Coast 1830-1847 including *Loriot* (1833-1835), *Bolivar, Fama,* and *Leonidas*. Died at St. Helena, California in 1878, aged 76.

Olney, James N. Second in command of the military organization of the San Francisco Committee of Vigilance of 1856. In 1860 his address was the Washoe Stock Exchange and he boarded with Mrs. Isabel Swearingen.

Parker, Francis Edward. Law partner of Richard Henry Dana, Jr. in Boston, 1856-1861.

Parsons, Levi. Attorney-at-law, San Francisco in 1859-1860.

Pico, Andrés (1810-1876). Commanded the Californian force at the Battle of San Pasqual, 1846. He was state Senator from Los Angeles, San Bernardino, and San Diego Counties in 1860-1861.

Poor, Charles H. Commander, U. S. Navy in 1859.

Popoff, A. A. Commodore, Russian Imperial Navy in 1859.

Pringle, Edward J. Partner in the firm of Whitcomb, Pringle and Felton, attorneys-at-law, San Francisco in 1859.

Purdy, S. Elected Lieutenant Governor of California in 1853.

Quitman, John A. Brigadier General of U. S. Volunteers, 1846.

Ripley, The Rev. George (1802-1880). Resident of Cambridge. Associated with Brook Farm experiment.

Robinson, Alfred. A native of Massachusetts, he came to California in 1829 at the age of 23 as clerk in *Brookline*. He was agent in California for Bryant, Sturgis and Co. 1830-1837. From 1849 onward he resided in San Francisco and Santa Barbara. He died in 1895.

Robles, Secundino. Born in 1813, he was a large landowner. In 1859 he was living on the Rancho Santa Rita in Santa Clara County.

Russell, Thomas. An American sailor picked up by *Pilgrim* in Santa Barbara and landed to supervise the hide house in San Diego. He became a permanent resident of the latter town. In 1840 he was 37 years old, was working as a carpenter, and was married to a native.

Ryan, James T. In 1860 he was a member of the California Senate from Humboldt and Trinity Counties.

Santa Ana, Antonio Lopez de (1795?-1876). A Mexican military man and politician.

Sawyer. There are five Sawyers in the Boston directory for 1834 who might qualify as the shipping master mentioned by Dana. Perhaps the most likely is Phineas Sawyer, proprietor of a victualling cellar at 1 Long Wharf in 1836.

Sedgwick, Mrs. This was probably Elizabeth Dana Ellery (1799-1862) who married Robert Sedgwick, a New York attorney who died in 1841.

Sedgwick, Elizabeth. Daughter of Robert and Elizabeth Sedgwick.

Sedgwick, Ellery. Son of Robert and Elizabeth Sedgwick.

Shattuck, George Cheyne (1783-1854). Boston Physician.

Shields, James. Brigadier General, U.S. Volunteers, 1846.

Smith, Persifor F. Colonel, U.S. Army in 1846 and Brigadier General in 1856. Died in 1858.

Stanly, Edward L. Member of the firm of Stanly and Hayes, attorneys-at-law, San Francisco in 1859.

Stearns, Abel. Came to California in 1829, and became a very wealthy and prosperous merchant in Los Angeles. He died in 1871 at the age of 72.

Stewart, Mrs. Mary L. Resident of Sacramento in 1859.

Stimson, Benjamin Godfrey (Dana spells his name Stimpson throughout the ms.) (1816-1871). Born and resident of Dedham, Massachusetts according to *Pilgrim's* crew list. He was an ordinary seaman, and transferred to *Alert* as Dana did. In 1834 he was 18 years of age, 5 ft. 10 in. tall, of light complexion and light hair.

Stone, Sherrold D. Commission merchant, San Francisco in 1859.

Sturgis, William (1782-1863). Boston mariner, shipowner, and merchant.

Sumner, George. Boston. Brother of Senator Charles Sumner.

Taylor, Edward Thompson (1793-1871). "Father Taylor' 'was a remarkably successful preacher to seamen in Boston. His Seamen's Bethel was built in 1833.

Temple, John. Came to California in 1827. He married and settled in Los Angeles in 1830 and died there in 1866 at the age of 68.

Terry, David Smith (1823-1889). Chief Justice of the California Supreme Court, 1857-1859. He resigned after the killing of Senator David Broderick in a duel in 1859.

Thompson, Alpheus B. Came to California in 1825 and was settled in Santa Barbara from 1834 onward. He was active in maritime and mercantile affairs. Brother of Francis A. Thompson. He died in 1869 at the age of 74.

Thompson, Francis A. Born in Maine about 1804. He came to California as master of *Roxanna* in 1832-1833 and in *Pilgrim* in 1835. He returned to Boston in *Alert*. Died of fever in Sumatra in 1837.

Thompson, Francisca Carrillo. Married Alpheus Thompson in 1834; died in 1841.

Thompson, Lydia. Mother of Alpheus, Francis, and Wildes Thompson.

Thompson, R. A. A member of the firm of Thompson, Irving and Pate, attorneys-at-law, San Francisco in 1859.

Thompson, Wildes B. Brother of Alpheus B. and Francis A. Thompson.

Thrall, The Rev. Stephen C. Rector of Trinity Church, San Francisco in 1859.

Townsend, Edward D. Major, U. S. Army in 1859.

Tracy, T. P. Republican politician in California in 1860.

Tukey, Francis. Resident of Sacramento, 1857. From Massachusetts.

Turner, Daniel. Chief Engineer at Mare Island Navy Yard in 1859.

Vallejo, Mariano Guadalupe (1808-1890). A great ranchero at Sonoma in 1859.

Vallejo, Salvador (1814-1876). Living with his brother, Mariano Guadalupe, at Sonoma in 1859.

Warner, Jonathan Trumbull. Came to California as a trapper in 1834 and settled in Los Angeles where he was living in 1859.

Washington, Benjamin F. Collector of the Port of San Francisco in 1859.

Weller, John B. U. S. Senator from California, elected in 1852. Governor of California, 1858-1860.

Wells, Alexander. Elected Associate Justice of the California Supreme Court in 1852 and remained on the bench until his death in 1854.

Wildes, Dixey. Resident of Boston in 1834. Captain.

Williams, Thomas H. Attorney General's Office, Sacramento in 1859.

Wilson, Benjamin Davis. Came to California in 1841 and became a prosperous ranchero and fruit raiser in the region of Los Angeles. Died in 1878 at the age of 67.

Wilson, John. A Scottish shipmaster and trader. He was master of *Ayacucho* (1831-1837), *Index, Fly,* and *Juanita*. He settled on a ranch at San Luis Obispo in 1845 and lived there until his death in 1860 at the age of 65.

Wilson. Three attorneys by this name, Charles A., James, and John are listed in the San Francisco *Directory* for 1859.

Woods, Mr. This may have been Leonard Woods (1807-1878) who had been Dana's tutor at Andover and was editor of the *Literary and Theological Review* in New York, 1833-1836.

Yount, George C. Came to California in the Wolfskill Party in 1831. He obtained a land grant in the Napa Valley in 1836 and lived there until his death at the age of 71 in 1865.

Zabriskie, J. C. Attorney-at-law, Sacramento in 1859. Compiler of the *Land Laws,* United States. Father of Mrs. J. Neely Johnson.

Members of the Dana Family.

Entries are those by which individuals are referred to in the journal or letters.

Baby. Angela Henrietta Channing Dana (1857-1928). Daughter of Richard Henry Dana, Jr.

Betsy, Aunt. Elizabeth Ellery Dana (1789-1874).

Charlotte. Ruth Charlotte Dana (1814-1901). Sister of Richard Henry Dana, Jr.

Charlotte. Ruth Charlotte Dana (1844-1903). Daughter of Richard Henry Dana, Jr.

Dana, Alexander Hamilton (1807-1887). Distant cousin of Richard Henry Dana, Jr. A resident of New York.

Dana, Aunt and Uncle (see Francis Dana).

Edward, Cousin. Probably Edward Everett Ellery, or Edward Tyrrell Channing.

Ellery, Mr. William Ellery (1761-1836). Great-uncle of Richard Henry Dana, Jr. or Frank Ellery (1794-1871).

Father. Richard Henry Dana (1787-1879).

Frank, Cousin. Francis Dana III (1806-1872), son of Francis Dana.

Frank, Uncle. Francis Dana (1777-1853).

Harriet, Cousin. Harriet Ellery, or Henrietta Ellery Channing, wife of E. T. Channing.

Lilly. Elizabeth Ellery Dana (1846-1939). Daughter of Richard Henry Dana, Jr.

Martha, Aunt. Martha Remington Dana Allston (1784-1862).

Mary, Cousin. Mary Russell of Milton, Massachusetts, or Mary Smith of Providence, Rhode Island.

Ned. Edmund Trowbridge Dana (1818-1869). Brother of Richard Henry Dana, Jr.

Ned, Uncle. Edmund Trowbridge Dana (1779-1859).

Richard. Richard Henry Dana III (1851-1931). Son of Richard Henry Dana, Jr.

Rosamund. Mary Rosamund Dana (1848-1937). Daughter of Richard Henry Dana, Jr.

S., Aunt. Sarah Ann Dana (1791-1866).

Sally. Sarah Watson Dana (1814-1907). Married Richard Henry Dana, Jr. in 1841.

Sally. Sarah Watson Dana (1842-1902). Daughter of Richard Henry Dana, Jr.

Sophia, Cousin. Sophia Willard Dana Ripley (1803-1861).

William, Uncle. William Smith of Providence, Rhode Island. Maternal uncle of Richard Henry Dana, Jr.

Wife. See Sally.

[These crew lists were prepared by Richard Henry Dana III for the 1911 edition of *Two Years before the Mast*. They were based on Custom house records which seemingly have been destroyed.]

List of Persons Composing the Crew of the Brig PILGRIM of Boston, whereof is Master Francis A. Thompson, bound for California

Names	Stations	Places of Birth	Places of Residence	Citizenship	Age	H'ght	Com-plexion	Hair	
Francis A. Thompson[1]	Master			U.S.A.					
Andrew B. Amazeen	1st Mate	Epsom	Portsmouth	Do.	28	5-8½	Light	Brown	Dischg'd
George Foster[2]	2nd Mate	Scituate	Scituate	Do.	23	5-6½	Light	Brown	Deserted
	3d Mate[3]								
John Holtz	Carpenter	Germany	Germany	Germany	37	5-11	Light	Dark	Dead
William Warren	Steward	Great Britain	Boston	Great Britain	28	5-6	Light	Dark	
Thomas Curtis	Cook	Weston	Boston	U.S.A.	40	5-7½	Black	Woolly	
James Hall[4]	Seaman	Pittston	Boston	Do.	21	5-10	Light	Brown	
Samuel Sparks[5]	Seaman	Westmoreland Co., Virginia	Boston	Do.	25	5-9½	Sallow	Dark Brown	
John Linden[6]	Seaman	Sweden	Sweden	Sweden	27	5-7	Light	Light	
William Brown	Seaman	Baltimore	Boston	U.S.A.	24	5-6½	Light	Light	
Henry Mellus[7]	O. Seaman	Dorchester	Dorchester	Do.	18	5-7¾	Dark	Dark	Dischg'd
Richard Henry Dana[8]	O. Seaman	Cambridge	Cambridge	Do.	19	5-5	Dark	Dark	Transf'd
Benj. G. Stimson[9]	O. Seaman	Dedham	Dedham	Do.	18	5-10	Light	Light	"
Samuel Hooper 2nd	O. Seaman	Marblehead	Marblehead	Do.	12	4-2½	Light	Light	"
George Bellamer[10]	Seaman	Boston	Boston	Do.	21	5-4	Light	Brown	Dead

PILGRIM

[1] Born in Maine about 1804. Transferred as Capt. of ALERT on return voyage. [2] Lowered to rank of seaman and deserted. [3] There was no third mate. [4] Promoted to second mate. [5] Flogged. [6] Flogged. [7] Left to be agent's clerk on shore. [8] Transferred to the ALERT. [9] Same as 8. [10] Lost overboard.

List of Persons Composing the Crew of the Ship ALERT, of Boston, whereof is Master E. H. Faucon, bound for California, 1834

Names	Stations	Places of Birth	Places of Residence	Citizenship	Age	H'ght	Complexion	Hair
Edward H. Faucon[1]	Master	Boston	Boston	U.S.A.	28	5-6	Dark	Dark
Richard Brown	1st Mate	Marblehead	Marblehead	Do.	25	5-4	Light	Brown
David Evans	2d Mate	Baltimore	Salem	Do.	30	5-9	Light	Sandy
James B. Hatch	3d Mate	Springfield	Springfield	Do.	19	5-7	Dark	Dark
M. Lilljequist[2]	Carpenter	Holland	Boston	Holland	35	5-8	Dark	Dark
James Luyck[3]	Steward	Boston	Boston	U.S.A.	27	5-7	Black	Woolly
James Williams[4]	Cook	New York	Boston	Do.	19	5-6½	Yellow	Woolly
Reuben Herriot[5]	Sailmaker & Seaman	New York	Boston	Do.	26	5-10½	Light	Brown
Henry White	Seaman	Boston	Boston	Do.	28	5-6½	Light	Brown
William H. Meyer[6]	Seaman	Newburyport	Boston	Do.	29	5-8	Light	Brown
Thomas Harris[7]	Seaman	Charlestown	Boston	Do.	40	5-8½	Dark	Dark
Joseph Brewer	Seaman	New Orleans	Boston	Do.	28	5-8½	Dark	Dark
Joseph E. Libby[8]	Seaman	Gardiner	Boston	Do.	23	5-10½	Dark	Dark
Henry Bennet[9]	Seaman	New York	Boston	Do.	31	5-6	Light	Brown
Cotton L. Pratt[10]	Seaman	Weymouth	Boston	Do.	28	5-8½	Light	Brown
William Harris[11]	O. Seaman	Boston	Boston	Do.	19	5-5	Light	Dark
Nathaniel B. Prouty[12]	O. Seaman	Hingham	Hingham	Do.	18	5-2	Dark	Dark
Ben Roubauds[13]	O. Seaman		Boston	Do.				
James Nye	O. Seaman	Dover	Dover	Do.	16	5-4	Dark	Light
George W. H. Somerby[14]	O. Seaman	New York	Boston	Do.	15	5-3	Dark	Dark
Henry R. May[15]	O. Seaman	Philadelphia	Boston	Do.	16	5-2	Light	Light

[1]Transferred from the ALERT to the PILGRIM in California. [2]Called "Chips" and became 3d Mate on next voyage of the ALERT. [3]Also given as Laych. [4]Called "Doctor." [5]Age 26 must be a mistake. He had been at sea 22 years, called "Sails," also "oldest man on board." Capt. Faucon said he was "fine looking"; a regular man-of-war's man at least 40 years old. [6]Full name William Hyson Meyers. Son of James & Abigail Meyers. Born Feb. 9, 1801. [7]Called Englishman. Birthplace given as Charlestown must be wrong. [8]Also spelt Libbey on later list & "station bill," is probably the other Kennebec man, and either he or Brewer the "Joe." [9]If the "oldest man" of the crew must have been more than 31. According to Capt. Faucon he was 40 at least. [10]Did not sail. Capt. Faucon could not remember such a man & Mr. Hatch wrote, "The Cotton Pratt I never heard of before." Probably "John the Frenchman" or Jack Stewart was taken in his place, or presented his papers as sailors sometimes did. Pratt's name was not in the ALERT's "station bill."

"John the Frenchman" so often mentioned does not appear on this crew list. There is no John and no one born in France. John C. Stewart is not on the regular crew list, but was on another and on the "station bill." [11]The later list says he "ran away at Callao" on the outward voyage. [12]Called the "Bucket-maker" & "Cape Cod Boy," also "Nat." b. Jan. 17, 1817, son of a blacksmith Nathaniel Prouty and Matilda B. Gregory his wife, both of Hingham. He married in Quincy, Nov. 18, 1847, Hannah Brown of Hingham. He died in Quincy 21 April, 1868. [13]Always mentioned as English. [14]Went out again in the ALERT Nov. 29, 1836. He died about 1838. The physician who saw to him was the Dr. George Parkman for whose murder Prof. Webster was convicted and hanged. [15]Called "Harry Bluff." George P. Marsh, an "Englishman" whose real name was George Walker Marsh, was shipped on board the ALERT at San Pedro in the Fall of 1835.

A Gallery of Photographs

especially grouped to show

the City and Bay of San Francisco in 1856

and in 1867, as well as views of

some of the places visited by Richard Henry Dana, Jr.

on his return trip to California, 1859-1860

View of the Waterfront from Rincon Point, 1856

Photograph by George R. Fardon. Courtesy Kodak Research Library

View from Stockton Street showing Washington Street, 1856

Photograph by George R. Fardon. Courtesy Kodak Research Library

North side of Montgomery Street, from California to Sacramento, 1856

View of the Plaza, Portsmouth Square, 1856

Steamboat Point showing early boatbuilders' yards, 1867

Photograph by George R. Fardon. Courtesy Kodak Research Library

View of North Beach from Telegraph Hill, 1856

View of Alcatraz Island, showing Meiggs Wharf, 1856

The City Hall, formerly the Jenny Lind Theatre, 1856

Photograph by George R. Fardon. Courtesy Kodak Research Library

Telegraph Hill, from Stockton and Sacramento Streets, 1856

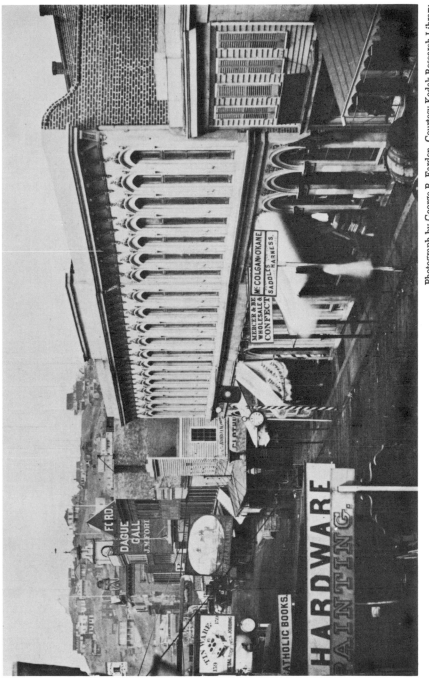

Kearny Street, 1856

Photograph by Edward Muybridge. Courtesy San Francisco College for Women

First and Brannan Streets, Pacific Mail Steamship Co. Docks, 1867

Photograph by George R. Fardon. Courtesy Kodak Research Library

The old Post Office at the Plaza, Portsmouth Square, 1856

Battery Street, showing the commission merchants stores, 1856

The India Dock, Davis Street, 1867

Photograph by Edward Muybridge. Courtesy San Francisco College for Women

View of the waterfront showing a P.M.S.S. Co. sidewheeler, 1867

Photograph by Edward Muybridge. Courtesy San Francisco College for Women

Beale Street docks showing U.S. Marine Hospital, 1867

Photograph by George R. Fardon. Courtesy Kodak Research Library

West side of Montgomery Street, towards Pacific Street, 1856

View showing Happy Valley, 1856

513

Fort Vigilance, headquarters of the Vigilance Committee, 1856

View of San Francisco between California and Bush Streets, 1856

515

Photograph by George R. Fardon. Courtesy Kodak Research Library

View over the City from Harrison Street, 1856

Photograph by Edward Muybridge. Courtesy San Francisco College for Women

Firewood schooners from Mendocino in the Bay near Meiggs Wharf, 1867

Photograph by Edward Muybridge. Courtesy San Francisco College for Women

The Waterfront near the North Point Dock Warehouse, 1867

Photograph by George R. Fardon. Courtesy Kodak Research Library

View of the Bay looking down Sacramento Street, 1856

Photograph by Edward Muybridge. Courtesy San Francisco College for Women

View of the docks from Telegraph Hill, 1867

The Merchant's Exchange, Battery Street, 1856

East side of Montgomery Street at California Street, 1856

California Street, showing the board streets, 1856

The Montgomery Block, Montgomery Street, 1856

South Park, San Francisco, 1856

Photograph by George R. Fardon. Courtesy Kodak Research Library

The Monumental Fire Engine House on the Plaza, 1856

Photograph by George R. Fardon. Courtesy Kodak Research Library

Kearny Street, the Orphan's Asylum in the foreground, 1856

Ship

Bark

Full-rigged Brig

Hermaphrodite Brig

Top-sail Schooner

Fore & aft Schooner

THE RIGGING OF SAILING VESSELS
Richard Henry Dana, THE SEAMAN'S FRIEND, *Boston, 1841*

APPENDIX C
GLOSSARY OF NAUTICAL
TERMS USED IN *TWO
YEARS BEFORE THE MAST*

*[Whenever possible, the definitions and explanations given are those
which Dana used in the "Dictionary of Sea Terms" which was included
in* The Seaman's Friend *which he published in 1841, the year after*
Two Years before the Mast *appeared.]*

Aback. The situation of a sail when the wind acts on its forward surface. Sails are caught aback or taken aback by a shift of wind or by
inattention at the helm.

Afterguard. Men who are stationed on the quarter deck or poop to
man the gear. Generally composed of landsmen and not required to
go aloft except to loose and furl the mainsail.

All standing. Fully equipped.

Anchor. The machine by which, when dropped to the bottom, the
vessel is held fast.

Athwart. Across.

Back-rope. A rope which fits over the dolphin striker with a cuckold's
neck, and sets up to the bows on each side. A cuckold's knot or neck
is a hitch by which a rope is secured to a spar; the two parts of the
rope cross each other, and are seized together.

Back-stays. Stays running from a masthead to the vessel's side, slanting
a little aft.

Balance-reef. A reef in a spanker or fore-and-aft mainsail which runs
from the outer head-earing, diagonally, to the tack. It is the closest
reef, and makes the sail triangular or nearly so.

Battens. Thin strips of wood put on masts, yards, or rigging to prevent
chafing. Also thin strips of wood put around the hatches to keep the
tarpaulin down.

Beam. A direction to windward or leeward, at right angles to the keel.
Also the breadth of a vessel.

Beam ends. A vessel is said to be on her beam ends when turned over
so that her beam ends are inclined toward the vertical.

Beating. Going toward the direction of the wind by alternate tacks.

Before the wind. A vessel having the wind aft is before the wind. The
yards are squared, and as the mainsail becalms the foresail and causes
the ship to steer badly, it is generally taken in.

Bend (verb). To bend a sail is to make it fast to the yard. To bend a cable is to make it fast to the anchor.

Bends (noun). The strongest part of a vessel's side, to which the beams, knees, and foot-hooks are bolted. The part between the water's edge and the bulwarks.

Best bower. The larger of the two bow anchors. In early days they were of different sizes, and the larger, called the best bower, was carried on the starboard bow; the other was known as the small bower. These designations were retained even after the anchors became of equal size.

Between-decks. The space between any two decks of a ship.

Bight. A bend in the shore, making a small bay or inlet. The double part of a rope when it is folded. Any part of a rope may be called the bight except the ends.

Bilge. That part of the floor of a ship upon which she would rest if aground; being the part near the keel which is more in a horizontal than a perpendicular line.

Bilge-water. Water which settles in the bilge.

Billet-head. Simple carved work, bending over and out, at the prow of a vessel.

Binnacle. A box near the helm containing the compass.

Bitts (Bits). Perpendicular pieces of timber going through the deck, placed to secure anything to. The cables are fastened to them if there is no windlass. There are also bitts to secure the windlass, and on each side of the heel of the bowsprit.

Block. A piece of wood with sheaves or wheels in it through which the running rigging passes to add to the purchase.

Board (To board the main tack). The stretch a vessel makes upon one tack when she is beating.

Boatswain. A warrant officer in the navy who has charge of the rigging and calls the crew to duty.

Boatswain's mate. Chief petty officer of the watch. He passes all the orders of the officer of the watch.

Bobstay. A rope or chain extending from the bowsprit to the cutwater. Used to counteract the strain of the head-stays.

Bolt-rope. The rope which goes round a sail and to which the canvas is sewed.

Bonnet. An additional piece of canvas attached to the foot of a jib or a schooner's foresail by lacings. Taken off in bad weather.

Boom. A spar used to extend the foot of a fore-and-aft sail or studding sail.

Boom-iron. Iron rings on the yards through which studding sail booms traverse.

Bower. A working anchor the cable of which is bent and reeved through the hawse-hole.

Bowline (Prounced bo-lin). A rope leading forward from the leech of a square sail to keep the leech well out when sailing close-hauled. A vessel is said to be on a bowline when she is close-hauled.

Bowse. To pull upon a tackle.

Bowsprit. A large spar projecting over the bows to support the fore-mast and extend the head-sails.

Brace (noun). A rope by which a yard is turned about.

Brace (verb). To brace a yard is to turn it about horizontally. To brace up is to lay a yard more fore and aft. To brace in is to lay it nearer square.

Brail (verb). To brail up is to pull on the brails and thereby spill the sail and haul it up for furling.

Brails (noun). Ropes by which the foot or lower corners of the fore-and-aft sails are hauled up.

Breast-backstays. Ropes which extend from the head of an upper mast, through an out-rigger, down to the channels forward of the standing backstays, for supporting the upper spars from to windward. When to leeward, they are borne abaft the top-rim.

Breast-hooks. Knees placed in the forward part of a vessel across the stem to unite the bows on each side.

Brig. A two-masted vessel, square-rigged on both masts.

Broad-pennant. A swallow-tailed piece of bunting, the distinctive mark of a commodore. Flying one in the *Alert* would indicate that the captain regarded her as the senior vessel on the coast.

Bulls-eye. A porthole. A piece of thick glass inserted in a hole in the deck or side to let light below.

Bumpkins. Pieces of timber projecting from the vessel to board the fore tack to, and from each quarter for the main brace-blocks.

Bunt. The middle of a sail.

Bunt gaskets. Gaskets at the bunt. Bunt gaskets cross each other.

Bunt jigger. A small purchase for rousing up the bunt of heavy sails.

Buntlines. Ropes used for hauling up the body of a sail.

Buoy. A floating cask or piece of wood attached by a rope to an anchor to show its position. To stream a buoy is to drop it in the water before letting go the anchor.

By the run. To let go by the run is to let go altogether instead of slacking off.

Cable's length. Usually 120 fathoms (720 feet).

Capstan. A machine placed perpendicularly in the deck and used for a strong purchase in heaving or hoisting. Men-of-war weigh their anchors by capstans. Merchant vessels use a windlass.

Carlines (or carlings). Short and small pieces of timber running between the beams.

Cat (verb). To hoist the anchor up to the cat-head.

Cat-block. The block of the tackle used to hoist the anchor up to the cat-head.

Cat-fall. The rope hauled upon when the cat-block is secured to the anchor in hoisting it to the cat-head.

Cat-harpin. An iron leg used to confine the upper part of the rigging to the mast.

Cat-head. A large timber projecting from the vessel's side to which the anchor is raised and secured.

Catspaw. A peculiar twisting hitch in the bight of a rope, making two smaller bights, into which a tackle is hooked.

Cat-tackle. The tackle used in hoisting an anchor. It includes the cat-block, cat-fall, and the sheaves in the cat-head.

Chafing gear. The stuff put upon the rigging and spars to prevent their chafing.

Chain cable. A large, strong chain used to retain a ship in place when at anchor. Chain cables are 120 fathoms long.

Chain plates. Plates of iron bolted to the side of a ship to which the chains and dead-eyes of the lower rigging are connected.

Channels. Broad pieces of plank bolted edgewise to the outside of a vessel. Used for spreading the lower rigging.

Chimes. The ends of the staves of a cask where they come out beyond the head of the cask.

Chock. A wedge used to secure anything with or for anything to rest upon. The long-boat rests upon two large chocks when it is stowed.

Chock-a-block. When the lower block of a tackle is run close to the upper one so that you can hoist no higher. This is also called hoisting up two-blocks.

Chronometer. A time piece of superior construction having adjustments and compensations for changes in temperature. Used in the determination of longitude at sea.

Clew (noun). The lower corner of a square sail and the after corner of a fore-and-aft sail.

Clew up (verb). To haul up the clew of a sail.

Clipper-built. A vessel with a sharp hull designed for fast sailing. Built on the model of a clipper.

Close hauled. Applied to a vessel which is sailing with her yards braced up so as to get as much as possible to windward. The same as "on a taut bowline," "full and by," "on the wind," etc.

Close-reef. The last reef in a sail.

Cock-bill. To cock-bill the anchor is to suspend it from the cat-head preparatory to letting go. To cock-bill the yards is to top them up at an angle from the deck—the symbol of mourning.

Companion. A wooden covering over the staircase to a cabin.

Corposant. St. Elmo's Fire. The luminous brush discharge frequently seen on the extremities of masts and yards at sea when atmospheric electricity of low intensity induces electricity on the ship or other objects which happens to be under its influence. This induced electricity concentrates at the extremities of structures where it becomes visible.

Corvette-built. Applied to naval vessels between a frigate and a brig. In the U.S. Navy generally called a sloop-of-war.

Courses. The common term for the sails which hang from a ship's lower yards. The foresail is called the fore course and the mainsail the main course.

Cringle. An eye or grommet in the head, leech, or clew of a sail. It is generally worked around a metal thimble, and serves as a convenient means of attaching the bowline-bridles, earings, etc. to the sail.

Cross-jack (pronounced crojack). The cross-jack yard is the lower yard of the mizzen mast.

Cross trees. Pieces of oak supported by the cheeks and trestle-trees at the mast-heads to sustain the tops of the lower mast, and to spread the topgallant rigging at the topmast-head.

Dead. "Dead before the wind" is directly before the wind.

Dog. A short iron bar with a fang or teeth at one end and a ring at the other. Used for a purchase, the fang being placed against a beam or knee, and the block of a tackle hooked to the ring.

Dog's ear. A small bight made in the leech-rope of a sail in reefing, making up, etc.

Downhaul. A rope used to haul down jibs, staysails, and studding sails.

Dunnage. Loose wood or other matters placed on the bottom of the hold, above the ballast, to stow the cargo upon.

Earing. A small line used to fasten the upper corners of a sail to the yard or gaff.

Eye. A loop or ring. Eye of a shroud is the part that goes over the mast-head. Thus the eyes of the royal rigging would be the point at which the royal shrouds pass over the head of the royal mast.

Fake. One of the circles or rings made in coiling a rope.

Fall. The rope of a tackle or purchase.

Fast. A rope by which a vessel is secured to a wharf. There are bow (or head), breast, quarter, and stern fasts.

Fathom. Six feet.

Fish (verb). To raise the flukes of an anchor upon the gunwale. To strengthen a spar when sprung or weakened by putting in or fastening on another piece.

Fish-davit. The davit used for fishing an anchor.

Fish-tackle. The tackle used for fishing an anchor.

Fist (verb). To lay hold of; to seize.

Flemish-eye. An eye used for the collar of a stay.

Flowing sheet. When a vessel has the wind free and the lee clews eased off.

Flying jib. The outermost jib or sail on the bowsprit, used as a jib to turn the ship's head. It is one of the light sails and is generally taken in and set with the royals.

Flying kites. Those lofty sails carried above the royals as sky-sails, moon-sails, star-gazers, etc.

Foot-rope. The rope stretched along a yard upon which the men stand when reefing or furling.

Forecastle. The forward part of the vessel under the deck where the sailors live in merchant vessels.

Foremast. The forward mast of all vessels.

Fore peak. The part of the hold in the extreme forward part of the ship, occupied by paint room, etc.

Foul hawse. When the two cables are crossed or twisted outside the stem.

Frap. To bind tightly with a rope or piece of small stuff.

Free. A vessel is going free when she has a fair wind and her yards braced in.

Furl. To roll a sail up snugly on a yard or boom and secure it.

Futtock plates. Iron plates crossing the sides of the top-rim perpendicularly. The dead eyes of the topmast rigging are fitted to the upper ends and the futtock shrouds to their lower ends.

Futtock shrouds. Short shrouds leading from the lower ends of the futtock plates to a bend around the lower mast just below the top.

Gaff. A spar to which the head of a fore-and-aft sail is bent.

Gaff topsail. A light sail set over a gaff, the foot being spread by it.

Gaskets. Ropes or pieces of plaited stuff used to secure a sail to the yard or boom when it is furled. They are called a bunt, quarter, or yard-arm gasket according to their position on the yard.

Gear. A general name for ropes belonging to any particular spar or sail. Also for the implements used in any operation.

Gig. A long, narrow boat used by the commanding officer. Generally clinker-built and single banked.

Girt-line (or gant-line). A rope rove through a single block aloft making a whip purchase. Commonly used in hoisting the rigging in the process of fitting out.

Grain. An iron with four or more barbed points to it; used for striking small fish.

Gripe (verb). A vessel gripes when she tends to come up into the wind.

Grog. Diluted spirits. Introduced into the Royal Navy in 1740 by Admiral Vernon and said to have been named from his grogram coat.

Ground-tackle. A general term for anchors, cables, warps, springs, etc.; everything used in securing a vessel at anchor.

Halyards. Ropes or tackles used for hoisting and lowering yards, gaffs, and sails.

Handspike. A long wooden bar used for heaving at the windlass.

Hanks. Rings or hoops of wood, rope, or iron around a stay and seized to the luff of a fore-and-aft sail.

Harness-cask. A large conical tub for containing the salt provisions intended for present consumption.

Hatch. An opening in the deck to afford a passage up and down. The coverings over these openings are also called hatches.

Haul wind. Said of a vessel when she comes up close upon the wind.

Hawse. The situation of the cables before a vessel's stem when moored. Also the distance before the water a little in advance of the stem: as, a vessel sails athwart the hawse or anchors in the hawse of another.

Hawse-hole. The hole in the bows through which the cable runs.

Hawser. A large rope used for various purposes as warping, for a spring, etc.

Head. The name applied to that portion of a ship, on either side of the bowsprit, which is set aside for the convenience of the ship's company. It served the purpose of the water closet of less hardy times and places, and the name is still used to denote the sections of a ship set aside for these purposes.

Head-pump. A small pump fixed at a vessel's bow, its lower end communicating with the sea; it is mostly used for washing decks.

Head sails. A general name given to all sails that set forward of the foremast.

Head sea. The name given to waves when they oppose a ship's course.

Head stays. The stays on the foremast.

Head yards. The yards on the foremast.

Heave to. To put a vessel into the position of lying-to. That is, to stop her progress at sea either by bracing the yards or by reducing sail so that she will make little or no headway, but will merely come to and fall off by the counteraction of the sails and helm.

Heel of the bowsprit. The lower or inner end of the bowsprit.

Hermaphrodite brig. A vessel with a brig's foremast (square rigged) and a schooner's mainmast (fore-and-aft rigged).

Hold. The interior of a vessel where the cargo is stowed.

Holystone. A large stone used for cleaning a ship's deck.

Hounds. Those projections at the mast-head serving as shoulders for the top or trestle-tree to rest upon.

Horse latitudes. The area of sea between the higher latitudes and trade winds, notorious for tedious calms. The name arose from mariners often throwing horses overboard which they were transporting to American and the West Indies when the voyage became over-long and stores and water ran short.

Irish pendants. Rope-yarns hanging about the rigging; loose reef-points or gaskets flying about; fag-ends of ropes.

Jack. An athwartship bar of iron at the topgallant mast-head to give spread to the royal shrouds.

Jack-cross-trees. Iron cross-trees at the head of long topgallant masts.

Jib. A triangular sail set on a stay forward.

Jib-boom. The boom rigged out beyond the bowsprit to which the tack of the jib is lashed.

Jigger. A small tackle used about decks or aloft.

Jolly-boat. A small boat usually hoisted at the stern.

Kedge (noun). A small anchor with an iron stock used for warping.

Kedge (verb). To warp a vessel ahead by a kedge and hawser.

Keelson. A timber placed over the keel on the floor timbers and running parallel with it.

Kettle-bottomed. A name applied to a vessel with a flat floor.

Kid. A small wooden tub. Used for dispensing food from the galley.

Knees. Crooked pieces of timber having two arms used to connect the beams of a vessel with her timbers.

Knight-heads. The timbers next the stem on each side and continued high enough to form a support for the bowsprit.

Knots. The log line is divided into knots, each of which bears the same proportion to a mile as 30 seconds does to an hour. Hence, in speaking of a vessel's speed the term "knot" is used, meaning nautical miles.

Larboard. The left side of a vessel looking forward.

Launch. A large boat. The long boat.

Leech (or leach). The border or edge of a sail at the sides.

Leeward. The side opposite to that from which the wind blows; as, if a vessel has the wind on her starboard side, that will be the weather and larboard will be the lee side.

Lifts. Ropes or tackles going from the yard-arms to the masthead to support and move the yard.

Log. A line with a piece of board, called the log-chip, attached to it, wound upon a reel, used for ascertaining the ship's rate of sailing.

Long boat. The largest boat in a merchant vessel. When at sea it is carried between the fore and main masts.

Luff tackle. A purchase composed of a double and single block.

Mainmast. The principal mast—the second from the bow.

Mainsail. The lower sail on the mainmast.

Man-ropes. Ropes used in going up and down a vessel's side.

Marline. Small, two-stranded stuff used for marling; a finer kind of spun-yarn.

Marline-spike. An iron pin, sharpened at one end and having a hole at the other for a lanyard. Used both as a fid and a heaver.

Martingale. A short, perpendicular spar under the bowsprit end used for guying down the head stays.

Mizzen (mizen) mast. The aftermost mast of a ship. The spanker is sometimes called the mizzen.

Nettings. A network of ropes or small lines used for stowing away sails or hammocks.

Nipper. A short piece of soft rope used in binding the chain to the messenger in heaving up the anchor.

Oakum. Stuff made by picking rope-yarn to pieces. Used for caulking and other purposes.

Old junk. Remnants or pieces of old cable or condemned rope, cut into small portions for the purpose of making points, mats, swabs, gaskets, sennit, oakum, and the like.

On the wind. Close to the wind. Close-hauled.

Overhand knots. Knots made by passing the end of a rope over its standing part and through the bight.

Painter. A rope attached to the bows of a boat, and used for making her fast.

Parcel. To wind tarred canvas around a rope.

Parcelling. Narrow strips of old canvas daubed with tar and wound around a rope like a bandage previous to its being served.

Pawl (noun). A short bar of iron which prevents the capstan or windlass from turning back.

Pawl (verb). To drop a pawl and secure the windlass or capstan.

Pay off. When a vessel's head falls from the wind.

Pea-jacket. A heavy coat worn by sea-faring men in cold weather; generally made of pilot-cloth.

Pinnace. A boat, in size between a launch and a cutter.

Plank-sheer (or shear). The pieces of plank laid horizontally over the timber-heads at the top-heights for the purpose of covering the top of the sides. Sometimes called covering-boards.

Pointings. To point a rope. To unlay, taper, weave some of the outside yarns of the end of a rope—for neatness, to prevent fagging out, and for convenience in reeving through a block.

Points. The compass card is divided at its circumference into 32 points. Four points would equal 45°.

Preventer. An additional rope or spar used as a support.

Quaker guns. False or wooden guns.

Quarter. The part of a vessel's side between the after part of the main chains and the stern. The quarter of a yard is between the slings and the yard-arm. The wind is said to be quartering when it blows in a line between the keel and the beam and abaft the latter.

Quarter-boat. Any boat is thus designated which is hung to davits over the ship's quarter; it is used as a lifeboat.

Quarter-deck. The part of the upper deck abaft the mainmast.

Ratlines. Small lines traversing the shrouds parallel with the water. They are from 14 to 16 inches apart and serve the purpose of a ladder.

Rattle down. To hitch and seize the ratlines in their proper places.

Reef. To reduce a sail by taking in upon its head if a square sail, and its foot if a fore-and-aft sail.

Reef-band. A band of stout canvas sewed on the sail across with the reef-points in it, and earings at each end for reefing.

Reef-points. Short lengths of line fitted to the reef-band at equal distances from each other, and used to secure the reef-band to the yard.

Reef-tackle. A tackle used to haul the middle of each leech up toward the yard so that the sail may be easily reefed.

Reeve. To pass the end of a rope through a block or any aperture.

Relieving tackle. A tackle hooked to the tiller in a gale to steer by in case anything should happen to the wheel or tiller-ropes.

Ringtail. A kind of studding sail hoisted beyond the after end of those sails which are extended by a gaff and boom over the stern.

Robands (or rope bands). Small pieces of two or three yarn, spun-yarn, or marline used to confine the head of a sail to the yard or gaff.

Rolling-ropes. Used on a light yard to support it in heavy rolling.

Rolling-tackles. Tackles used to steady the yards in a heavy sea.

Rope-yarn. A thread of hemp or other stuff of which a rope is made.

Rounding. A service of rope hove round a spar or larger rope.

Royal. A light sail next above the top-gallant sail.

Royal-mast-head. The spar above the topmast spar. The masthead is the part of the mast above the hounds.

Run (noun). The after part of a vessel's bottom which rises and narrows in approaching the stern-post.

Runner. A rope used to increase the power of a tackle. It is rove through a single block which you wish to bring down and a tackle is hooked to each end or to one end, the other being made fast.

Running large. A vessel sailing with a fair wind so that her sails receive its full effect.

Running rigging. The ropes that reeve through blocks and are pulled and hauled such as braces, halyards, etc.; in opposition to the standing rigging, the ends of which are securely seized, such as stays, shrouds, etc.

Scuppers. Holes cut in the water-ways for the water to run from the decks.

Scuttle. A small opening in the deck of a vessel not over two feet square; they are generally made flush with the decks without coamings.

Scuttled butt. A cask with a hole cut in its bilge and kept on deck to hold water for daily use.

Seizings. The fastenings of ropes that are seized together.

Seizing-stuff. Small-stuff is used for seizings; foxes and rope-yarns for temporary seizings; marline, hambroline, houseline, round line, etc., for permanent seizings. Seizing-stuff is 9-, 6-, or 4-thread stuff of tarred hemp yarns.

Sennit (or sinnet). Flat cordage formed by plaiting rope-yarns together.

Serve. To wind small-stuff, as rope-yarns, spun-yarn, etc., around a rope to keep it from chafing. It is wound and hove round taut by a serving-board or mallet.

Service. The stuff wound round a rope to keep it from chafing.

Serving-board. A flat piece of hard wood having a handle attached used in serving small ropes.

Sextant. A portable instrument for measuring angles by reflection and very generally used by navigators and surveyors for measuring the altitude of heavenly bodies and thereby latitude.

Shackle. An iron link, one end of which is closed by a movable bolt.

Shear pole. An iron rod, fastened to the shrouds just above the dead-eyes to which the ratlines are parallel.

Sheet. A rope used in setting a sail to keep the clew down to its place. With square sails, the sheets run through each yard-arm. With boom sails, they haul the boom over one way and another. They keep down the inner clew of a studding sail and the after clew of a jib.

Sheet home. The sheets are said to be home when the clews are hauled chock out to the sheave-holes.

Ship. A vessel with three masts with tops and yards to each.

Ship shape and Bristol fashion. In seamanlike manner; neatly and thoroughly done.

Shrouds. A set of ropes reaching from the mast-heads to the vessel's sides to support the masts.

Sky-sail mast. The upper portion of a royal mast when used for a sky-sail. Sometimes it slides on the royal mast like a sliding gunter.

Sky-sail. The light sail next above the royal.

Slings. The ropes used for securing the center of a yard to the mast.

Slip. To let a cable go and stand out to sea.

Slip-rope. A rope bent to the cable just outside the hawse-hole and brought in on the weather quarter for slipping.

Slops. Ready-made clothes and other furnishings for seamen.

Slush. To grease the spars after scraping them.

South-wester. A storm-hat of painted canvas, oiled cloth, silk, or rubber, with broad brim or flaps to protect the neck.

Spanish burton. A kind of purchase.

Spanker. The after sail of a ship or bark. It is a fore-and-aft sail setting with a boom and gaff.

Spencer (spenser). A fore-and-aft sail with a gaff and no boom and hoisting from a small mast called a spencer-mast, just abaft the fore and main masts.

Spencer mast. A trysail mast stepped abaft the principal mast.

Spilling-line. A rope used for spilling wind from a sail.

Splice. To join two ropes together by interweaving their strands.

Sprit-sail yard. A yard lashed across the bowsprit or knight-heads and used to spread the guys of the jib and flying jib-boom. There was formerly a sail bent to it called a sprit-sail.

Spring. To crack or split a mast.

Spun-yarn. A cord formed by twisting together two or three rope-yarns.

Squared yards. Yards are squared when they are horizontal and at right angles with the keel. To square a yard in working a ship means to bring it square by the braces. Squaring by the lifts makes them horizontal, and by the braces makes them at right angles with the vessel's line.

Squilgee. A small swab.

Stage. A plank platform or single plank used to support men while working.

Stanchions. Upright posts of wood or iron placed so as to support the beams of a vessel. Also, upright pieces of timber placed at intervals along the sides of a vessel to support the bulwarks and rail and reaching down to the bends, by the side of the timbers, to which they are bolted.

Standing rigging. That part of a vessel's rigging which is made fast and not hauled upon.

Starboard. The right side of a vessel looking forward.

Starbowlines. The familiar term for the men in the starboard watch.

Start. To ease off a little.

Stays. Large ropes used to support masts and leading from the head of some mast down to some other mast or to some part of the vessel. Those which lead forward are called fore-and-aft stays; those which lead down to the vessel's sides, backstays.

Staysail. A sail which hoists upon a stay.

Staysail nettings. A rope or canvas receptacle on the bowsprit for the fore-topmast staysail.

Stay tackles. Any tackle put on a stay for hoisting out or moving weights.

Steerage. That part of the between-decks which is just forward of the cabin.

Stern-sheets. The after part of a boat, abaft the rowers, where the passengers sit.

Stopper. Rope, or more frequently chain or mechanical contrivance, serving to arrest the motion of a cable or prevent its running out when at anchor.

Storm-jib. The inner jib of square-rigged vessels. A strong jib, bent in bad weather.

Storm-sail. A sail of heavy canvas bent and set during a storm when lying to.

Strap. A piece of rope spliced around a block to keep its parts well together. Some blocks have iron straps in which case they are called iron-bound.

Streak (or strake). A range of planks running fore and aft on a vessel's side.

Studding-sail. Light sails set outside the square sails on booms rigged out for that purpose. They are only carried with a fair wind and in moderate weather.

Studding-sail boom. A spar rigged out for the purpose of setting a studding-sail and taking its name from the sail above it.

Supercargo. A person in the merchant service charged with the sale of the cargo and other commercial transactions.

Swab. A mop formed of old rope, used for cleaning and drying decks.

Swift. To bring two shrouds or stays close together by ropes.

Swifter. The forward shroud to a lower mast. Also ropes used to confine the capstan bars to their places when shipped.

Swinging boom. A long spar used at sea to stretch the foot of a lower studding-sail, and in port for the boats to hang on to.

Tack (noun). A vessel is on the starboard tack, or has her starboard tacks on board, when she has the wind on her starboard side. The rope or tackle by which the weather clew of a course is hauled forward and down to the deck. The tack of a fore-and-aft sail is the rope that keeps down the lower forward clew. The tack of the lower studding-sail is called the outhaul. Also that part of a sail to which the tack is attached.

Tack (verb). To put a ship about so that from having the wind on one side you bring it round to the other by way of her head. The opposite of wearing.

Taffrail. The rail around a ship's stern.

Tally. To haul the sheets aft.

Taut. Tight.

Taut bowline. A ship is said to be on a taut bowline when she is close-hauled as the bowlines are then taut.

Thole-pins. Pins on the gunwale of a boat between which an oar rests when pulling instead of a rowlock.

Three turns round the long-boat and a pull at the scuttled-butt. See "Tom Cox's traverse."

Tie. The part of the purchase for hoisting a topsail yard which is attached to the yard and passes through the sheave-hole in the mast, or the tie-block at the mast-head.

Tiller. A bar of wood or iron put into the head of a rudder by which the rudder is moved.

Timber-heads. The ends of the timbers that come above the decks. Used for belaying hawsers and large ropes.

Toggle. A pin placed through the bight or eye of a rope, block-strap, or bolt, to keep it in its place, or to put the bight or eye of another rope upon and thus secure them both together.

Tom Cox's traverse. To work Tom Cox's traverse signifies the efforts made by a skulker to avoid work. It has been described as "Up one hatchway and down another"; also, "Three turns around the long-boat and a pull at the scuttle."

Top. A platform of semicircular form resting upon the trestle-trees of the lower mast of a square-rigged vessel. It gives spread to the top-mast rigging, which is set up to the rim of the top. It is used as a landing place from which the light-yard men start in loosing or furling. The breadth of a main-top is equal to one half the breadth of beam of the vessel.

Top-gallant breeze. A fair wind light enough for the setting of top-gallant sails.

Top-gallant forecastle. A short deck in the bows of a vessel above the spar deck.

Top-gallant mast. The third mast above the deck.

Top-gallant sail. The third sail above the deck (unless the vessel carry double topsails).

Top hamper. Unnecessary spars and rigging kept aloft.

Topsail. The second sail above the deck. In the later 19th century generally divided in large vessels into upper and lower topsails.

Topsail haliards (halyards). Topsail yards have a permanent purchase, variously rigged according to the size of the yard. Haliards, the rope or purchase employed to hoist a yard or sail on its mast or stay.

Trade winds. The name given to the atmospheric currents of the northern and southern hemispheres which have a general direction from the northeast in north latitudes and southeast in south latitudes. Blow steadily.

Traverse. The various courses made by a vessel in beating against the wind, or the irregular track made by a vessel sailing on different courses. Solution of traverse sailing consists in obtaining an equivalent course and distance from the several courses and distances actually sailed.

Trice up. To haul up by means of a rope.

Trim the yards. To arrange the sails by the braces with reference to the wind.

Trip the anchor. To raise an anchor clear of the bottom.

Truss. The rope by which the center of a lower yard is kept toward the mast.

Trysail. A fore-and-aft sail set with a boom and gaff and hoisted on a small mast abaft the lower mast. This name is generally confined to the sail so carried at the mainmast of a full-rigged brig; those carried at the foremast and mainmast of a ship or bark being called spencers, and those at the mizzenmast of a ship or bark, spankers.

Trysail gaff. The gaff to which a trysail is bent.

Tye. A rope connected with a yard to the other end of which a tackle is attached for hoisting.

Twig. To pull upon a bowline.

Unlay. To untwist the strands of a rope.

Waist. The part of the upper deck between the quarter-deck and the forecastle.

Wall-sided. A vessel is wall-sided when her sides run up perpendicularly from the bends. In opposition to tumbling home or flaring out.

Watch-tackle. A small luff-purchase with a short fall, the double block having a tail to it, and the single one a hook. Used for various purposes about decks.

Water-ways. Long pieces of timber, running fore and aft on both sides, connecting the deck with the vessel's sides. The scuppers are made through them to let the water off.

Wear. To turn a vessel round so that from having the wind on one side, you bring it upon the other, carrying her stern round by the wind.

In tacking the same result is produced by carrying a vessel's head round by the wind.

Weather. In the direction from which the wind blows.

Weather-bit. To take an additional turn with a cable round the windlass-end.

Whale-boat. A long, narrow boat from 20 to 30 feet in length, sharp at both ends, and admirably fitted for all uses at sea. These boats are best in the surf and should be steered with a long oar rather than a rudder.

Wheel-ropes. Ropes or chains leading from the tiller or helm through blocks in the decks and trunks under the beams to the barrel or the steering wheel where they are fastened.

Whip (noun). A purchase formed by a rope rove through a single block.

Whip (verb). To hoist by a whip.

Wind ahead. Wind from directly ahead or against the course.

Windlass. The machine used in merchant vessels to weigh the anchor by.

Worm. To fill up between the lays of a rope with small stuff wound round spirally. Stuff so wound is called worming.

Yard. The long piece of timber, tapering slightly toward the ends, and hung by the center to a mast to spread the square sails upon.

Yard-arm. The extremities of a yard.

Yard tackle. A heavy tackle hooked to the lower yards and used in hoisting heavy articles in and out.

Yoke. A piece of wood placed across the head of a boat's rudder, with a rope attached to each end, by which the boat is steered.

INDEX

This index was prepared by Anna Marie and Everett Gordon Hager

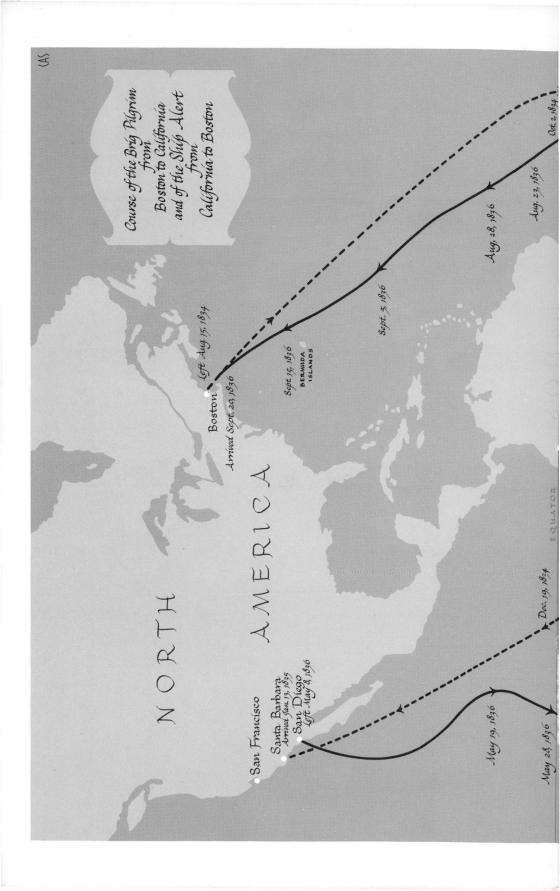

Course of the Brig Pilgrim
from
Boston to California
and of the Ship Alert
from
California to Boston

N O R T H

A M E R I C A

San Francisco

Santa Barbara
Arrived Jan. 13, 1835

San Diego
Left May 8, 1836

Boston
Left Aug. 15, 1834
Arrived Sept. 20, 1836

Sept. 15, 1836

BERMUDA
ISLANDS

Sept. 5, 1836

Aug. 28, 1836

Aug. 23, 1836

Oct. 2, 1834

Dec. 19, 1834

May 19, 1836

May 28, 1836

EQUATOR